Greenhill
Books

War in the
Fourth
Dimension

War in the Fourth Dimension

US Electronic Warfare, from the Vietnam War to the Present

Dr Alfred Price

With a Foreword by
General Charles A. Horner

Greenhill Books, London
Stackpole Books, Pennsylvania

War in the Fourth Dimension
first published 2001 by

Greenhill Books, Lionel Leventhal Limited,
Park House, 1 Russell Gardens, London NW11 9NN
and

Stackpole Books,
5067 Ritter Road, Mechanicsburg, PA 17055, USA

Copyright © The Association of Old Crows, 2001
The moral right of the author has been asserted

British Library Cataloguing in Publication Data
Price, Alfred, 1936-
    War in the fourth dimension : US electronic warfare :
    Vietnam War to the present
    1. Electronics in military engineering - United States
    2. Military art and science - United States - Automation
    3. Information warfare - United States - Case studies
        I. Title
        355.8

ISBN 1-85367-471-0

Library of Congress Cataloging-in-Publication Data
A catalog record is available

Edited and designed by Donald Sommerville

Printed and bound in Great Britain
by MPG Books Ltd., Bodmin, Cornwall

Contents

List of Illustrations

7

Preface

This book leans heavily on the use of material from declassified documents, and on unclassified interviews with numerous participants in the events described. Nevertheless the need to observe the requirements of US national security has precluded detailed discussion of several aspects of the story. As might be expected, the problem became more onerous during the final chapters of this book.

Quite separate from the problem of security, there is the no less serious problem of shortage of space. This book covers a thirty-seven year time frame, which means hard editorial choices were necessary to produce an account that follows the main areas of the story.

During the research for this book I interviewed 127 people involved in US electronic warfare at all levels. Where I quote people it should not be inferred that the individual played a leading or even a major part in the events described. In many cases he or she was speaking on behalf of the team or organization involved.

Where this book is successful, credit is due to the people listed in the Acknowledgements. I am deeply grateful to those who patiently led me round, over, and in some cases out of, the traps awaiting the chronicler of this complex subject. If, despite their efforts, some errors have insinuated their way into the account, I alone am responsible.

Alfred Price
2001

Foreword

By General Charles A. Horner

An old saying assures us that, "Those who fail to learn from history, are doomed to repeat its mistakes." That statement was never more true than in the world of electronic warfare. After each conflict the lessons learned include major findings by land, sea, air and space forces, regarding failures to exploit the electromagnetic environment for offense and defense. I know this to be true from personal experience. In Vietnam I flew missions against radar guided defenses, without either a radar warning receiver or a self-protection electronic countermeasures system. We should have known better, given the pioneer efforts of the old crows from World War II and Korea. But we didn't pay attention. We played catch-up, from that day in August 1965 when an SA-2 downed an F-4C. When we went after the offending missile site, we lost six jets.

Too often, catch-up has been the name of the game when it comes to electronic warfare. To be sure, there is a need to respond rapidly. Measures require countermeasures, and the enemy does not open his kimono until the shooting starts. But more likely, we enter the fray ignoring the past and what was learned at such a cost in lives in combat. For example, in the late 1950s our peacetime training emphasized low level flying as the way to avoid enemy radar-guided defenses. This head-in-the-sand approach did not serve us well when the bullets started flying.

The Vietnam War proved to be a good teacher. After it many returned to the foolish old ways, though the voices of reason maintained a foothold. The land forces concentrated on electronic deception and targeting the enemy command and control systems. Intelligence assets integrated their ELINT missions directly into combat operations, as we turned data and awareness rapidly into knowledge and understanding of the enemy. We got so we could control the electronic environment, misleading the enemy while hiding entire fleets of ships at sea. Airmen from all our Services, and those of our foreign allies, tested themselves in complex electronic environments during the realistic Green Flag exercises. This emphasis on electronic warfare came from military and civilian leaders who would not be shouted down by the ignorant, as had happened after the Korean War.

The lessons stuck. As a result, we entered the Gulf War of 1991 with well-trained and equipped forces. The Iraqi Air Defenses were dense and deadly, and electronic warfare was critical to success in this war. Air Force leaders like Larry Henry and John Corder, who were schooled in the arcane science of

EW and experienced in combat, showed us how to fight. Men and women who had trained in Green Flag exercises exploited the superb equipment provided by electrical engineers from the Services' acquisition corps and civilian industries. EW networks from the logistical community, and specialized talent from organizations such as the Tactical Air Warfare Center, provided the depth of knowledge needed to handle the unforeseen that characterizes the electronic battle. Most important of all, our forces had grown up in the peacetime environment in the 1980s, where EW was taken seriously. It was a pass-fail item during our readiness inspections. But, that golden age did not last.

The end of the Cold War ravaged our hard-won EW readiness. In 1999, during the war in Kosovo, our forces were tested over the Serbian countryside. We succeeded, but the cracks in our EW readiness were showing. The enemy had learned from the Gulf War, and had applied the lessons accordingly. We remained strong in some areas, but we had lost the force structure needed for robust electronic combat operations. In the air war only two aircraft were lost in combat, but we should not take solace from that low number. "Force protection" had become the goal and the strategy. Effectiveness was measured in "aircraft not lost," versus how well we inflicted our will on the enemy. The real lesson is that we had forgotten about EW in peacetime. Signals intelligence is interesting, but uninspiring. Pictures get our attention. We are inclined to renew our ardor for the bright and shiny aircraft, and find it easy to shun the unseen power of the electronic jammer or the HARM missile. The fact is that EW is a battle fought in the mind. Electronic combat is about what is seen and not seen, what is known and unknown, what is real and imagined. During peacetime it holds little attraction. But in war it spells the difference between life and death.

The Korean War is ancient history. The Vietnam War is not far behind. Even the Gulf War is rapidly receding out of our corporate memories. Will the warriors of the future go into battle and find that they are ill equipped, inadequately trained and poorly led to survive in the complex electronic environment that characterizes modern war? It should not happen, the lessons of the past were paid for in blood. As a nation we are the masters of the electron, whether it is used to aim a missile or to power a computer. The Association of Old Crows* has laid before us, in vivid detail, the history we should study if we are to avoid the mistakes of the past. How well we learn these lessons will determine if we are true caretakers of our nation's future, or louts who confuse loud talk with the ability to win a fight.

Charles A. Horner
General, USAF (Retired)

---

* The Association of Old Crows is an international association of those active in, or supportive of, electronic warfare and related fields of military electronics. It commissioned, funded and supported the three-volume *History of US Electronic Warfare*, Volume III of which is the basis of this book. *See also page 267.*

Acknowledgements

The author wishes to record his grateful thanks to the following for granting interviews or supplying material used in the preparation of this book. Ranks are given only for those who reached general officer/flag rank.

Dave Adamy
Dan Allred,
Stan Alterman
Bob Annen
Mark Ashton
Charles Atkins
Bill Bahret
Chris Bakke
Joseph Bert
John Black
Gil Bouffard
Tony Brees
Dave Brog
Ted Brown
Susan Browning
Farrel Bryant
H. Lee Buchanan
Dennis Buley
Roc Caldarella
Bill Cannon
Rear Admiral Martin Carmody
Mike Casey
Ed Chapman
Charles Christman
Maj Gen John Corder
Monte Correll
Dick Curtis
Joe Digiovanni
Butch Erickson
Frank Ernandes
Roy Fair
Jeff Fischer
Basil Foy
Maj Gen Jim Freeze

William Gardner
Mike Gilroy
Jim Goslar
Gerald Green
Tony Grieco
John Grigsby
Maj Gen Bert Harbour
Lowell Haskins
Rich Haver
Ingwald Haugen
Jim Henning
Brig Gen Larry Henry
Art Hepler
William Hickey
Jeff Huang
Lee Ilse
Maj Gen Kenneth Israel
Rear Admiral Grady Jackson
Craig Johnson
Don Jones
Hon. Dr Paul Kaminski,
Joe Kearney
Michael Kemmerer
Chip Kochel
Donald Kilgus
Frank Klemm
William Knarr
Kenneth Krech
Danny Kuehl
Mike Kulera
Vic Kutsch
Rear Admiral Julian Lake
Fred Levian
Pierre Levy

Garry Long
Jerry Long
Vern Luke
Kathleen Maloney
Dale Marchand
Maj Gen John Marks
Jim Massaro
Thomas Mathews
Pete McGrew
Joe McLain
Lt Gen Paul Menoher
Glen Miller
Dennis Millsap
Antonio Mitchell
Creed Morgan
Rick Morgan
Sherm Mullin
George Nicholas
John O'Brien
Jim Odom
Tofie Owen
Barnie Parker
Fred Paxton
Vic Pheasant
John "Rusty" Porter
Gene Poteat
Hugo Poza
Jerry Proctor
Tom Reader
Tom Reinkober
Walter Rice

Butch Schimmel
Pat Scott
Bob Seh
Marty Selmanowicz
J.P. Sheehan
Richard Short
Bob Simmen
Gene Simmons
Dave Sjolund
Rudy Smart
Mark Smith
Ron Smith
Jerry Sowell
Gene Starbuck
Jack Stevens
John Stevens
John Stevens III
John Strabian
Bill Strandberg
Rear Admiral Bill Studeman
James Sullivan
Jim Talley
Maj Gen Chuck Thomas
Maj Gen John Thomas
Pepper Thomas
Marv Thompson
Gary Torre
Alfred Victor
Andy Vittoria
Paul Westcott
Jerry White

Author's Note

To maintain the relevance of the account it has been necessary to stick closely to the usually accepted short definition of electronic warfare: any military action involving the use of electromagnetic and directed energy to control the electromagnetic spectrum or to the attack the enemy.

For simplicity the AN prefixes of US equipments have been omitted, thus AN/ALT-71 is referred to as ALT-71, etc. During the period under review the US system of letter designators for frequency bands changed. The author has used the current A through M band designation system, as follows:

A band	100 to 250 MHz
B band	250 to 500 MHz
C band	500 to 1000 MHz
D band	1000 to 2000 MHz
E band	2000 to 3000 MHz
F band	3000 to 4000 MHz
G band	4000 to 6000 MHz
H band	6000 to 8000 MHz
I band	8000 to 10000 MHz
J band	10000 to 20000 MHz
K band	20000 to 40000 MHz
L band	40000 to 60000 MHz
M band	60000 to 100000 MHz

The military ranks are those held at the time described in the text. When describing Soviet systems the author uses the NATO designation, with the Soviet designation when known given in parentheses. Miles are in nautical miles (1 nautical mile equals 1.15 statute miles), weights are in pounds and US tons and volumes are in US gallons.

The author has taken pains to avoid the overuse of acronyms and jargon words. On the other hand a few abbreviations—such as USN, USAF, SAC, CIA etc.—are familiar to everyone and the author has used these where appropriate. A Glossary of Abbreviations and Electronic Warfare Terms is included on pages 19–21.

Current Definitions

In this book the terms and definitions used are those appropriate to the time frame described. The current military definitions for electronic warfare and related areas are given below. Readers should note, however, that as the subject evolves these definitions are liable to change.

ELECTRONIC WARFARE (EW)
Any military action involving the use of electromagnetic and directed energy to control the electromagnetic spectrum or to the attack the enemy. The three major subdivisions within electronic warfare are:

Electronic Attack (EA)
That division of electronic warfare involving the use of electromagnetic or directed energy to attack personnel, facilities or equipment with the intend of degrading, neutralizing or destroying enemy combat capability. The term includes those aspects of the subject that previously came under the heading of Electronic Countermeasures (ECM).

Electronic Protection (EP)
That division of electronic warfare involving actions taken to protect personnel, facilities and equipment from any effects of friendly or enemy employment of electronic warfare that degrade neutralize and destroy friendly combat capability. The term includes those aspects of the subject that previously came under the heading of Electronic Countermeasures (ECCM).

Electronic Warfare Support (ES)
That division of electronic warfare involving actions tasked by, or under direct control of, an operational commander to search for, intercept, identify and locate sources of intentional and unintentional radiated electromagnetic energy for the purpose of immediate threat recognition. Thus, electronic warfare support provides information required for immediate decisions involving electronic warfare operations, threat avoidance, targeting and other tactical actions. The term includes those aspects of the subject that previously came under the headings of Electronic Warfare Support Measures (ESM) and Signals Intelligence (SIGINT).

COMMAND AND CONTROL WARFARE (C²W)
The integrated use of operations security (OPSEC), military deception, psychological operations (PSYOP), electronic warfare (EW) and physical destruction, mutually supported by intelligence, to deny information to,

influence, degrade or destroy adversary command and control capabilities, while protecting friendly command and control capabilities against such actions. C^2W applies across the operational continuum and all levels of conflict. C^2W is both offensive and defensive. The term includes those aspects of the subject that previously came under the heading of Command, Control and Communications Countermeasures (C^3CM). The two major subdivisions within Command and Control warfare are:

Counter-C^2
To prevent effective C^2 of adversary forces by denying information to, influencing, degrading or destroying the adversary C^2 system.

C^2 Protection
To maintain effective command and control of own forces by turning to friendly advantage or negating adversary efforts to deny information to, influence, degrade or destroy the friendly C^2 system.

INFORMATION OPERATIONS (IO)
Actions taken to access and/or affect adversary information systems, while defending one's own information and information systems.

INFORMATION WARFARE
Information Warfare: Information Operations conducted during time of crisis or conflict to achieve specific objectives over a specific adversary or adversaries.

Abbreviations and Electronic Warfare Terms

AAA   Anti Aircraft Artillery.

ABM   Anti-Ballistic Missile system.

AI   Airborne Intercept (radar).

Apogee   Highest point reached by a satellite during its orbit.

ARM   Anti-radiation missile.

ASE   Aircraft Survival Equipment; Army term for self-protection electronic warfare systems fitted to its aircraft.

Big Eye   Lockheed EC-121D aircraft providing radar and other types of surveillance to support US fighters operating over North Vietnam. Also known as College Eye.

Brigand   Passive system for plotting the returns from non-cooperating (usually enemy) surveillance radars.

B Scope   Radar display with range measured as the vertical distance from the base of the display, and azimuth or elevation angle measured by the displacement of the blip to left or right of the center line running vertically from the base of the display.

Burnthrough range   The slant range from the radar to the target, at which a radar operator is able to see the skin echo from the incoming target (usually an aircraft) which had previously been obscured by noise jamming from that target or from a stand-off source. At all distances greater than the Burnthrough range, the target is concealed by the jamming. At ranges less than the Burnthrough range, if the radar is handled correctly, the radar operators should be able to see the target through the jamming.

BWO   Backward Wave Oscillator, a source of power for countermeasures and other transmitters. Also called the Carcinotron.

Carcinatron   See BWO.

Chaff   Metal foil, or more recently metal coated fiberglass dipoles, employed to produce spurious echoes on radars or break radar lock-on.

College Eye   See Big Eye.

COMINT   Communications Intelligence.

Compass Call   Lockheed EC-130H fitted with Rivet Fire communications jamming system.

Coronet Solo   Lockheed EC-130H fitted with equipment to transmit radio and TV broadcasts while airborne, usually used to pass propaganda messages to unfriendly or hostile forces.

DARPA   Defense Advanced Research Projects Agency.

Deception Repeater   Countermeasures system which picks up signals from enemy radar, applies a deceptive modulation to these, amplifies the signals and re-radiates them back to the radar either to break the lock-on or mislead the latter regarding a plane or ship's position or velocity.

DF   Direction Finding.

DMZ   Demilitarized Zone. Buffer zone intended to separate North Vietnam from South Vietnam.

ECCM   Electronic Counter-Countermeasures.

ECM   Electronic Countermeasures.

ECMO   ECM Officer (Navy).

ELINT   Electronic Intelligence.

EOB   Electronic Order of Battle.

EW   Electronic Warfare.

EWO   Electronic Warfare Officer (Air Force).

FTD   Foreign Technology Division, Air Force intelligence division based at Wright-Patterson AFB.

GCI   Ground Controlled Intercept (radar).

IFF   Identification Friend or Foe equipment.

Inverse Conical Scan   Angle deception technique used against Conical Scan radar. The power radiated is inversely proportional to the strength of the signal picked up, thereby inducing major errors into the radar's automatic tracking system.

IP   Initial Point. Final navigational check point used before an aircraft commences its attack run.

IR   Infrared.

IRCM   Infrared Countermeasures.

Iron Hand   Generic term to describe attacks on enemy ground-to-air defensive system.

MAC   Military Airlift Command.

Main Lobe Blanking   Countermeasures technique applicable to search and track- while-scan radars having periodic scan, also to monopulse radars working in the acquisition mode. The repeater radiates return pulses only when the radar's side lobes pass through it, but not when it is in the main lobe. This technique is similar to inverse gain.

MIGCAP   Combat Air Patrol, fighters operating primarily in the air-to-air role.

Monopulse   Type of tracking radar which radiates two or four parallel beams simultaneously, and compares differences in the strengths of the return signals to align itself on the target. Monopulse tracking is a powerful ECCM, since it is impervious to most types of angle-track deception jamming.

Noise Jamming   Countermeasures technique, in which the jammer
   attempts to radiate sufficient power on the victim radar's frequency to
   screen the return echoes from the airplane, ship, etc.

PACAF   Pacific Air Forces.

Perigee   Lowest point reached by a satellite during its orbit.

PRF   Pulse repetition frequency.

PRI   Pulse repetition interval (inverse of PRF).

QRC   Quick Reaction Capability. System of issuing contracts to build new
   equipments or modifications to older ones, without going through the
   lengthy full procurement process.

Range Gate Pull Off   Deception method to counter the range measuring
   system of a radar operating in the automatic tracking mode.

RHWR   Radar Homing and Warning Receiver.

RWR   Radar Warning Receiver.

Rivet Top   RC-135V SIGINT collection aircraft.

SADS   Soviet Air Defense Simulator. SADS-1 was a working replica of the
   Soviet Fan Song Model B radar, SADS-2 was a replica of the Fan Song
   Model C/E radar.

SAM   Surface-to-Air Missile.

SEA   South East Asia.

SEAD   Suppression of Enemy Air Defenses

Shoe Horn   Navy operation to install the ALQ-51 deception system in
   small tactical fighters that had not been designed to carry it.

TFW   Tactical Fighter Wing.

TFS   Tactical Fighter Squadron.

TWT   Travelling Wave Tube. Power source and amplifier system employed
   in many countermeasures and other systems.

VTM   Voltage Tuned Magnetron. Power source employed in some
   countermeasures systems.

Wild Weasel   Code name for dedicated Air Force units sent to attack
   enemy SAM sites.

WSO   Weapon Systems Officer (Air Force).

Yankee Station   Code name for area of sea off the coast of North
   Vietnam, in which US warships operated during the conflict there.

Chapter 1

THE INTELLIGENCE ATTACK: 1

Pre-1964 to 1965

"Give every man thine ear, but few thy voice."
Shakespeare, *Hamlet*

The Cold War, the ideological conflict between the United States and its Allies on one side and the Communist Bloc on the other, lasted forty-one years. It had no clearly defined start, though by the summer of 1948 it was well established.

In the fall of 1962 the Cuban missile crisis brought the world to the brink of Armageddon. The US and Soviet governments faced each other down, each with its strategic bomber and missile forces at their highest state of readiness short of war. A single miscalculation on either side could have led to an all-out nuclear conflict. That never happened, but the high-stakes poker game had nearly run out of control. In the decades to follow US and Soviet forces would glower at each other in many parts of the world, but both sides took pains to ensure they did not meet in direct conflict. Throughout that time, each side sought to gain intelligence of the opposing side's military capabilities and intentions.

During the late 1950s and early 1960s, the US intelligence agencies ran numerous operations to gather information on Soviet air operations. One such was the Air Force Security Service's Flight Wolf operation.

Due to the poor network of landlines in remote areas of the Soviet Union, many Soviet surveillance radars passed track plots to their control centers using high frequency radio and Morse code. The messages were encrypted, but in cryptographic terms it was a simple matter to break the ciphers.[1] US planes were routed past coastal sites on tracks where they were sure to be observed. The radio track plots from the Soviet radars gave the planes' location, speed, heading, altitude and the number present. US monitoring stations picked up the encrypted Soviet reports, then cryptographers had the relatively easy task of stripping away the cipher protecting a message whose content they already knew. Thus US intelligence could follow each change made in the Soviet reporting system.

US monitoring stations made regular use of Soviet radar plots to track the movements of Soviet planes, and also those of US and allied aircraft flying within range of Soviet radars. As we shall observe later, Flight Wolf played a key role in other US intelligence operations.

Throughout the Cold War the Central Intelligence Agency (CIA) frequently commissioned systems to assist with the collection of intelligence. One such device, used early in the 1960s, was a miniature hand-held radar receiver to pick up signals from the Fan Song control radar used with the Soviet SA-2 (S-75) missile system. That receiver was about the size of a modern micro-cassette recorder and ran off a dry battery. An audible tone, heard through a hearing-aid earpiece, allowed the listener to hear the radar's distinctive scan pattern. The small directional antenna, about six inches across, was mounted on a flat piece of composite insulating material. The receiver and antenna were small enough to fit into a large purse or coat pocket.[2]

This novel receiver had its moment of glory during the Cuban missile crisis in the fall of 1962. After U-2 aircraft photographed the Soviet intermediate range ballistic missile sites on the island from high altitude, the Department of Defense decided it needed low altitude close-up photographs of the sites. Navy and Marine RF-8 Crusader reconnaissance aircraft based at Key West were sent on high-speed low altitude photographic runs past the sites, but in common with other tactical aircraft at that time, the RF-8s had no radar warning receiver.[3]

To correct this deficiency Gene Poteat from the CIA's Science and Technology Directorate at McLean arrived at Key West with a small team and four radar receivers. He described the installation of the receivers in the RF-8s:

> "We went shopping in Key West to buy the items we needed to hold the systems in place. The receiver was strapped to the pilot's leg using a dog's collar, with Kotex napkins to provide the necessary padding. The wire carrying the audio output from the receiver ran to an earpiece in the pilot's helmet, held in place by duct tape. The antenna was wedged in the corner of the windshield, held in place by more tape."[4]

The RF-8s flew their low altitude missions and returned with the required close-up photos. No plane was lost. One RF-8 pilot heard signals from a missile control radar and his evasive turns caused the radar to lose contact.[5] Almost certainly those RF-8s were the first tactical aircraft ever to carry radar-warning receivers during an operational mission.

The CIA also mounted special operations to collect specific items of information on Soviet radar systems. One of these, Project Melody, ran for several years.

In the 1950s Gene Poteat worked at Cape Canaveral, assisting with the testing of Thor and Titan ballistic missiles. From colleagues he heard that these big missiles were good reflectors of radar signals. Signals from tracking radars more than one thousand miles down range were often picked up by radars at the Cape, having bounced off a missiles on the way.[6]

After Poteat joined the CIA, he saw an intelligence application for this phenomenon.

"The CIA ran an ELINT and COMINT collection site at Beshar in Iran, on the south shore of the Caspian Sea. This picked up telemetry signals from missiles launched from the Soviet sites at Tyuratam and Kapustin Yar. New Soviet radars were located deep inside the Soviet Union, where our ELINT stations or aircraft could not pick up their signals. But it occurred to me that the big Soviet missiles would reflect their radar signals, as our [missiles] had at Cape Canaveral. We would use the missile's beacon to keep our antenna trained in the right direction. We did some calculations, which proved to our satisfaction that the system would work."[7]

The special receivers and antennas were set up at Beshar and in the years to follow Melody scoured the frequency spectrum for Soviet radar signals. Signals were received from ground radars more than one thousand miles away, and in the decades to follow the method yielded a wealth of useful intelligence on Soviet radar developments.

Information on Soviet rocket technology was another item high on the US intelligence agencies' list of priorities. Operation Landboom Special, which began in the late 1950s, was a joint Army-Navy program to collect telemetry signals from Soviet missile tests. Ground stations on the southern shores of the Black Sea in Turkey and the Caspian Sea in Iran kept a close watch on the tests.

A Soviet surface-to-surface ballistic missile's trajectory would carry it high above the radio horizon from the US monitoring sites, allowing them to track the missile's transponder beacon. That gave an indication of the missile's flight range, and when the signals ceased it indicated that the flight had terminated either as planned or prematurely.

The US ground stations also picked up telemetry transmissions from the Soviet missiles. These transmissions were not encrypted, probably because the Soviets believed it was impossible to identify the individual channels so the information was of little value.[8] That proved not to be the case, however. Engineers at the Electronics Defense Laboratories at Mountain View,

California, plotted the telemetry signals on graphs. Joe Bert from EDL recalled:

"I went with Bill Perry to see the rocket experts at the Jet Propulsion Laboratory at Pasadena, California. We talked to people working on US guided missiles, and showed a senior scientist one of our curves. He said 'That looks just like the acceleration curve for our Corporal missile!' After a bit of analysis, we found that was the acceleration curve of the Soviet missile. After applying some mathematics, we found the velocity channel. Then we found the channel giving the positions of the missile's control surfaces, and another giving the amount of fuel remaining in each tank. We did not identify all the channels, but we got a lot of significant ones.

Once we were able to analyze the information from the telemetry, we could say 'This guided missile must weigh about w pounds, it must have about x amount of thrust, after take off it accelerates at y feet per second per second and the motor cuts off at z velocity.' We could probe very deeply into the missile systems, we could even get a good idea of their accuracy."[9]

It is difficult to exaggerate the intelligence value of the data from this source. The information was highly detailed and manifestly true.[10] Thus was born the science of telemetry intelligence collection, later known as TELINT.

Due to limitations imposed by the radio horizon, ground stations in Turkey and Iran could not collect the full train of telemetry signals from Soviet intercontinental ballistic missiles. To extend the coverage, three Boeing B-47 Stratojet bombers were modified for the telemetry collection task. These aircraft, EB-47Es, were usually referred to as "Tell Two" planes. Each carried the normal front-end crew of three (aircraft commander, co-pilot and navigator) plus two EW officers in a pressurized capsule in the bomb bay with their radio receivers and tape recorders. Externally the only difference from a regular B-47E bomber was a 15-foot-long horizontal rod antenna with streamlined supports, mounted on each side of the nose.[11]

The Tell Two B-47s, flown by the 55th Strategic Reconnaissance Wing, operated from Incerlik in Turkey. When a Soviet long-range missile shot was planned, a recognizable pattern of radio signals indicated that the range was being prepared. When the missile launch was imminent, an EB-47E took off and headed for its patrol line over northern Iran, some 700 miles from the Tyuratam launch site.[12] The EB-47E carried four receivers to cover the primary interest telemetry frequencies of 25, 61, 66 and 100 MHz. Two other receivers covered the specific frequencies of 19.995 and 20.995 MHz, which were linked to the de-orbiting of satellites and the passing of intelligence data to their ground stations. The presence of a 25 MHz signal indicated a space capsule launch.

Captain Roy Fair flew as an EW Officer on two Tell Two deployments, in the fall of 1964 and the summer of 1965. He recalled:

"On occasions during my two deployments, I witnessed the 25 MHz signal, and others, come up strong, fluctuate violently and immediately disappear back into the grass. That was a sure-fire indication of a failure and sometimes a human tragedy."[13]

Over several decades, the ground and airborne monitoring of Soviet missile TELINT yielded a cornucopia of intelligence on that nation's steadily improving rocket technology.

During a normal ELINT operation, listening to a radar's signals provides the operating frequency, pulse repetition frequency, type of scan and the location of the radar and its likely purpose. For a noise jamming attack, that information is sufficient.

Deception repeater systems like the Sanders ALQ-49 and ALQ-51 equipments developed for the US Navy were more demanding. They required detailed information on the victim radar if they were to function effectively. A particular target for this type of jamming was the Fan Song radar associated with the SA-2 surface-to-air missile system. If the repeater moved the Fan Song scan pattern away from the aircraft, its designers needed to know if that was far enough to put the plane outside the lethal range of the missile's warhead. They needed to know the exact width of the Fan Song scanning sectors in azimuth and elevation and the power radiated in each beam.[14]

To get that information, early in the 1960s the CIA launched its airborne Power and Pattern Measurement Systems (PPMS) program.[15] The Air Force's 7499th Support Group based at Wiesbaden in Germany operated a specially modified C-97 transport plane with the necessary receivers. Air Force Captain David Brog joined the program in 1964 and commanded the C-97 operating team:

"We flew up and down the corridors to Berlin, going past SA-2 sites in East Germany. Once we were in the air corridor we would extend the antennas and begin looking for signals. We would fly the route in the morning, land at Templehof [Berlin] and go back in the evening. We flew along the regular cargo routes from Frankfurt or Wiesbaden into Berlin and back.

The Fan Song radars did not necessarily have to track us. They had to transmit when their crews were training, and we could pick up their signals. If they were tracking another airplane, we could still get useful information."[16]

One good pass on a working Fan Song radar pointing in the direction of the aircraft would produce the required data, but the Soviets were past masters in radiation security.[17] It took several months before the necessary data could be collected.

Following that success, PPMS became a regular aspect of US ELINT collection activities. A modified RB-47 aircraft, operated by the 55th Strategic Reconnaissance Wing, flew similar missions in the Far East.

During the late 1950s the CIA planned a replacement for the U-2 aircraft conducting deep penetration reconnaissance flights over the Soviet Union. Two competing programs were considered: Project Corona, a photographic reconnaissance satellite; and Project Oxcart, a manned aircraft designed to fly at Mach 3.3 at altitudes around 90,000 feet.

Modern readers will have no doubts that the reconnaissance satellite was the better system, but in 1960 that issue was far from certain. There was apprehension whether a photographic satellite could deliver photographs from space, and between February 1959 and June 1960 the Corona program suffered twelve consecutive failures before it flew a successful mission.

Meanwhile, the construction of the prototype Oxcart aircraft went ahead at Lockheed's Skunk Works at Burbank, California. The single seater was designated the A-12 (it was the predecessor of the better-known two-seat SR-71 Blackbird). Oxcart was the first manned aircraft to incorporate a range of stealth features from the initial design stage, and large parts of the airframe incorporated radar-absorbent material.[18]

Oxcart had a radar echoing area smaller than any previous aircraft of its size. Yet the question remained, was it sufficiently stealthy to avoid detection by Soviet air defense radars? CIA analysts were particularly interested in the principal Soviet early warning equipment, the high powered Tall King (P-14) A-band radar which employed a huge openwork reflector 112 feet across. Also, as always, they were interested to learning as much as possible about the Fan Song missile control radar.[19]

Thanks to the PPMS program, CIA analysts knew the effective radiated power and spatial coverage of the Tall King and the Fan Song radars. The next step was to discover their receiver sensitivity and get an idea of the proficiency of the operators.

To answer those questions the CIA launched Project Palladium. By some clever electronic sleight of hand, Palladium generated a false aircraft target electronically and injected it into a victim radar. To achieve that aim the "ghost echo" had to look plausibly like a real aircraft and move across the radar screen in a realistic manner. Gene Poteat wrote:

"Basically, we received the radar's signal and fed it into a variable delay line before transmitting the signal back to the radar. By smoothly varying the length of the delay line, we could simulate the false target's range and speed. Knowing the radar's power and coverage from the PPMS project, we could now simulate an aircraft of any radar cross section. That might range from an invisible stealth airplane, to one that made a large blip on Soviet radar screens. We could make anything in between, flying at any speed and altitude and along any path...

Now the real trick was to find some way of knowing which of our blips the Soviets could see on their radar screens—the smallest size blip being a measure of sensitivity of the Soviets' radars and the skill of their operators."[20]

A small-scale monitoring and deciphering operation along the lines of Flight Wolf provided the required information. The monitors listened to the Soviet operators' track plots by radio on the "ghost" aircraft. From these, analysts determined the threshold size of radar echo the operators could see.

The Palladium equipment was small enough to operate from a medium size van on the deck of a frigate, or it could be carried inside a submarine. The operating team comprised two operatives to man the "ghost generator", and a five-man team from the National Security Agency (NSA) or the Naval Security Group to monitor and de-crypt the Soviet track reports.[21]

CIA operatives examined lists of known Tall King and Fan Song sites to select those suitable to receive the Palladium treatment. It was important that no other radar of the same type was in the vicinity, otherwise the signals would produce "running rabbits" interference on the other sets and arouse suspicion. The Palladium operations were run at night to reduce the chances of a Soviet plane intruding on the proceedings.[22]

The parameters of the Tall King early warning radar were easy enough to measure, since the equipment radiated for long periods. It was far more difficult to get the Fan Song missile control radar to radiate, and to achieve this the CIA mounted a Palladium operation off Cuba.[23]

One night a US destroyer carrying Palladium equipment moved into position off the north coast, remaining below the radar horizon. The repeater then generated a "ghost aircraft" on a Spoon Rest (P-12) surveillance and missile acquisition radar, looking as if it was about to make a high speed run towards Havana. A US submarine lay just outside Havana Bay, and at a predetermined time it surfaced and released several balloons carrying calibrated metal spheres of different sizes. The plan was to let the Spoon Rest radar track the incoming "ghost" aircraft. As the latter neared the coast it was hoped the Fan Song would switch on and initiate a missile engagement. The smallest calibrated sphere reported seen by the Fan Song operators would indicate the radar cross section of the smallest target they could observe.[24]

Although the operation produced the required information, there were moments of excitement. Cuban fighters were scrambled and directed to the point where the submarine had launched the balloons. To draw the fighters away from the submarine, the Palladium crew ran their "ghost aircraft" out of the area at high speed then turned off the repeater. In the meantime the submarine had dived. The baffled fighter pilots scoured the area for several minutes then, finding nothing, they returned to base.[25]

Palladium had been initiated to determine the capability of the Soviet air defense radars against the Oxcart stealth aircraft. The program established that the Tall King and Fan Song radars were better at detecting and tracking small targets than had previously been supposed. The vulnerability analysis concluded that Oxcart could be detected and tracked by the Soviets.[26]

Despite that finding, the CIA continued with the Oxcart program. A reconnaissance aircraft that could sustain speeds in excess of Mach 3.5 at altitudes around 90,000 feet would still be a valuable asset. The Lockheed A-12 aircraft made its maiden flight in April 1962 from the remote Groom Dry Lake airfield in the Mojave Desert in California. We shall return to this aircraft in a later chapter.

In the early 1960s Chuck Christman was a civilian engineer attached to Navy reconnaissance squadron VQ-1 based at Atsugi in Japan. There he ran the Special Configurations workshop, making non-standard changes to the electronic receiver suites of the unit's Lockheed EC-121 Warning Star ELINT planes. If someone wanted to do non-standard collection, the workshop would try to produce the required hardware by modifying what was available.

Chuck Christman's *tour de force* was the imaginative Brigand system for "capturing" the plan position indicator picture from a non-cooperating (i.e. hostile) radar. The principle of operation was as follows. When a high powered radar's transmissions strike an object—a plane, a ship, a coastline or a hillside—a minute proportion of the energy returns to the radar. The reflected energy travels in several other directions, however. If there is a sufficiently sensitive receiver aboard a plane up to two hundred miles from the radar, it can also pick up that reflected energy. By running a rotating time base in synchronism with the victim radar's scanner, and with a dash of electronic trickery, the victim radar's picture can be recreated on the Brigand screen. [27]

Brigand worked only against surveillance radars whose antennas rotated through the full 360-degree scan pattern. It showed topographical features such as hillsides or coastlines and large objects such as warships, but could not provide continual tracking on small objects such as aircraft. The ability to reproduce the victim radar's ground clutter pattern proved extremely useful, however, allowing the location of static radars with greater speed and accuracy than was possible using triangulation methods. The operator tuned Brigand to the victim radar's frequency and performed a few adjustments, then took a long exposure photograph of the screen during one full rotation of the time base—about ten seconds. The scope picture carried distortions, but using a computer program these could be corrected mathematically on the ground.[28]

As has been said, Brigand worked only against a surveillance radar whose antenna rotated through the full 360-degree scan pattern. The system did not work with radars operating in the sector-scanning mode, which ruled out airborne intercept radars, nodding height-finders and most types of missile and gun control radar.

By mid-1964, Brigand was fully operational aboard the Navy EC-121 planes of VQ-1 operating over the Pacific, and VQ-2 operating over the

Atlantic and the Mediterranean. Then an extensive program was launched to re-locate the position of every observable surveillance radar throughout the territory of the Soviet Union and her allies.[29]

It must be stressed that Brigand gathered its information completely passively. The aircraft carrying it did not need to radiate, or do anything else that might betray its position.

Several items of intelligence amassed by programs described in this chapter would soon find application. For, as we shall observe, the war in Vietnam was escalating rapidly and there was increasing involvement by US forces. The US electronic warfare community was about to face its sternest challenge since the end of World War II.

References to Chapter 1

1. Interview Pat Scott
2. Interview Gene Poteat
3. *Ibid.*
4. *Ibid.*
5. *Ibid.*
6. *Ibid.*
7. *Ibid.*
8. Interview Joe Bert
9. *Ibid.*
10. *Ibid.*
11. Interview Roy Fair
12. *Ibid.*
13. *Ibid.*
14. Interview Dave Brog
15. *Ibid.*
16. *Ibid.*
17. *Ibid.*
18. Poteat Interview
19. *Ibid.*
20. *Ibid.*
21. *Ibid.*
22. Poteat, Gene, "Stealth, Countermeasures, and ELINT, 1960–1975", unclassified article in classified US intelligence journal
23. *Ibid.*
24. *Ibid.*
25. *Ibid.*
26. *Ibid.*
27. Interview Chuck Christman
28. *Ibid.*
29. *Ibid.*

Chapter 2

CRISIS IN A DISTANT LAND

August 1964 to October 1965

"The canons have their bowels full of wrath
And ready mounted are they to spit forth
Their iron indignation."
Shakespeare: *King John*

By the summer of 1964 the US military involvement in South Vietnam was increasing rapidly. What had started with a few hundred US Special Forces troops and military advisors had grown into a major military commitment.

On 5 August 1964, following an inconclusive skirmish involving US warships and North Vietnamese patrol boats,[1] President Johnson ordered retaliatory air strikes against naval facilities in North Vietnam. Sixty-four Navy planes attacked the port at Quang Khe and the fuel storage area at Vinh. AAA shot down two aircraft, and two others returned with battle damage.[2]

In the months that followed the guerrilla war in South Vietnam intensified, as did the US retaliatory air strikes. In March 1965, US forces in the theater commenced Operation Rolling Thunder, a program of sustained air attacks on targets in North Vietnam. On 2 March more than a hundred F-100s, F-105s and B-57s attacked the ammunition depot at Xom Bong causing serious damage. Two F-100s and three F-105s were shot down by AAA.[3]

Intelligence officers at Pacific Air Force (PACAF) headquarters had carried out their first analysis of the North Vietnamese air defense system in November 1961. The early warning radar chain then consisted of a few old Soviet-built RUS and Knife Rest (P-8 and P-10) equipments.[4] By August 1964 the radar network had expanded to about twenty-two early warning sets and four Whiff (SON-4) gun control radars. Early in 1965 Navy EC-121 aircraft of VQ-1 ran a Brigand operation to plot the positions of surveillance radars in North Vietnam.[5]

The first North Vietnamese fighter unit, the 921st "Red Star" Fighter Wing, completed training with MiG-17 fighters in the summer of 1964. Following the initial US attacks the unit began flying patrols, but kept clear of US raiding forces.[6]

Meanwhile the Soviet and Chinese governments began sending large numbers of AAA weapons to North Vietnam, and several Whiff and Fire Can (SON-9) gun control radars.[7] Neither radar was modern, but the AAA losses testified to their accurate fire direction. During the first seven months of 1965 fifty-one Air Force and Navy jets were lost over North Vietnam, mostly to AAA.[8] The US attack fighters were the most advanced in the world, yet they were falling to relatively unsophisticated weaponry.

To keep pace with these developments, six Douglas RB-66C aircraft deployed to Tan Son Nhut near Saigon in May 1965. This aircraft carried a crew of six; pilot, navigator and four EWOs. There were four radar receiver positions, and the plane carried nine jamming equipments and a chaff dispenser. RB-66Cs accompanied strike forces flying into North Vietnam, providing threat warnings and jamming gun control radars.[9]

On paper the US Air Force already possessed a jamming system that could counter the Soviet-made gun control radars, one designed to fit on an underwing weapons pylon of a fighter plane. Produced under a Quick Reaction Capability contract, the QRC-160-1 jamming pod was 8 feet 4 inches long, had a diameter of 10 inches at its widest point and weighed less than 100 pounds. The QRC-160-1 operated in the D/E band and was optimized for use against ground-based gun and missile control radars.[10] General Electric produced about 150 QRC-160-1 pods for Tactical Air Command (TAC). The Command showed little interest in the pods, however, and shipped most of them to Kadena AB, Okinawa, where they went straight into storage.

Over North Vietnam the aircraft type at greatest risk from AAA was the RF-101C Voodoo reconnaissance plane. Flying singly or in pairs, these made high speed photographic runs through target areas at low or medium altitude and often drew heavy fire. In June 1965 a small batch of QRC-160 pods arrived in South Vietnam for fitting to RF-101s of the 15th Tactical Reconnaissance Squadron at Tan Son Nhut.[11]

Captain Tony Brees was on assignment at Ton San Nhut from HQ Thirteenth Air Force, having previously served as an electronic warfare officer with Strategic Air Command. The QRC-160 project was not part of his job, but he was one of the few people on the base who knew anything about electronic warfare. He soon learned at first-hand of PACAF's antipathy to electronic warfare systems:

> "PACAF had no great desire to have the pods in the first place, they had been pushed on them. The attitude was, 'Another inch of throttle and another bomb, and I'll go any place in the world. Just tell me where the

target is.' The pods were built as a QRC equipment, they never went through any fault testing. They had been stored on Okinawa, ready for use on F-100s and F-105s flying their wartime nuclear penetration missions. The guys figured that when the pods were needed they would just bring them out of store, clamp them straight on the planes and off the pilot would go… "[12]

That failed to recognize the fact that electronic systems, like airplanes, deteriorate if they are left unused for any length of time. There were other problems. When the jamming pods arrived at Ton San Nhut there were no trained maintenance personnel or test equipment at the base. Working from unfamiliar manuals, ground crews fitted three RF-101 Voodoo reconnaissance planes each with four pods, two each on a pylon under each wing. The intention was for a pod-fitted aircraft to accompany a "clean" RF-101 which was to take the photographs. As the pair approached the target, the photographic aircraft was to accelerate to maximum speed to make its photographic run. The trailing plane, slowed by the drag from the four pods, then jammed the gun control radar.[13]

When the tactic was tested over North Vietnam, pilots reported that AAA fire was just as vicious and no less accurate. To discover whether the QRC-160-1 pods radiated effectively, a podded RF-101 was flown against a US surveillance radar in South Vietnam. Tony Brees continued:

"The first mission was launched, and they got no jamming power. They couldn't duplicate the fault on the ground, and on the next mission, there was still no power. In the meantime, inoperable pods were collecting in the repair facility and nobody knew how to fix them. Somebody opened one up, and found several capacitors and resistors that had broken off the cards. The low frequency vibration, caused when planes taxied out over uneven concrete, had shaken them off. No wonder they couldn't get any power out of those pods!"[14]

To get the pods fit for action, Logistics Command sent a team of experts from Wright-Patterson AFB. The working pods were filled with a potting material that solidified and held the electronic components in place. Yet the reliability of the QRC-160 remained poor, and finally PACAF rejected the pods and returned them to the US. [15]

Initially AAA had been the only air defense system facing US aircrews over North Vietnam. Then, in April 1965, the MiG-17 force went into action. This obsolescent subsonic interceptor, armed with cannon and with no search radar, seemed no match for the modern supersonic US fighters it sought to engage. However, other factors tilted the balance in the MiGs' favor.

US attack fighters carrying bombs cruised at subsonic speeds, so they were vulnerable to attack from their subsonic opponent. The MiG-17 was nimble and small, and its smoke-free engine made it difficult to detect. It operated under tight ground control and took off only when the controller saw a favorable opportunity to engage. The MiGs usually delivered a single snap attack, then broke away and headed for home.

On the morning of 3 April, six MiG-17s scrambled from Noi Bai to engage Navy planes attacking the Than Hoa bridge. In the ensuing combat the North Vietnamese pilots claimed the destruction of two F-8s. In fact only one Crusader suffered damage. No MiG was hit, though one nearly ran out of fuel and made a forced landing.[16]

On the following day the MiG-17s went into action again. The striking force comprised forty-eight F-105Ds escorted by F-100D Super Sabres and Navy F-4Bs, and again the target was the Than Hoa bridge. Eight MiG-17s engaged and they shot down two F-105s. AAA brought down another Thunderchief. The escorting Super Sabres then retaliated and claimed one MiG-17 probably destroyed. In fact they shot down three MiGs and harried a fourth until it nearly ran out of fuel and made a forced landing in open country.[17]

An obvious way to warn US aircraft of the approach of MiGs was to provide radar surveillance of the combat area. A radar near Nakhon Phanom AB, close to the Thai/Laos border, gave useful cover over North Vietnam at medium and high altitudes. It could not observe MiGs flying at low altitude, however.[18]

In a move to resolve this problem, in April 1965 a small force of Lockheed EC-121D Big Eye radar picket planes arrived at Tan Son Nhut AB. The plane carried the big APS-20 surveillance radar with a theoretical maximum range of about 130 miles, and a height finder. Both radars were elderly, however, and they were much affected by ground clutter.

The EC-121Ds followed the movements of US planes by interrogating their IFF (identification friend or foe) transponders. The EC-121Ds observed MiGs flying above 8,000 feet, but their information was not precise enough for accurate fighter control.[19]

In July 1965 the USS *Independence* arrived on Yankee Station (the Navy operational area off South Vietnam), and Attack Squadron VA-75 took the Grumman A-6A Intruder into action for the first time. The A-6 carried the Sanders ALQ-51 and would be the first type to fly in combat with a deception countermeasures system. [20]

At this time Navy Captain Julian Lake held the post of OP 352 at the Pentagon, responsible for overseeing the Navy's air electronic warfare systems. Like many others, he saw that small attack planes like the A-4 Skyhawk needed electronic warfare protection to survive over defended areas. The ALQ-51 fitted into boxes with a total volume of 2.3 cubic feet, and Lake found room for it in the A-4's gun bay, in place of half the 20-mm ammunition.[21] Satisfied with the feasibility of the scheme, Lake drafted a proposal to build a prototype installation in an A-4.

On 5 April 1965 a Navy RF-8A Crusader returned to the carrier *Coral Sea* after a photographic mission to the Hanoi area. Its pictures revealed the distinctive "Star of David" road pattern of an SA-2 missile site under construction some 15 miles southeast of the capital.[22] Air Force and Navy staff officers planned an air strike on the missile site, but President Johnson vetoed the idea. The fear was that such an attack might cause deaths among the Soviet or Chinese advisors at the site, and provoke increased intervention from their respective nations.[23]

Work on the sites around Hanoi continued without pause. By 4 July four sites were ready or nearly ready for occupation. On 23 July an RB-66C ELINT aircraft picked up signals from a Fan Song missile control radar undergoing testing.[24]

On 24 July eight F-4C Phantoms of the 47th Tactical Fighter Squadron were escorting F-105s attacking the explosives manufacturing plant at Kangchi northwest of Hanoi.[25] Suddenly the pilot of Leopard Two noticed a "flying telephone pole" emerge from cloud and streak towards the right side of the formation. He pulled his aircraft out its path just in time. "Before I could press the mike button," the pilot later recalled, "it had detonated under the formation."[26] The warhead went off close to Leopard Four, and only the pilot ejected from the tumbling fighter. The three other Phantoms in the flight suffered minor damage. Another missile then emerged from the undercast but the alerted fighter crews outmaneuvered it relatively easily.

Before describing the moves to counter the new threat, we need to look at the SA-2's "kill chain". Each link in the chain had to be intact if a missile battery was engage successfully. The process began when a surveillance radar detected the aircraft and determined its range, bearing, approximate altitude and approximate flight path. Usually a Spoon Rest radar performed that task. The information was passed to the Fan Song narrow-beam missile control radar, to point it in the right part of the sky to find the aircraft. Once the Fan Song had picked up the aircraft, its operators tracked the machine to determine its precise position and flight path. During the tracking process the missile control computer calculated the impact point ahead of the plane, where the missile needed to go to achieve a kill. Provided the desired impact point lay within range, a pair of Guideline missiles would then be launched.

The Guideline missile had no means of homing on an aircraft. It was command guided, in much the same way as a radio-controlled model airplane is steered in flight. Each missile carried a radar beacon so it could be tracked in flight. Knowing the position of the aircraft and each missile, the control computer generated commands to steer the latter on to the predicted impact point. If the target aircraft turned to evade, the computer recalculated the impact point and transmitted revised guidance signals to correct the missiles' flight paths. The Guideline missile carried a radar proximity fuse, which detonated the warhead when it detected an aircraft within lethal range.

The SA-2 kill chain was vulnerable at several points, but it required specialized systems to attack many of these and they would take time to develop. Meanwhile, tactical fighter units operating over North Vietnam had to cope with the new threat with the equipment they had.

Initially only high priority targets were to be attacked in missile-defended areas, and aircraft were routed clear of the latter whenever possible. An RB-66C or EA-3B ELINT aircraft accompanied each raiding force, to warn the fighters if it picked up Fan Song radar signals. In missile-defended areas fighters kept below 4,000 feet, where the SA-2 was relatively ineffective. These tactics held down losses from missiles, but they placed aircraft in the engagement envelope of medium caliber AAA weapons. As a result, losses from these weapons rose.

An obvious point of vulnerability was the SA-2 missile site itself, and following the loss of the Phantom the ban on attacking these was rescinded. The first such attack, Operation "Iron Hand", took place on 27 July. Fifty-four F-105s set out to hit the two SA-2 sites thought to have fired at Leopard flight. Flying one of the F-105s was Captain Chuck Horner serving with the 18th TFW based at Korat:

> "The first indication of trouble came as we headed north toward the target. 'Buick Lead in the river' informed all that the Lead Takhli Thud (F-105) was down. To my left I saw Bob Purcell's F-105 rise up out of a cloud of dust with its entire underside on fire, roll over and go straight in. We were doing 650 knots, carrying cans of napalm that were limited to 375 knots. I looked out to the left and saw anti-aircraft artillery lined up in rows with their barrels depressed, fire belching forth from their ends. Looking up, I saw the familiar black, greasy clouds with orange centers as the shells burst over our jets, which were now scraping banana and palm trees. Emergency beepers began to fill our radio as we scanned the ground for the target. Seeing something, we let go of our ordnance and broke left to safety, west of the Red River. Ahead of us, Capt. Bill Barthelmus asked Maj. Jack Farr to look over his jet as they crossed the Mekong River, but Bill's flight controls failed just as Jack positioned himself over the stricken F-105. The jets collided, killing both."[27]

This disastrous attack cost six F-105s and an RF-101 reconnaissance plane, none of them to a missile. Returning pilots reported considerable damage at both missile sites. Later, however, photographic reconnaissance established that the "radars" and "missile launchers" attacked were wooden dummies. Expecting such an attack, the North Vietnamese had moved the precious new hardware well clear of the sites.[28]

11 August, the Navy lost an A-4E to a missile. On the following two
ines from the carriers *Midway* and *Coral Sea* scoured the area for the
g missile site. They failed to find it, but lost five aircraft to AAA in the
attempt.[29]

To complicate the process of locating SA-2 batteries, North Vietnamese
firing units shuttled between a number of prepared sites within a few miles of
each other. From the initial order to move, a firing unit took about three
hours to close down at one site and between four and six hours to set up at a
new site.

Those early attacks on SAM sites produced several lessons. The sites were
difficult targets, well-protected by AAA which caused more losses than the
missiles. The AAA and missile units worked in close co-ordination and their
commanders had shown tactical imagination. The SAM sites were well
camouflaged and to deliver an effective first-pass attack, aircrews needed a
means to locate these targets from a distance. Also the North Vietnamese
exploited the SA-2's mobility; once an active missile site was found it had to
be hit quickly, because in a few hours it would be empty. In the next chapter
we shall observe US reactions to this development.

References to Chapter 2

1. Bowman, John S, ed., *Vietnam War*, World Almanac, New York, 1985, pp 83–84
2. Dorr, Robert, *Air War Hanoi*, Sterling Publishing New York, 1988, p 10
3. Dorr p 20
4. Pierson, James, *Electronic Warfare in SEA 1964–1968*, USAF Security Service, 1973, p 9
5. Correspondence Chuck Christman
6. Buza, Zoltán, "MiG-17 over Vietnam," published in *Wings of Fame*, Volume 8, p 100
7. Pierson, p 10
8. USAF and US Navy Official Loss List, declassified official document
9. Pierson, p 67
10. Seefluth, August, "The Birth of Pods," *Air Force*, February 1992
11. Interview Tony Brees
12. *Ibid*
13. *Ibid*
14. *Ibid*
15. *Ibid*
16. Toperczer, Istvan, *Air War Over North Viet Nam, The Vietnamese Peoples' Air Force 1949–1977*, Squadron/Signal Publications, Carrollton, Texas, 1998, pp 10-11
17. *Ibid*

18. Michel, Marshall, *Clashes*, Naval Institute Press, Annapolis, Maryland, 1997, p 46 *et seq*
19. *Ibid*
20. Interview Admiral Julian Lake
21. *Ibid*
22. Barker, Captain Patrick, USAF, "The SA-2 and the Wild Weasel", MA Degree Thesis, Lehigh University, Pennsylvania, pp 9–10
23. Kearns, Doris, *Lyndon Johnson and the American Dream*, quoted in Barker, *op cit*, p 10
24. Pierson, p 14
25. Barker, p 10
26. Interview Pierre Levy
27. Horner, Charles, "First Person Singular," *Journal of Electronic Defense*, January 1999
28. *Ibid*
29. Barker, pp 72–3

Chapter 3

FIGHTING OFF THE SAMs

August 1965 to July 1966

*"Courage alone is not enough—in technical warfare
of this nature we must also have the best possible
weapons and, above all, be so well trained as to be
able to use those weapons effectively."*
General Douglas MacArthur

The shock waves from the loss of the Phantom over North Vietnam caused ripples of apprehension that spread far and wide. In its first engagement during this conflict, the SA-2 had knocked down one of the world's most advanced fighter planes.

On 13 August 1965, less than three weeks after the shoot-down, USAF Chief of Staff General John McConnell ordered the formation of a "SAM Task Force" to investigate ways to counter the Soviet missile system.[1] He appointed Brigadier Géneral Kenneth ("KC") Dempster, Deputy Director of Operational Requirements, to establish a high-powered committee to consider the matter. It was to include representatives of the Air Staff, the major air commands, industry and the scientific community.[2]

In the spring of 1965 Applied Technology Inc at Palo Alto had a workforce of about three hundred and was engaged in producing items of electronic equipment for US government "black" programs.

Ed Chapman, an ex-Air Force EWO, had recently joined the marketing department and knew the shortcomings of the aging APS-54 radar warning receiver carried in the B-52. He suggested that a new receiver with a cathode ray tube to show the threat bearing, and some means of identifying its frequency band, might interest SAC.[3]

Robert Johnson, a talented engineer at the company, took up the gauntlet. Earlier, for the CIA, the company had built the System XII lightweight radar warning receiver for installation in the U-2 spyplane. That receiver used state-of-the-art electronic miniaturization techniques and was far in advance of any other radar-warning receiver in existence at that time.[4]

Johnson re-designed the System XII to work as Chapman had outlined. The new receiver, called the Vector, covered 2 GHz to 12 GHz in three bands. The 3-inch diameter scope showed the direction of the threat as a strobe originating from its center. To assist radar identification, the operator could listen to its scan pattern. The Vector receiver had no moving parts and was considerably smaller and more effective than the APS-54.[5]

Ed Chapman arranged to show the new receiver to an Air Force buddy working in the B-52 Project Office in the Pentagon. Between the original request and the presentation itself, the F-4 had been shot down by an SA-2. Ed Chapman arrived at the Pentagon with Robert Johnson expecting to meet some junior ranking B-52 people. The reality was rather different:

> "Bob and I walked into the conference room and there was General Dempster at the head of the table with about twenty officers. Andy had convinced the general that he might like to hear our presentation. It was a marketing man's dream: a room full of senior officers all willing to listen. This was not the meeting I had requested; it was much better.
>
> We set up a signal generator and antenna system on a pedestal in the middle of the conference table. I gave an introduction saying what we were about to do. Then Bob proceeded to tell them how the Vector receiver worked. Then we walked around the room with the prototype, to demonstrate the equipment's direction-finding capabilities."[6]

The AT representatives answered several questions, then they were dismissed. They thought they had made a good impression.

The demonstration for General Dempster and his staff established a valuable line of communication between his office and Applied Technology. That line also carried details of the company's new IR-133 panoramic scanning receiver, for homing on radars operating in the 2–4 GHz band. Like the Vector, the IR-133 drew heavily on previous work for "black" programs.[7]

General Dempster's staff conceived the idea of using the IR-133 to hunt for SAM launching sites, by homing on emissions from their missile control radars. As originally envisioned a plane would mark the missile site with smoke rockets, then accompanying attack fighters would deliver more lethal ordnance.

Having devised what looked like a workable solution, no time was wasted in bringing this to reality. Dr John Grigsby, AT's Vice President for Engineering at the time, recalled:

> "At the end of August, Major Pierre Levy from General Dempster's office called me. It was almost 5 p.m. our time, so it was nearly 8 p.m. Pierre's time in the Pentagon. He said 'I want to buy a couple of those IR-133 receivers that [a company representative] told us about.' I said 'We priced them out, a pair will cost $80,000.' Pierre said 'I've only got $40,000 but I

need two of them.' I said 'Two will cost you $80,000, Pierre.' His comment was 'If you do this for us, you won't get hurt in the long run.'

I went to see Bill Ayre, the company president, and told him what the Air Force wanted. I said I thought we ought to go along with them, and Bill agreed. So I went back to my office, picked up the phone and said, 'Pierre you've got a deal, two receivers for $40,000.'"[8]

A few days later Ed Chapman was summoned to a meeting in the Pentagon with Major Levy and his immediate boss Colonel Williamson. For the first time, he learned how the Air Force intended to use the Vector warning equipment:

"They said they were going to take some F-100s and put together some sort of EW system to home on enemy missile control radars. I was asked how soon we could have Vector systems available—we had only the one prototype. Those F-100s were to carry not only the Vector receiver, but also the IR-133 homing receiver."[9]

The requirement was for two sets of receivers to be built and installed in a pair of F-100Fs, code-named Wild Weasels, within forty-five days. After consulting his company president, Chapman said it would be possible to meet the harsh deadline.[10]

Early in 1965 the Army's Harry Diamond Laboratory at Washington delivered a SADS-1 equipment to the Eglin test range. The acronym stood for Soviet Air Defense Simulator #1, a working surrogate of the Fan Song Model B radar built using the best available intelligence. The external appearance of SADS-1 was nothing like a Fan Song as Marvin Thompson, one of those working on the radar, explained:

"Ours was not a van system like the real Fan Song, it was housed in a building. The antennas were under a radome, primarily for security but also because the antennas were not watertight. It was a complete radar with a transmitter and a receiver. The display was as much like that of the SA-2 as we knew at that time. SADS-1 was a fully instrumented system, and we were able to collect data for analysis. Our data was compared with that from an FPS-16 precision radar that tracked the aircraft's beacon, so we knew exactly where the aircraft was at any time. As a result we were able to measure missile miss distances, errors introduced by jamming, etc."[11]

As new intelligence on the Soviet system trickled in, SADS-1 was continually modified to conform with it. Following the Phantom shoot-down the simulator was in heavy use to test the various counters to the Soviet missile system.

The Navy was first to fit a small tactical aircraft with an active electronic system to counter the SA-2, and get it into action. Project "Shoe Horn" arose from Captain Julian Lake's proposal to install an ALQ-51 deception jamming system into an A-4 Skyhawk. Engineers from Sanders Associates, Douglas Aircraft and the Navy built a prototype installation and by the end of August 1965 it was ready for testing.

Navy Air Development Squadron 5 (VX 5) evaluated the effectiveness of the modified A-4, flying runs against the Navy's "Flint Stone" Fan Song surrogate radar at the Sanders Merrimack Test facility.[12] The ALQ-51 employed angle gate deception against Fan Song. When it received signals from the track-while-scan radar, the ALQ-51 re-transmitted pulses into the radar's side lobes but left the main lobe untouched. That induced errors into the radar's angle tracking system, making it appear that the target aircraft was some distance from its true position.

Following successful tests, at the end of September 1965 Sanders and Navy engineers flew to NAS Cubi Point in the Philippines with a batch of ALQ-51s and installation kits. In the following month, Skyhawks aboard the USS *Constellation* went into action carrying the equipment. Once sufficient A-4s had been fitted with the deception system to cover initial needs, F-4s and F-8s were similarly modified.[13]

Navy aircrews usually flew with the ALQ-51 in the standby mode, until they observed signs that a gun or missile battery was engaging them. Then they turned on the repeater and its deception signals caused the radar's automatic angle tracking system to wander. Missiles launched under those conditions received a series of over-corrections that made them miss the target. To overcome the problem Fan Song operators could switch to manual operation and track the aircraft's skin echo on their scopes. That increased the missile system's reaction time, however, and a moderate turn by the aircraft was usually sufficient to throw off the missile. If that failed, the pilot would jettison external stores and resort to a more violent evasive maneuver.[14]

Initially the ALQ-51's reliability was poor, though when the equipment functioned properly it proved its worth. For planes with operable deception systems, the loss rate to SAMs was about one plane per fifty missiles fired. That compared with one plane per ten missiles fired if no ALQ-51 was fitted or if the equipment malfunctioned. There were insufficient ALQ-51s to equip every front-line unit, so as an air group left the combat zone its systems were cross-decked to the air group replacing it.[15]

At this time the Navy lacked an effective carrier-based standoff jamming aircraft. The only plane equipped for the task was the old piston-engined Douglas A-1 "Queer Spad" (later redesignated the EA-1F), which lacked the performance to survive over defended areas in North Vietnam.

Casting around for an aircraft to fill the requirement, Julian Lake's eyes fell on the twinjet Douglas A-3 Skywarrior (the Navy version of the Air Force's

Fighting Off the SAMs

B-66). This one-time heavy attack plane no longer operated in its original role and there were plenty in storage. Under the TACOS (tanker countermeasures) program, thirty-seven A-3s were converted to the EKA-3B configuration with a suite of jamming equipments and receivers, and a hose-and-drogue refueling unit in the bomb bay. Work began on the first conversions, but several months would elapse before the aircraft were ready for operations. [16]

The Marine air units operating over North Vietnam were rather better off than their Navy counterparts. Based at Da Nang about 100 miles south of the Demilitarized Zone (DMZ), Marine Composite Reconnaissance Squadron One (VMCJ-1) operated EF-10B Skyknight planes to provide jamming support to strike forces attacking targets in the DMZ and in the southern part of North Vietnam. The two-seater Skyknight had started life as a carrier-based night fighter and now carried up to six jammers, ALT-6Bs and ALT-2s, feeding high gain antennas mounted in the nose. It also carried passive receivers to provide electronic surveillance of the area and to set jammers on the radars' frequencies.[17]

In October 1965 the nine EB-66Cs (previously known as RB-66Cs) at Takhli, Thailand, were formed into the 41st Tactical Reconnaissance Squadron. Soon afterwards five EB-66Bs arrived from Europe to join the unit. Although externally it resembled the RB-66C, the EB-66B had no ELINT capability. In what previously had been the bomb bay it carried a pallet with twenty-three noise jammers. The frequency and bandwidth of each jammer was preset before take-off, and the operator had only an on/off control for each.[18]

Over North Vietnam the EB-66Cs continued with their previous task of providing warning of Fan Song transmissions. They and the EB-66Bs also provided jamming to cover the F-105s' ingress and egress routes. In addition the EB-66Bs jammed the IFF transmissions from MiG fighters in an attempt to complicate the task of fighter control.[19]

General Dempster wanted a radar-warning receiver in every USAF combat plane operating over North Vietnam, but first he needed to be sure that the system chosen was the best available. So he asked Major Levy to arrange a "fly before buy" competition at Eglin. Several companies took part. Each company fitted its receiver in a jet fighter, which flew a set number of sorties over the radar test range during a three-day period. Applied Technology's Vector receiver won the competition and was ordered into production as the APR-25.[20]

Throughout 1965 the construction of prepared sites for SA-2 firing units proceeded apace throughout North Vietnam. By the end of the year US reconnaissance planes had located sixty-four. Between ten and fifteen missile firing units played a deadly version of the Shell Game, moving erratically between the prepared sites. Between July and the end of December 1965 an estimated 194 missiles were launched at Air Force and Navy planes, and shot down eleven.

At the end of 1965 there were five F-105D squadrons in Thailand each with a nominal strength of eighteen aircraft, giving a total of ninety fighters. These aircraft bore the brunt of the air operations against North Vietnam, and the losses they suffered provide a barometer of effectiveness of the enemy defenses.

From the beginning of August to the end of 1965 twenty-nine F-105Ds were lost to enemy action over North Vietnam, nearly one third of the force's established strength. Missiles accounted for three fighters, while two fell to unknown causes. The other twenty-four Thunderchiefs fell to AAA fire, usually in areas where the threat of missile attack had forced the fighters to transit at low altitude.[21]

The difficulties confronting pilots at this time are exemplified by those experienced during the attack on the Lang Met bridge northwest of Hanoi on 5 October. Twenty-four F-105s of the 23rd Tactical Fighter Wing took off from Tahkli, each carrying two 3,000-pound bombs. The fighters were divided into six flights, with five-minute separation between each. As each flight neared the missile-defended area, it descended to 2,000 feet for the low altitude run-in. The Thunderchiefs accelerated to 520 knots but were hotly engaged by light and medium caliber AAA. At the Initial Point, three miles short of the target, each flight pulled into a steep climb to 7,000 feet to identify its target, then commenced its dive attack. After bomb release the F-105s returned to low altitude until they were clear of the missile-defended area. The attackers dropped one span of the bridge but took a pummeling from AAA. Two F-105s were shot down, fourteen others suffered battle damage and had to divert to Da Nang or Udorn.[22]

US fighter pilots soon discovered how to outmaneuver an upcoming Guideline missile, provided they saw it early enough. When a pilot saw a missile coming in his direction he turned to position it in the 10 o'clock or the 2 o'clock position from his cockpit, to give the best possible view of it. Then he applied full power and pushed the stick forward so the plane entered zero gravity and achieved maximum acceleration. Then he waited until the missile was about one mile away. Pilots were assured "Don't worry about that. When it's one mile away, you'll know!" At that point the pilot looked for the side of the missile. If he could see it, the missile was not heading for him and he need not worry about it further. If he could not see the side of the missile, the pilot made a turn and watched the missile to see if it adjusted its trajectory to follow him. If it did, that was the time for drastic measures. The pilot would haul on the stick to make a maximum rate pull-up, at about 6G. That gave the missile a maneuvering problem when it tried to follow, and usually the weapon flashed harmlessly past its intended victim.[23]

Provided it was executed in good time, that evasive maneuver was usually effective. However, to achieve the required agility F-105 pilots usually had to jettison their bombs. Also such maneuvers caused the raiding flight to scatter, leaving individual planes vulnerable to fighter attack.

Late in 1965 the F-105 force abandoned the policy of transiting through missile defended areas at low altitude. From then on the fighters would fly through these areas at around 18,000 feet, out of reach of most AAA. If a missile was seen approaching, the threatened F-105 flight would split up and the planes would react individually.

Although a lot was known about the SA-2, some aspects of its operation remained unclear. It was known that radio command signals guided the missiles in flight, but there had been only one tantalizingly short look at those signals by a monitoring station in Berlin. The so-called "uplink" and "downlink" beacon signals were still a mystery. These signals, transmitted from the Fan Song to a transponder in the missile, and from the missile transponder to the ground, enabled the Fan Song computer to track each missile in flight. A further area of uncertainty concerned the transmissions from the missile's radar proximity fuse.

The characteristics of these transmissions made interception difficult. The only place to be certain of picking them up was in the target aircraft during a successful missile engagement—shortly before the plane was blasted out of the sky!

To discover the answers to these important questions the CIA put together an intelligence operation, "United Effort". A few Ryan 147E drones were fitted with receivers covering the frequency bands thought to be used by the missile guidance signals, the transponder beacon and the missile fusing radar. The drones also carried transmitters to re-transmit any signals found. To make the drones attractive targets, each carried a radar echo enhancer.[24]

The first United Effort mission was early in October 1965, when a Lockheed DC-130 mother plane launched a drone into a missile defended zone in North Vietnam. Orbiting over the Gulf of Tonkin, a Boeing RB-47H ELINT aircraft of the 55th Strategic Reconnaissance Wing stood ready to collect signals relayed by the drone. It waited in vain, the missile batteries failed to respond.

The second mission, about a week later, was partially successful. A missile battery engaged the drone which picked up and relayed the pitch, yaw and roll guidance signals to the missile, as well as the downlink signals. Just before the missile's fusing radar came on, however, the drone ceased transmitting. A third United Effort mission, later that month, produced a similar result. Later, Ryan engineers ascribed the failures to overheating of part of the drone's equipment.[25]

On 13 February 1966 a DC-130 launched a modified Ryan 147E drone into the Thanh Hoa missile zone. This, the fourth United Effort mission, went according to plan. An SA-2 battery launched a pair of missiles which detonated close to the drone. Before it went down, however, the small plane had fulfilled its duty. The waiting RB-47H received not only the full sequences of guidance and downlink signals, but also the long-sought signals from the radar proximity fuse.

Some information yielded by United Effort would soon be exploited. The guidance signals, which came on within four seconds of missile launch,[26] provided clear evidence that a missile was on its way. A relatively simple receiver would warn crews of the threat. In the case of the downlink signals, as we will see later, nearly two years would elapse before that part of the system came under attack.

The proximity fuse signals, the most difficult of all to secure, were also the most difficult to jam effectively. Several schemes were proposed, but there was little time to initiate countermeasures between the start of transmissions and the time the warhead came within lethal range of the target. There was even a risk that triggering the warhead might increase rather than decrease the damage inflicted on the aircraft.[27]

Working with engineers from North American Aviation, Applied Technology installed Vector and IR-133 receivers in two Wild Weasel F-100F Super Sabres and completed the work in the stipulated forty-five day period. Once the equipments had been shown to work, two further F-100Fs were similarly modified.[28]

Following initial flight testing, the four F-100Fs flew to Eglin AFB where they were united with their crews. The pilots selected for the program had considerable flying time on the F-105 and the EWOs were experienced operators from SAC B-52 units. The men, all volunteers, had no idea of what they had let themselves in for.

After a few familiarization flights, training for the new role began in earnest. The crews flew test runs against the SADS-1 Fan Song surrogate at Eglin, with everybody on a steep learning curve. After the disastrous attempts to hit missile sites in North Vietnam, people knew which tactics did not work. The problem was, nobody knew for certain which tactics would work. The Wild Weasel crews devised procedures as they went along, and tested them during training flights. Nobody knew more about the subject than the trainees themselves.[29]

On learning details of the signals transmitted on the SA-2 command guidance channel, Applied Technology designed a further warning receiver to pick up those signals. If the guidance channel was active, that meant that enemy missiles were probably on their way and crews would get vital additional seconds in which to initiate countermeasures.

John Grigsby and Ed Chapman visited Major Levy in the Pentagon to discuss the proposed receiver. Levy agreed that if it could be made to work, the Air Force would certainly want to fit it into the Wild Weasel planes. The conference continued into the evening, after most of the administrative staff had gone home. It was important to begin detailed design work as soon as possible, but the company needed an official order. Accordingly, John Grigsby drew a block diagram of the new receiver on the blackboard in Pierre Levy's office. Levy chalked an order to the company to build a prototype receiver along those lines, and signed it. Then Grigsby wrote in his agreement to build such a receiver, and signed that. To provide an air of formality for what was probably an unenforceable contract, Levy then took a couple of Polaroid photographs of the contract and gave one to Grigsby and kept the other for himself.[30]

The new receiver carried the Applied Technology designation WR-300. Within a few days, the first hand-built examples had been delivered to the Air Force for installation in the F-100Fs.[31]

In November 1965 the Wild Weasel unit was judged ready for combat, and the four modified F-100Fs set out from Eglin for 60 days temporary duty in Thailand. The ground support party went out by Military Airlift Command. The Super Sabres reached Korat on Thanksgiving Day, in time for their crews to join the celebratory supper. Once established at Korat, the small force made final preparations to begin operations.

On 28 November, the F-100Fs made their first orientation flights over enemy territory. Teamed with an RB-66C and keeping outside SAM range, the EWOs in the converted fighters observed and recorded the mass of radar signals coming from North Vietnam and China. On that day and the next two, the F-100Fs flew eight orientation sorties.[32]

On 1 December 1965 the Wild Weasels set out on their first Iron Hand mission over North Vietnam. Major Williard and Captain Lifsey in one F-100F, and Captains White and Sandelius in another, each led a flight of F-105s to "troll" past a missile site. Each Super Sabre carried two pods of 2.75-inch unguided rockets, the F-105Ds carried various armament loads. The mission failed to stir any response from SA-2 sites, however, nor did several similar missions in the weeks to follow.

Wild Weasel F-100Fs had their first serious encounter with enemy defenses on 20 December. Accompanying an attack force heading for the Vu Chua railroad bridge northeast of Hanoi, Captains Pitchford and Trier led twelve F-105s. In another F-100F, Captains Schwartz and Donovan led eight more. Low cloud forced the raiders to descend below 4,000 feet. Trier picked up Fan Song signals and commenced a homing, but then the Super Sabre took hits from AAA and caught fire. The crew ejected, Pitchford was taken prisoner but Trier was killed. It was a sobering moment; the Wild Weasel unit had suffered its first losses before it delivered a successful attack. It was a bad day for all concerned. One F-105 was also shot down and the bridge remained standing.[33]

A contributory factor to the loss of the Wild Weasel F-100F had been the presence of a low overcast, which forced the crew to descend to low altitude within lethal range of AAA. Under new rules of engagement, Iron Hand operations needed clear skies up to 8,000 feet above ground level on approach and exit routes where an active SAM site was suspected. Unless that condition was met, F-100Fs were not to attempt to engage a missile site.[34]

Over North Vietnam the Wild Weasel operation was far more difficult than on the range at Eglin. The enemy radars were small, usually well hidden and liable to cease transmitting at any time. Moreover, the presence of AAA defenses around missile sites made repeat runs hazardous.

The Weasel force soon exacted revenge for the initial shootdown. On 22 December Captains Al Lamb and Jack Donovan led four F-105s in a strike on a suspected missile site, in support of an F-105 attack on the Yen Bai rail yard northwest of Hanoi. Donovan later described the action:

"Right after we crossed the border, the Vector started picking up a Fan Song. The NVA [North Vietnamese Army] were alerted but hadn't found us yet. Lamb started down to both mask our presence and increase our speed. We would pop up over the next hill and I'd get a new bearing, then roll over and down into the valley. Up—'12 o'clock!', then back down. After about five minutes of this we hit a long, flat valley area leading directly to the Red River. Bang! The Vector scope had a 2½-ring strobe. The Fan Song was now in Hi PRF, meaning they were looking right at us.... There was one long hill left between us and the Fan Song and Al dropped down behind it. But instead of going up over it, Al turned down its length and began to go around it. As we passed around the hill, the Vector lit up all three rings but now at six o'clock. 'Six o'clock! Six o'clock!' I yelled. Lamb popped up from 300 feet to about 1300 and started looking for the site visually. Nothing there—some fields, a tiny village and some rice paddies. Oops! Now we had a second Fan Song to our right, and a few Fire Can signals thrown in for good measure. The Vector scope started looking like a Christmas tree."[35]

Lamb pulled the Super Sabre up to 2500 feet and caught sight of the Fan Song control van sitting in the village itself. Nearby he spotted three white-painted missiles protruding from under thatched roofs. He aligned himself on the missile launchers and fired both pods of rockets. Then he ran in to strafe the site with 20-mm cannon.

Donovan continued:

"The rockets hit short but the 20 mm fire walked right into one of the missiles, exploding it. The F-105 flight picked out the smoke and fire and started their runs. Spruce Two's rockets also hit short but his 20-mm fire hit the control van. Spruce Three's rockets hit the van squarely and the Fan Song went off the air. Spruce Four fired his rockets, one pod at a time, aiming at the hut covering the SA-2s on their launchers. Spruce Five spread his rockets all over the village area."[36]

The five aircraft strafed the missile site, inflicting severe damage. Then, unscathed, the flight returned to Korat. Al Lamb and Jack Donovan received the Distinguished Flying Cross for their parts in the action.

Initially Wild Weasel planes employed unguided rockets, napalm, cluster bombs and cannon fire during attacks on missile sites. In the spring of 1966 the AGM-45 Shrike, the first successful antiradiation missile, appeared in the operational theater. Shrike was first used on 18 April 1966, during an Iron Hand operation by three F-105Ds led by a Wild Weasel F-100F. The Wild Weasel crew picked up signals from a Fire Can AAA control radar near Dong Hoi and launched the missile in its direction. Shortly afterwards the radar fell silent and was not heard to resume transmissions.[37]

Shrike was a considerable advance over the unguided ordnance used previously, but against SA-2 its performance left much to be desired. Launched horizontally, Shrike had a maximum range of about 8 miles and it attained a speed of about Mach 2. The SA-2, in contrast, had a maximum range of about 13 miles and reached maximum speeds around Mach 3. To bridge part of the gap, fighter crews delivered Shrike in lofted attacks in which the aircraft pulled into a high speed 30-degree climb to impart maximum energy to the missile before launch. The lofted attack increased the range of Shrike to about 12 miles, and its steeper trajectory increased its angle of impact and increased its chances of damaging the radar.[38]

Even if a Shrike homed accurately, its 50-pound blast-fragmentation warhead inflicted damage only in the immediate vicinity of the Fan Song radar van. To knock out the entire firing unit required a far greater weight of explosive.[39]

In January 1966 General Dempster took stock of the Wild Weasel project. Despite the loss of a Super Sabre and crew, the operational tests demonstrated the potential of the new tactic. Of the methods considered to counter enemy missile sites, this offered the greatest prospect of success. Yet if crews were to survive in the new role they needed the best possible equipment, and the F-100F was less than ideal. With external stores it cruised about 100 knots slower than the accompanying F-105s. The latter were unwilling to reduce speed while over defended areas, so had to weave from side to side to maintain station on the F-100F lead ship.[40] General Dempster accordingly secured funding for a small number of F-105F two-seaters to be modified for the Wild Weasel role.

The General also saw that crews needed specialized training, and recommended that a unit be formed for this purpose. Accordingly the 4537th Fighter Weapons School, the "Wild Weasel College", was established at Nellis AFB. Initially the course lasted four weeks, later extended to six weeks. Crews who had taken part in the early operations instructed at the school. By now people knew that, although the mission was difficult, it was do-able.[41]

During May 1966 the first ten Weasel-modified F-105Fs arrived at Korat, some with a further additional receiver to provide warning of impending missile launch. The See-Sams equipment, carried in addition to the WR-300, illuminated a warning light when the aircraft was centered in the azimuth and elevation beam patterns of a Fan Song radar. That meant final tracking had begun and missile launch was imminent.[42]

The next batch of F-105Fs went to the Takhli Wing. Captain Mike Gilroy, an F-105F back seater, arrived there to find a welcome that was less-than-wholehearted:

> "It was a pretty rocky start, we were not well accepted when we got out there. The other pilots didn't know what the Wild Weasels were for, didn't think they were needed. Although the F-105s were taking heavy losses, their pilots didn't see us as a solution to their problem. And at the start we didn't do a lot to build respect, because we didn't know a lot about the role."[43]

On 3 June the F-105F flew its first Wild Weasel mission over enemy territory, led by an F-100F. On 6 June F-105Fs led an Iron Hand mission for the first time, without success. On the next day, the F-105F flew its first successful operation and attacked a GCI radar station.

During its early missions the F-105F was armed with two pods of 2.75-inch rockets, later supplemented by a pair of Shrikes. On occasions the accompanying F-105Ds carried Shrikes, in which case the Wild Weasel aircraft led the Shrike carrier into the lofted attack and told the pilot when to launch the missile. Crews saw their role as "hunter-killers", the more genteel term "defense suppression" had yet to enter their tactical lexicon.[44]

SAMs and AAA were not the only hazards confronting the Wild Weasel crews. On 29 June a flight struck at a Fan Song radar but then came under attack from four MiG-17s. One F-105F took hits but the aircraft all returned safely.[45]

On 5 July 1966 a Wild Weasel fought the wildest action to date. Majors Bill Robinson and Peter Tsouprake in an F-105F led three F-105Ds of Eagle flight. North of Hanoi Tsouprake picked up signals from six different missile sites. Robinson headed for the strongest signal and launched a Shrike. The missile vanished into a cloud bank, and when the F-105F emerged on the other side the pilot picked out the missile site. The Shrike had been launched at too great a range and the receivers indicated that the Fan Song was still radiating. Shortly afterwards the site launched a pair of missiles at the Thunderchiefs which the latter evaded. One F-105D fired two pods of rockets at the site. Another missile site joined in the fight and Robinson launched his remaining Shrike at it. At the same time Eagle Two came upon yet another SAM site and launched two pods of rockets at the radar van, causing secondary explosions. Yet another SA-2 site launched more missiles, which the F-105s evaded. Finally, the Thunderchiefs closed on that last site and used the remainder of their ordnance against it. All the planes returned safely.[46]

During July the last F-100F Super Sabre departed Korat. Though the F-105F Thunderchiefs which took over had a far better performance, that did not render them immune to losses. During the next six weeks four F-105Fs were lost in action. It required no great mathematical brain to calculate that a Weasel crew's chances of completing a tour of one hundred combat missions were disconcertingly close to zero.

From then on, however, Weasel losses fell and during the remainder of 1966 only one more F-105F was lost in action.[47] Several factors contributed to this change. The crews that survived the initial bout of losses had quickly gained in experience. They also became more diligent in applying the hard-won lessons, and less inclined to take needless risks.

As the Wild Weasel units established themselves in the theater, they made life progressively more hazardous for those manning the North Vietnamese missile and gun control radars.

Meanwhile a different and more effective counter to the SA-2 had been developed in the US. Yet, for doctrinal reasons it would take several months to introduce it. Until that happened, US attack fighter units operating over North Vietnam were condemned to further heavy losses.

References to Chapter 3

1. Quoted in Barker, Patrick, "The SA-2 and the Wild Weasel", MA Degree Thesis, p 49
2. *Ibid.*, p 9–12
3. Interview Ed Chapman
4. *Ibid.*
5. *Ibid.*
6. *Ibid.*
7. Interview John Grigsby
8. *Ibid.*
9. Chapman
10. *Ibid.*
11. Interview Marvin Thompson
12. Ward, Ed, *History of Airborne ECM*, unpublished monograph produced by Sanders Associates Inc, undated, p 13.
13. Pierson, James, *Electronic Warfare in SEA 1964-1968*, USAF Security Service 1973, p 150
14. Ward
15. Interview Julian Lake

16. *Ibid.*
17. Ward
18. Pierson, 66 *et seq*
19. *Ibid*
20. Interview Pierre Levy
21. USAF and US Navy Official Loss List
22. Dorr, Robert, *Air War Hanoi*, Sterling Publishing, 1988, pp 36–7
23. Interview Donald Kilgus.
24. Wagner, William, *Lightning Bugs*, Aero Publishers Inc, Fallbrook, CA, 1982, p 102.
25. *Ibid*
26. Levy
27. *Ibid.*
28. Chapman
29. Davis, Larry, *Wild Weasel*, Squadron/Signal Publications, Carrollton, Texas, 1986, p 8
30. Levy
31. Grigsby
32. Barker p 105
33. *Ibid*, p 108
34. *Ibid*
35. Quoted in Davis, p 12
36. *Ibid*
37. Pierson, *op cit*, p 83
38. Barker p 118
39. *Ibid*
40. Davis pp 13–14
41. Interview Mike Gilroy
42. Interview Art Hepler
43. Gilroy
44. *Ibid*
45. Davis p 14
46. *Ibid*, p 15
47. Loss List

Chapter 4

THE SAGA OF THE JAMMING PODS

September 1965 to November 1966

"Keep a thing for seven years and you'll find a use for it."

Irish Proverb

Following the loss of the F-4C Phantom to a SAM over North Vietnam, anyone with ideas on how to counter the Soviet weapon found a ready ear. Lieutenant Colonel Ingwald "Inky" Haugen had retired from the USAF in 1961 after nearly twenty years experience in electronic warfare. Now he worked as a civilian project officer at the Electronic Warfare Test Division at Eglin AFB, Florida.

Haugen had addressed a nearly similar problem several years earlier, while serving in the Directorate of Requirements at the Pentagon. In 1955 he had seen the initial intelligence reports on the first Soviet surface-to-air missile system to go into service, the SA-1 (S-25). That system's Yo Yo missile control radar, like the Fan Song used with the SA-2, was a track-while-scan system which radiated two fan-shaped beams. One beam measured the target's position in azimuth, the other beam measured its position in elevation.[1] That posed a difficult target for the low-powered noise jammers then carried by SAC's bombers. As Haugen mulled over the matter he conceived the idea of a four-ship unit of bombers, B-47s or B-52s, with each plane occupying an adjacent resolution cell of the missile control radar. To counter an E band radar like Yo Yo (or Fan Song) required a lateral spacing of about 1,800 feet between planes and a similar spacing in altitude. If all the planes radiated noise jamming on the radar's frequency, the operators at the separate azimuth and elevation scopes would each see four closely spaced jamming strobes that merged into each other. The jamming would create a large volume of uncertainty around the force and if command guided missiles with high explosive warheads were fired at the group, they would stand little chance of destroying a bomber. Haugen wrote a paper on the jamming formation which did the rounds. He was told that, although his idea would probably work, it was not practical for the nuclear war SAC was preparing to fight. If the enemy launched a nuclear- tipped missile at the formation, a single burst would knock down all four aircraft.[2]

"Inky" Haugen kept the idea in the back of his mind during the years to follow. In 1965 the air fighting over North Vietnam was different from that which had governed SAC's tactics a decade earlier. He thought that four F-105s, each carrying a couple of QRC-160-1 noise jamming pods and correctly spaced in azimuth and elevation, could seriously degrade the SA-2 system.[3] Haugen discussed the matter with his boss, Colonel Joe Gillespie, who passed the idea up the chain of command. Shortly afterwards the Air Proving Ground Center and the Tactical Air Warfare Center, both at Eglin, received orders to evaluate the jamming formation tactic. The project received the code-name Problem Child.

A batch of jamming pods arrived at Eglin where each one was carefully checked and adjusted to ensure that it performed to specification. Then four F-105s were each fitted with two pods. The first instrumented test of the jamming pod formation took place in October 1965. The F-105 formation flew at between 15,000 and 20,000 feet against the facility's SADS-1 Fan Song surrogate radar. The flight path of each F-105 was observed using a separate, unjammed, FPS-16 high precision beacon tracking radar. Data from the four FPS-16s and the jammed SADS-1 were then fed into computers which calculated the tracking errors induced by the jamming.[4]

From the start, it was clear that the jamming formation idea was a winner. "Inky" Haugen commented:

"We found that the pods would screen the aircraft from all aspects, at most ranges, until the aircraft came broadside-on to the radar site. Then, for a short time, there was 'burn-through' and the aircraft could be seen through the jamming. That was long enough for a site to launch a missile, but not long enough to guide it in for a kill."[5]

The tests showed that full degradation of the Soviet missile system required four aircraft correctly positioned, each with at least one jamming pod working properly. The formation was less effective if there were three jamming aircraft, and much less effective if there were only two.

Colonel Gillespie passed on the results of the early tests and suggested that an operational test of the jamming formation be conducted over North Vietnam.[6] Fate now took an unexpected turn, however.

PACAF senior officers were not interested in the proposed new tactic. As far as they was concerned the QRC-160-1 jamming pod had been tried over North Vietnam, it had failed and been rejected. That was the end of the matter.

For those involved with Problem Child it was the start of a frustrating time. The tests showed that if the QRC-160-1 pods worked to specification and were used properly, they would bring an immediate drop in losses of US aircraft. The answer was to assemble the most powerful case possible in support of the jamming pod formation, and circulate it as widely as security allowed. That took time. The full Problem Child test program was completed in February 1966, the detailed report appeared at the end of April and distribution began in the following month.[7]

After reading the Problem Child report, Pentagon EW staff officers joined the clamor to test the jamming formation over North Vietnam. Still there remained the deep-seated opposition in the operational theater to the reintroduction of the pods, however. Captain Tony Brees, now at Takhli, observed the reaction there:

"There was a lot of 'Not invented here' and 'Don't understand it.' Also, 7th Air Force was reluctant to spare four aircraft to practice the jamming formation as a training mission over Thailand. At that time, the other side of the base was hollering for four sorties per airplane per day on the target. And they could launch only three or maybe two. So, the sortie generation requirement was driving them. The DO [Director of Operations] of the Fighter Wing was saying 'I haven't got time to learn this new thing, I've got to put iron on the target.' And the pilots were skeptical. They didn't want to carry pods on their planes because that meant having to leave a couple of bombs off. But throughout this time the loss rates were horrendous."[8]

At the 355th Tactical Fighter Wing at Takhli, losses peaked during July and August 1966. In that disastrous two-month period the wing's three F-105 squadrons, with a nominal establishment of 54 aircraft, lost exactly half that number of planes in action. Eighteen pilots were killed or taken prisoner.[9]

Finally Lieutenant General William Momeyer, Seventh Air Force Commander, directed that a further combat evaluation of the QRC-160-1 pod be made.[10] A batch of twenty-five carefully prepared pods was flown to Thailand for installation on F-105s of the Takhli Wing.[11]

Between 26 September and 8 October a four-ship flight of F-105s flying in jamming pod formation, with each plane carrying two jamming pods, accompanied raiding forces on nineteen occasions. At first the targets were in Route Package I, the relatively sparsely defended area in the southern part of North Vietnam. The pods were set to radiate jamming on the frequencies used by the Fire Can and Fan Song radars.

As each flight reached the IP (Initial Point before commencing its bomb run), it climbed rapidly to 10,000 feet to identify its target before commencing its attack dive.[12] Maintaining their special formation, the F-105s with jamming pods began their climbs a little earlier than the other fighters. Once at altitude, they were exposed longer before commencing their attack dives. No missile was fired at the jamming F-105s, though the aircraft in accompanying flights drew several. As a bonus, the jamming also defeated radar-controlled AAA.[13]

On 8 October there was the clearest possible proof of the value of the jamming pod formation. Two flights of podded F-105s formed part of a force attacking the fuel storage tanks at Nguyen Khe, in a high threat area. The podded aircraft drew little attention, while the non-podded planes received a hot reception from the defenses.[14] The North Vietnamese SAM crews made no attempt to engage the jammers, preferring to concentrate on the "silent" flights.[15]

Suddenly PACAF's wall of antipathy to electronic warfare collapsed in a heap of rubble. In sharp contrast to their previous indifference, pilots assigned to attack dangerous targets now *demanded* to have jamming pods on their planes. People became very enthusiastic about the pods, and in response to their demands another batch was rushed to Takhli. General Electric sent a strong contingent of engineers to maintain the pods.

At the same time, unused QRC-160-1 pods were recalled to the makers for modification and refurbishment. Those which had been stored in the open at Kadena AB, Okinawa, arrived in a particularly poor condition with varying degrees of salt spray corrosion.

There remained one valid criticism of the jamming pod formation: as originally devised it was too inflexible. The 1,500-foot lateral spacing placed aircraft closer together than was desirable when flying in areas where they might encounter enemy fighters. And the 1,500-foot vertical separation between adjacent planes, giving the formation a depth of 4,500 feet, made it difficult for an aircraft to support its neighbor if the latter came under fighter attack.[16] However, during operations crews found that the formation need not be as rigid as originally thought. Takhli pilots found that the altitude separation between the highest plane in the formation and the lowest could be halved, to 750 feet, without detrimental effect. That permitted better mutual cover against fighter attack.[17]

That October "Inky" Haugen flew to Takhli to brief pilots on the new tactic. When he arrived he was greeted with a sight he will remember as long as he lives: a long line of F-105s on the ramp, every one with a jamming pod under each wing.

Good news travels fast. When the other Thailand-based F-105 wing, the 388th at Korat, heard of the development it too demanded jamming pods. That posed a problem, because there were only about one hundred and forty QRC-160-1 pods in existence. If each plane carried two pods there were insufficient for the Korat wing. "Inky" Haugen continued:

"When I reached Takhli one of the first questions Colonel Scott [commander of the 355th Tactical Fighter Wing] asked me was 'Will it work as well if there is only one pod on each aircraft?' I could only answer 'I don't know.' With hindsight, it might seem strange that we had never tested this during Problem Child. But I had always assumed that with the deep belly of the F-105 protruding so far beneath the wing, there was bound to be considerable screening of the jamming on the opposite side. During Problem Child, we had plenty of pods at Eglin. We felt the main thing was to show that the technique worked and get it accepted by the operational flyers, rather than try to work out refinements."[18]

Haugen called Eglin on the "hot line" and asked for a test with each F-105 carrying only one QRC-160-1 pod, to see how that worked. Back came the answer, there was no observable difference on the radar if only a single pod was carried. When Colonel Scott received the news, he passed half of his jamming pods to Korat. From then on, the aircraft of both F-105 wings received jamming protection.[19]

There followed a period of experimentation, as each F-105 wing sought to get the best out of the pods and formation. The F-105s from Korat flew at altitudes between 15,000 and 18,000 feet, a two-minute spacing between succeeding formations. The extra altitude gave better protection against AAA, but bomb-laden F-105s were unwieldy at this height and the formation was difficult to maneuver. The F-105s from Takhli moved first to 6,500 feet, then went gradually higher, and flew with about one minute spacing between succeeding formations. Those tactics exposed the planes to more AAA fire, but the formations were more flexible and maneuverable.[20]

Although the QRC-160-1 pods performed far better than during their initial spell in combat the previous year, reliability remained poor by normal

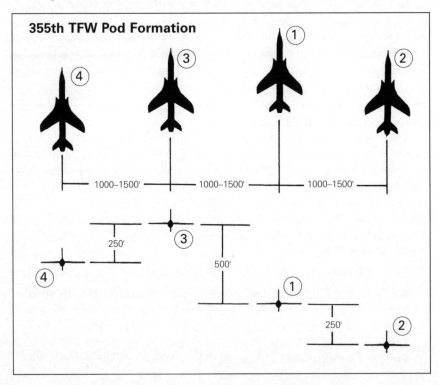

355th TFW Pod Formation

service standards. The pod had originally been designed for one-time use aboard a fighter delivering a nuclear weapon in a high-speed straight-and-level bomb run. Now the pods had to fly day after day, carried by aircraft employing the full range of combat maneuvers.

The jamming pod formation was not the only important electronic warfare innovation to reach the theater in the fall of 1966. Earlier in the year Applied Technology's WR-300 receiver, which picked up the missile guidance signals and was fitted in Wild Weasel planes, had been ordered into production as the APR-26. Both it and the APR-25 radar warning receiver were now coming off the production line in useful numbers, and when batches were ready they were flown to the F-105 bases in Thailand.

Tony Brees described the installation program:

"The APR-25 and the APR-26 started being installed in the F-105s at Takhli and Korat in September or October 1966—about the same time as the introduction of the jamming pod formation. The warning receivers were installed at the bases, with guys working on four planes at a time. It was quite a big job, they had to cut metal, put in the antennas in the nose and the tail, run wires into the cockpit. It took a week to ten days to turn around an F-105."[21]

Fighter pilots flying over enemy territory quickly came to appreciate the improved situational awareness provided by their warning receivers.

From the end of November 1966 all F-105s flying into missile-defended areas carried jamming pods. Paradoxically, that provided a further test of nerve for their pilots. No longer could the North Vietnamese missile batteries ignore the jamming aircraft and concentrate on those without jammers, for there were none of the latter. Now the jamming pod formations had to face determined attacks from the missile batteries.

For the jamming to produce the required "footprint" on the ground, the fighters were restricted to a maximum bank angle of 15 degrees. The jamming pattern from a pod can be likened to a huge inverted saucer (a rather chunky saucer) rigidly attached to the underside of the plane. If the aircraft applied bank, the "footprint" of the jamming on the ground shifted to the outside of the turn. Too great a bank angle would reduce the effectiveness of the jamming, and might cause it to miss the enemy radar altogether. As one fighter pilot remarked:

"The jamming pod formation was wide, it was stacked and it was awkward to fly. It you were in the high position and the leader went down or turned into you, you couldn't roll upside down and pull down like you normally would to keep positive G on the airplane. If you did that, your jamming would point way into the sky. You had to push on negative G to hold your place in formation, and that was uncomfortable. If the formation turned, it was either very slow and gentle, or else it was very aggressive and hard. Everything else was done with wings level, either pull back or push down. Judging distances was not difficult. The big deal was, don't get closer than 500 feet from the next guy, and don't get further away than 2,500 feet."[22]

Salvation lay in avoiding banked maneuvers and maintaining formation integrity. When a Guideline missile came towards the formation, pilots had to grit their teeth and hold a straight and level flight path. That, at a time when every natural instinct of survival told them to break formation and pull into tight diving turns. If it seemed the missile was heading for one aircraft in the formation, the leader would take all four down in a shallow descent.[23] Usually that was sufficient to avert the threat, and the missile passed harmlessly over the formation. If a missile corrected its trajectory to follow one of the planes, it meant that for some reason the jamming had failed. As a last resort pilots had then to jettison their bombs, break formation and revert to the old-style missile evasion maneuver. But only rarely would that prove necessary.

Early in 1967 HQ Pacific Air Forces conducted a study into the effectiveness of QRC-160-1 pods during the period September through December of the previous year. The report noted that during November and December, losses of F-105s carrying jamming pods flying over Route Package VI (the most heavily defended area, which included Hanoi and Haiphong) were less than one-third those suffered in the same area before the introduction of pods. The incidence of aircraft having to initiate missile evasive maneuvers was also much reduced. Between July and September, about half of F-105 combat missions had been forced to resort to such maneuvers. Between October and December, the number fell to less than 10 per cent.[24]

Crews reported seeing missiles start to guide toward their formation. But then, instead of singling out an individual aircraft, they usually flew erratic paths and sped past the formation before exploding harmlessly when well clear. Due to the wide spacing of the planes, there was ample room between adjacent machines for the missiles to pass through the formation without getting close enough to trigger the warhead's proximity fuse. Now, if an F-105 was lost to missile attack, it was usually because it had broken out of the pod formation to begin its attack dive or for some other reason, or because one or more planes in the formation had malfunctioning jamming pods.[25]

Once fighter pilots had became accustomed to the new of formation, the improvement in survivability was clear beyond doubt. With the zeal of a convert, Colonel William Chairsell commanding the 388th Tactical Fighter Wing at Korat informed the Director of Operations at Seventh Air Force:

"The introduction of the QRC-160-1 pod to the F-105 weapon system represents one of the most effective operational innovations I have ever encountered. Seldom has a technological advance of this nature so degraded an enemy's defensive posture. It has literally transformed the hostile air defense environment we once faced, to one in which we can now operate with a latitude of permissibility."[26]

Such unstinting praise for jamming pods from a PACAF wing commander, shows how far that force's mindset regarding electronic warfare had shifted during the previous few weeks.

The jamming pod formation became fully accepted by Seventh Air Force in October 1966. Yet, as we have seen, it could have been introduced several months earlier. The first phase of Problem Child had proved the effectiveness of the new tactic before the end of 1965. Given a degree of urgency, it should have been possible to introduce the pods and the jamming formation into F-105 units in Thailand by mid-April 1966. For the reasons outlined above, six months elapsed until mid-October when the pods and new tactics actually came into use. The tables show that during those six months, seventy-two F-105s were lost over North Vietnam to SAMs and AAA. In the six months following the introduction of the new tactics F-105 losses fell sharply, to twenty-three. It seems reasonable to conclude that the delays in introducing the new tactic cost the Air Force at least forty F-105s and about thirty pilots

F-105D Combat Losses over North Vietnam

Losses in six-month period, up to introduction of jamming pods

Cause	Apr 66	May	June	July	Aug	Sept	Total
AAA	8	9	9	15	15	14	70
SAM	1	0	0	0	1	0	2
Total	9	9	9	15	15	14	72

Losses in the six-month period, after introduction of jamming pods

Cause	Oct	Nov	Dec	Jan	Feb	Mar	Total
AAA	4	6	2	1	1	6	20
SAM	0	0	1	1	0	1	3
Total	4	6	3	2	1	7	23

Source: USAF and US Navy Official Loss List

When the jamming pod formation was introduced in October 1966, the tactic was employed only by F-105Ds. The tables above show the losses suffered from AAA and SAM by F-105Ds flying regular attack missions over North Vietnam, during six-month periods before and after the general introduction of the jamming pod formation in October 1966. In the period April through September 1966, 72 fighters were lost—an average of 12 per month. During the six-month period October 1966 through March 1967, when they employed the new tactic, 23 F-105Ds were lost, an average of just under 4 per month. During that latter period, the F-105s continued to fly at high sortie rates into heavily defended areas, and the defenses were strengthening with each month that passed.

killed or captured. The attack fighter units paid a heavy price for PACAF's long-standing prejudice against electronic warfare systems.

From October 1966, the jamming pod formation provided Air Force tactical aircraft with a useful degree of immunity from attack by SA-2 missiles. That immunity applied only as long as all the enemy missile batteries were equipped only with the Fan Song Model B radar, however. And, fortunately for US aircrews, that was the only type of missile control radar in use in North Vietnam. How long that situation would continue was anybody's guess. Newer variants of the SA-2, and more effective later systems, were already being deployed in quantity in the Soviet Union and Eastern Europe. Compared with Fan Song B, these systems operated on shorter wavelengths and had better target-resolution capability. If the new missile systems appeared in North Vietnam, US fighter crews could again face difficult times.

References to Chapter 4

1. Interview "Inky" Haugen
2. *Ibid*
3. *Ibid*
4. *Ibid*
5. *Ibid*
6. *Ibid*
7. *Ibid*
8. Interview Tony Brees
9. USAF and US Navy Official Loss List
10. Pierson, James, *Electronic Warfare in SEA 1964-1968*, USAF Security Service, 1973, p 36
11. *Ibid*, p 85
12. *Ibid*
13. Barker, Patrick, "The SA-2 and the Wild Weasel", MA Degree Thesis, p 122 *et seq*
14. *Ibid*
15. Haugen
16. Barker, p 122 *et seq*
17. *Ibid*
18. Haugen
19. *Ibid*
20. Michel, Marshall, *Clashes*, Naval Institute Press, Annapolis, Maryland, 1997, p 62
21. Brees
22. Interview General John Corder
23. Barker, p 121 *et seq*
24. *Ibid*
25. Haugen
26. Pierson, p 86

Chapter 5

MEASURE AND COUNTERMEASURE

December 1966 to October 1967

"When things are going badly in battle, the best tonic is to take one's mind off one's own troubles by considering what a rotten time one's opponent must be having."

Field Marshal Lord Wavell

At the end of 1966 the hard-fought electronic battle in the skies over North Vietnam reached its climax. On the one side were the defending gun and missile batteries, and the radars directing them and the MiG fighters into action. Arrayed against these was the gamut of electronic countermeasures systems carried by raiding planes and their supporters.

Except for the Wild Weasels, all Air Force attack fighters now carried radar-jamming pods. Navy and Marine attack fighters carried the ALQ-51A deception system. A significant and increasing proportion of attack fighters also carried radar-warning and missile-launch receivers. Teams of Air Force Wild Weasel or Navy Iron Hand aircraft sought to destroy enemy missile control radars, or at least force them to cease transmitting. Douglas EB-66B and EB-66C standoff jamming planes supported the raiding forces, though the need to keep out of threat areas reduced their effectiveness.

The construction of SA-2 sites continued without pause and by the end 1966 US planes had photographed more than 150. About thirty missile firing units shuttled unpredictably between these sites, moving between six and thirty miles each time.

Although the main countermeasure effort was directed against the SAM batteries, AAA caused the majority of losses. During the first three months of 1967 SAMs destroyed seven Air Force, Navy and Marine jet fighters.[1] In the same period AAA destroyed 29 fighters, four times as many as lost to missiles.[2] When attack fighters descended from medium altitude to deliver dive attacks, they were vulnerable to optically aimed fire. Electronic jamming could do nothing against that. With frequent processions of targets coming past their sites, the North Vietnamese gunners had every opportunity to gain proficiency in their lethal craft.

At this time the F-4C Phantom air superiority fighter carried neither a jamming pod nor a warning receiver. In the last four months of 1966, five had been lost to SAMs.[3] The recently introduced F-4D carried the Bendix APS-107 radar warning receiver as a baseline item, but earlier models lacked such equipment. To rectify this deficiency, APR-25 and APR-26 warning receivers were fitted into earlier versions of the F-4. F-4s without warning receivers were banned from entering the missile-defended areas.[4]

North Vietnamese radar operators quickly learned about the Iron Hand operations, and sought ways to reduce their effectiveness. The distinctive "lofted" attack maneuver with Shrike was easily recognizable on radar. And when a Shrike was launched, metal particles in the exhaust gave a distinctive blooming return on radar to show that the missile was on its way. If the Fan Song ceased transmitting at that point the Shrike was deprived of homing signals and "went stupid."

On the other hand, if the Fan Song ceased transmissions it could no longer control Guideline missiles in flight. If the use of Shrikes allowed an accompanying raiding force to pass through the defenses without coming under missile attack, that was a win for the attackers.

Fan Song radar operators learnt the need to keep transmissions as short as possible. Initially they had spent five minutes or longer "on air," but once Iron Hand operations began in earnest that extravagant use of radar ceased. Yet there were limits to what could be done in this respect. When switched to transmit, a Fan Song took nearly a minute for its azimuth and elevation beam transmitters to reach full power at 600 kW. That could be dangerous if Iron Hand aircraft were prowling nearby. To reduce the delay, operators employed their "dummy load" equipment. Part of the maintenance equipment for Fan Song, this could be plugged into the transmitter to draw off the power. The latter was dissipated as heat, working in much the same way as a microwave oven. With the dummy load inserted, the radar ran at full power with very little radiation to allow adjustments to be made. Now the device became part of an electronic counter-countermeasures technique. While waiting to go into action, a Fan Song radar fed its output into the dummy load. When a target aircraft came within engagement range, the output was switched to the antennas and the radar reached full power with minimum delay. Thus an experienced Fan Song crew could conduct a missile engagement with their radar "on air" for only about 30 seconds.[5]

When the Fan Song radar signals were fed into the dummy load, a small amount of power still leaked out. Enter Chuck Christman, with a further modification to Navy EC-121 ELINT aircraft of VQ-1 (*see also Chapter 1*). He rigged a system using the plane's APS-20 high gain radar antenna feeding signals into a state of the art amplifier, to produce a highly sensitive receiver. This picked up the feeble emanations from the Fan Song in dummy load, signifying the radar was ready for action. Chuck Christman commented:

> "The Fan Song operators would bring the radar up in dummy load, both beams, and they would run it for 15 to 20 seconds. We could see the Fan Song radar working in dummy load, no matter which way it was pointing. Then the two beams would go off the air, and the missile guidance signals would come on in dummy load. [My system] would see that. We could tell if it was a test, or if there were proportional guidance signals which meant a missile was in flight. We could hear the command arming signal to the missile, we could hear the command destruct signal."[6]

During these operations VQ-1 maintained two EC-121s on station off the coast of North Vietnam, to triangulate the positions of SAM batteries preparing for action and broadcast warnings on the radio guard channel.[7] The Spoon Rest, the Flat Face and the Bar Lock surveillance radars were frequently "Briganded" to assist in keeping track of the defenders' moves.[8]

There can be no doubting Chuck Christman's outstanding personal contribution to the effectiveness of the US Navy VQ squadrons. By developing the means to detect and locate Fan Song radars running in dummy load and about to go into action, to take just one of his many creations, he helped save numerous US aircraft flying over North Vietnam. In recognition of his work Chuck Christman received the Navy Distinguished Public Service Award, the highest award the Navy can present to a civilian.

In August 1967 the first Douglas EB-66Es arrived in theater to replace the older EB-66Bs. The new variant carried a crew of three and the bomb bay housed a battery of thirty-four jamming transmitters, mostly ALT-6Bs.[9] By the late fall there were fourteen EB-66Es in theater, giving a marked improvement in support jamming capability.[10] There was evidence that the operation of some early warning radars, notably the A-Band Knife Rest and Spoon Rest and the C-band Flat Face, suffered significant disruption from jamming. The E-band Rock Cake height finder and the Bar Lock multi-beam air surveillance equipment suffered to a lesser degree.[11]

The installation of active countermeasures systems in US attack fighters cut losses from missiles and AAA. In war things do not stand still, however, and the North Vietnamese fighter force now assumed a greater importance. Initially it had operated only obsolescent MiG-17s, but in the spring of 1966 the supersonic MiG-21 Fishbed with Atoll IR missiles made its appearance. At first these new fighters were content merely to threaten US attack planes and force them to jettison their bombs. Then, in the fall of 1966, the MiG-21s became more aggressive. During December 1966 several strike flights came under threat and were forced to jettison their bombs.[12] Also that month, MiGs shot down two F-105s.

Military tactics are usually a matter of compromise; a measure that is effective against one type of weapon sometimes leaves the user more vulnerable to another system. A clear example of this was the jamming pod formation. While it provided excellent protection against SA-2 missiles, planes using the formation were at a disadvantage if they confronted MiGs. As one F-105 pilot commented:

"Pod formation is not a good look-out formation in a MiG environment. It's the worst kind of formation you can fly. You have restricted visibility and restricted movement. If you have a MiG shooting at you, it's dangerous to break [make a defensive turn] from a pod formation [because the other aircraft were so close]. It also doesn't lend itself to mutual support."[13]

To reduce the MiGs' effectiveness, in mid-1966 the Navy established radar surveillance patrols in the Gulf of Tonkin. A cruiser operating about 25 miles off the coast, code-named Red Crown, kept watch over air activity with its surveillance radar. Two other warships operated in conjunction with it, one to the north and one to the south. If the MiGs remained at low altitude, however, they were unlikely to be seen by the ships' radars or the EC-121Ds.

The battle between the opposing fighter forces over North Vietnam has been covered in numerous other publications. This account will restrict itself to actions relevant to the history of electronic warfare.

The escorting F-4 fighters, assisted by tactical ELINT aircraft, did their utmost to bring the MiGs to battle but, directed by GCI radar, the North Vietnamese fighters made difficult targets. For political reasons, at this stage US planes were not permitted to attack enemy airfields. That handed the tactical initiative to the MiGs' ground controllers who decided when, where and if an aerial engagement took place.

Colonel Robin Olds commanded the 8th Tactical Fighter Wing based at Ubon in Thailand. Equipped with F-4Cs, the unit's primary task was to escort F-105s and prevent interference from defending MiGs. Frustrated at the ban on attacks on airfields, Olds decided to "teach the MiG jockeys a lesson."

Olds borrowed QRC-160-1 jamming pods from the F-105 units and had these fitted to his Phantoms, so that when seen on radar they resembled a raiding force of F-105s. The F-4Cs would radiate jamming and fly in the jamming pod formation, at typical F-105 speeds and altitudes and using their IFF settings, radio procedures and callsigns. Several flights of Phantoms armed for air-to-air combat were to fly down an ingress route often used by F-105s. If MiGs took off to engage, they would be in for a nasty shock.[14]

On 2 January 1967 Olds set his trap, code-named Operation Bolo. The Phantoms were divided into two forces. East Force, with seven four-plane flights of F-4Cs from the 366th Tactical Fighter Wing, was to head for Kep and Cat Bai airfields to the east of Hanoi. West Force, the bogus F-105 group comprising seven flights of F-4s from Colonel Olds' Wing, headed for Phuc Yen airfield. Supporting the Phantoms was an Iron Hand operation by six flights of F-105Ds and F-105Fs. EB-66C standoff jamming planes and an EC-121 Big Eye radar surveillance aircraft completed the cast.[15]

During the ingress East Force encountered high level cloud, which forced it to abandon the mission. West Force went on alone. That day its Phantoms had been allocated radio callsigns with names of automobile manufacturers: Ford, Rambler, Olds, etc. Olds chose the last of those for his flight. Although this ran counter to the dictates of security, there is no evidence the lapse affected the operation.

As the Phantoms passed Phuc Yen airfield cloud blanketed the area, concealing the composition of the force from ground observers. Above 10,000 feet the skies were clear, however.[16]

North Vietnamese records state that eight MiG-21s and twenty-two MiG-17s were scrambled to engage the "raiding force". The MiG-17s orbited below cloud, waiting to pounce on US planes descending through the overcast to attack their target.[17] The first four MiG-21s airborne climbed through the cloud layer and the leader emerged in front of Ford Flight. Thus warned, Colonel Olds turned to meet the threat. Then a couple more MiG-21s popped out of the undercast about 1½ miles in front of him. His WSO, Lieutenant Charles Clifton, locked his radar on one of the enemy fighters and Olds launched a pair of Sparrow missiles. By then the MiG was inside the Sparrows' minimum engagement range, and both weapons missed. Olds then launched a couple of Sidewinder missiles at the MiG, which promptly dived into cloud. It was the MiG pilot's lucky day—four missiles launched at him without effect. His companion was not be so fortunate. Olds gained a firing position on the second MiG and launched his remaining two Sidewinders. One scored a hit and blew off the MiG's right wing.[18]

The action became general and Olds, Ford and Rambler flights were hotly engaged. The F-4Cs claimed the destruction of six MiG-21s before they withdrew without loss.[19] North Vietnamese records reveal that all four MiG-21s in the leading flight were shot down. The second MiG-21 flight lost its leader, but the other three fighters escaped. All five MiG-21 pilots ejected safely. One of those shot down was Nguyen Van Coc, later the top scoring North Vietnamese fighter ace credited with nine victories.[20]

On 6 January there was another attempt to lure the MiGs into action. This time the 8th Tactical Fighter Wing sent two F-4Cs flying in very close formation, to appear on radar as a single aircraft, along a route sometimes used by the unarmed RF-4Cs. Four MiG-21s attempted to engage the "recon plane" northwest of Hanoi and lost two of their number when the trap was sprung.[21]

By March 1967 Captain Mike Gilroy had amassed eighty Wild Weasel missions and was one of the most experienced EWOs with the 355th TFW. Weasel losses had resumed, however, with two F-105Fs shot down during the first two months of that year.

That was the position on 10 March when Lincoln flight set out from Takhli, to support F-105s attacking the Thai Nguyen steel works north of Hanoi. Lincoln Lead was an F-105F, Lincoln Two was a single seat F-105D. Gilroy and his pilot, Captain Merlyn (Merle) Dethlefsen, were in Lincoln Three and Major Ken Bell in an F-105D was Lincoln Four. Each F-105F carried two Shrikes and two CBU-24 cluster weapons. Each "D" model carried two Shrikes and six 500-pound bombs. The operation got off to a bad start, as Mike Gilroy explained:

> "There were two SAM sites protecting the approach to the steel mill. We were supposed to keep these occupied. As we approached the target the leader was descending, we were at about 5,000 feet and descending too. The weather was good. Then suddenly, damn, we heard beepers. Lincoln Lead had taken a hit from AAA and both guys had bailed out. Then Two called and said he had also been hit real bad, so Merle told him to go home." [22]

Piloting the only F-105F left in the area, Dethlefsen now took the lead. With Lincoln Four in close trail, he entered a climb to avoid AAA while Gilroy searched for further radar signals.

> "As we climbed we got a radar on the scope. Merle ran in and fired a Shrike at it, so did the No 4. Nothing happened, the signal stayed up, so we had not hit the radar. We went off to the north, came back in and fired the other Shrike at it. Again the No 4 fired too. And again nothing happened. The radar was still on." [23]

All four Shrike missiles had been expended without effect. As the pair left the target after the second attack, two MiG-21s attempted to engage the Thunderchiefs. Dethlefsen evaded them by turning back into the flak bursts. The move succeeded, but as he emerged from the bursts on the other side two more MiGs were waiting for him. The determined pilot turned back into the maelstrom of flak.

As the last elements of the strike force left the target, Dethlefsen felt he had unfinished business. Mike Gilroy continued:

> "The flak was terrible, as bad as I had ever seen. Most of it was 37 mm and 57 mm. We took hits from fragments but nothing was that bad. The SAM site was not firing at us, but it was tracking us. We lined up on the site, but that run was too short and we had to break away. We went back out about 10 miles and lined up on the site again. We went in at 450 knots and made station passage on the site [passed over it]. As the signal dipped, I said to Merle 'OK, that's it!' He looked down, saw the missile site and said 'I got

it.' He lit the burner, got up to about 8,000 feet, came in a 45 degrees and dropped the CBUs [cluster bomb units]. Ken Bell in the D model was trailing us and he dropped his bombs. Then we both went back and strafed the site. No doubt we hit it, it went off the air. We could see flames on the ground where the CBUs and the 500 pounders had burst."[24]

Both Thunderchiefs limped into Udorn and landed with little fuel. The F-105F had 137 hits from missile fragments, the D model had nearly as many.

For his valor that day Merlyn Dethlefsen received the Medal of Honor, while Mike Gilroy received the Air Force Cross.

Early in 1967 the Air Force's EC-121 Big Eye radar picket force changed its name from Big Eye to College Eye. That May its planes received a new item of equipment, QRC-248, that would have a profound effect on future air-to-air engagements. When operated in the active mode, QRC-248 radiated pulses that interrogated the Soviet SRO-2 IFF set, which replied with a distinctive pulse train. The range and bearing of the MiG were then plotted using regular radar methods. Alternatively QRC-248 could operate in the passive mode, relying on enemy ground stations to trigger the MiG's transponders, but only bearing information was then available. Only MiGs carried the SRO-2 transponder which radiated the unique pulse trains, so QRC-248 provided unambiguous identification of hostile aircraft. Lieutenant Colonel George Anderson, Vice-Commander of the College Eye Task Force, stated:

> "With the advent of QRC-248 we were able to detect aircraft we had not previously seen. It was somewhat frightening to realize that in the past there had been so many aircraft we had not seen."[25]

As well as EC-121s, Navy EP-3 Orion aircraft and warships conducting radar surveillance off the coast of North Vietnam also carried QRC-248.

In the summer of 1967 the EC-121 force received a further important addition in the shape of a K model aircraft code-named Rivet Top. As well as the regular radar suite and QRC-248, Rivet Top carried equipment to interrogate the SRO-1 and SOD-57 transponders carried by MiGs. Rivet Top carried a surveillance crew of ten, which included a SIGINT intelligence team of four to monitor communications between MiG pilots and their GCI stations. The combination of ELINT and SIGINT allowed the crew to determine the location and movements of MiG fighters in real time.[26]

On 24 October 1967 Major William Kirk of the 433rd Tactical Fighter Squadron led a MIGCAP operation to cover a strike on Phuc Yen. The EC-121 overseeing the area located approaching MiGs on the QRC-248 and warned Kirk of attackers closing on him from behind. Afterwards the F-4 pilot reported:

> "I positioned my flight line abreast, high and to the left of the trailing F-105 flight. MiG calls were heard as we entered NVN. They proved to

be extremely accurate. When the MiG calls indicated that the MIGs were 6 o'clock at 8 miles, I turned our flight back into the attack. As I rolled out of the 180° turn my [back seater, Lt. Bongartz] acquired radar lock on a target 30° right at 4 miles. I immediately looked to that position and visually identified a MiG-21."[27]

After a hard maneuvering fight, during which Kirk launched two AIM-7s without effect, the F-4 pilot finally closed to within about 500 feet and destroyed the MiG with cannon fire.

The SIGINT operators in the Rivet Top aircraft provided much valuable information on enemy operations, but the picture was incomplete. Eavesdropping on enemy radio conversations revealed that MiGs were being vectored against part of a US raiding formation, yet it gave little idea of which part of the force was under threat. Another problem concerned security. While the North Vietnamese radio conversations themselves were not regarded as secret, the fact that US monitors were eavesdropping was highly classified. Senior service officers pressed hard to be allowed to use this information, but for much of the war front line units were not permitted to exploit it.[28]

By the end of 1965 all fifteen Lockheed A-12 high-speed reconnaissance aircraft had been delivered to the CIA, although two had been lost during flight testing. If one of these advanced planes was shot down it would be a major coup for the Communist propaganda machine. For that reason the A-12 was withheld from operational missions until there was a task of great importance only it could fulfil.[29]

In May 1967 Intelligence reports suggested that the Hanoi government was about to receive a shipment of surface-to-surface ballistic missiles. If true, that meant a serious escalation in the conflict. The A-12 unit received Presidential approval to fly reconnaissance missions over North Vietnam to search for evidence.[30]

Three A-12s moved to Kadena AB, Okinawa, and on 31 May 1967 CIA pilot Mele Vojvodich flew the first mission. As he neared the coast of North Vietnam he accelerated to Mach 3.1 and climbed to 80,000 feet.[31] With cameras turning and the plane's ELINT collection system running, the A-12 flashed past Haiphong on its way to Hanoi. The radar warning receiver indicated the plane was being tracked by more than one Fan Song radar, then that Guideline missiles were in flight. Vojvodich observed missiles streaking across the sky but none came close enough to bother him.

Covering nearly 35 miles per minute, the A-12 took about six minutes to cross North Vietnam. Then the pilot decelerated to subsonic speed and descended to medium altitude, to rendezvous with a KC-135 tanker. After refueling, the A-12 accelerated to operational speed and altitude for a second photo run over North Vietnam. Vojvodich continued on to Kadena, where he landed after three hours and forty minutes airborne.[32]

During 1967 the A-12s flew a further twenty-one sorties over North Vietnam. The combination of very high speed and ultra high altitude proved an effective safeguard against the missiles. The nearest the defenders came to success was on 30 October, when CIA pilot Denny Sullivan counted eight Guideline detonations in the vicinity of his plane. None seemed particularly close, but during the post-flight inspection at Kadena part of a missile's fusing system was found lodged in one wing.[33] The A-12s' photographs yielded no evidence that surface-to-surface ballistic missiles had arrived in North Vietnam.

The period reviewed in this chapter had seen the hardest-fought battle of electronic countermeasures versus counter-countermeasures since World War II. Yet while the focus of US electronic warfare activity was on the war in Southeast Asia, developments elsewhere also merit our attention. We shall examine these next.

References to Chapter 5

1. USAF and USN Official Loss Lost
2. *Ibid*
3. *Ibid*
4. Pierson, James, *Electronic Warfare in SEA 1964–1968*, USAF Security Service 1973, p 89
5. *Ibid* p 83
6. Interview Chuck Christman
7. Pierson, p 117
8. Christman
9. Interview Roy Fair
10. Pierson, p 118
11. *Ibid*, p 117–9
12. Michel, Marshall, *Clashes*, Naval Institute Press, Annapolis, Maryland, 1997, p 46
13. Red Baron report quoted in Michel, p 177
14. *Ibid*, p 63
15. Glasser, Jeffrey, *The Secret Vietnam War*, McFarland & Company, Jefferson, North Carolina, 1995 p 86
16. *Ibid*
17. Nordeen, Lon, *Air Warfare in the Missile Age*, Smithsonian Institution, Washington, 1985, p 24 *et seq*
18. Glasser, p 86
19. *Ibid*
20. The details on the North Vietnamese side of the action come from the Hungarian air historian Zoltán Buza, who gained access to official records held at the Defense Ministry in Hanoi
21. Quoted in Futrell, R. Frank *et al*, *Aces and Aerial Victories*, Office of Air Force History, 1976, p 39

22. Interview Mike Gilroy
23. *Ibid*
24. *Ibid*
25. Michel, p 100
26. *Ibid*
27. Futrell, p 68.
28. Michel, p 115
29. Crickmore, Paul, *Lockheed SR-71*, Reed Books London, 1993, p 26 *et seq*
30. *Ibid*
31. *Ibid*
32. *Ibid*
33. *Ibid*

Chapter 6

FAR AND WIDE

1967 to 1972

"The best scale for an experiment is 12 inches to a
   foot."
                    Admiral of the Fleet Sir John Fisher

We now leave the conflict in Southeast Asia and return to the US, to review developments in countermeasures systems taking place there. Some of these would find application in the war zone, others were destined for branches of the armed forces operating elsewhere.

All US fighting services now devoted sizeable funds to electronic warfare, but Strategic Air Command retained its position as the largest single player in this field. By 1967 its manned bomber force consisted of 588 B-52s and 81 B-58s.[1] At this time the B-52s were being fitted with the Phase V ECM suite, with the following systems:[2]

Sensors	Jammers	Dispensers
• ALR-20	• Four ALT-6B	**Chaff**
• APR-25	• Six ALT-28	• Eight ALE-24
• ALR-18	• Two ALT-32H	• Two ALE-25
	• One ALT-32L	**Flares**
	• Two ALT-16	• Six ALE-20

To suppress the enemy air defenses, the B-52 force had available 477 Hound Dog air-launched attack missiles and 448 Quail radar decoy missiles.[3] The B-58 was being phased out of service and has no further relevance to this account.

By 1972 the manned bomber force comprised 402 B-52s and sixty FB-111As. A large proportion of the B-52 force now carried the Phase V ECM suite.[4] The Quail radar decoy missile and Hound Dog air launched attack missile remained in service in reduced numbers, and the force now possessed 227 Short Range Attack Missiles (SRAMs).

The FB-111A carried the Sanders ALQ-94 DECM system, the Dalmo Victor ALR-62 threat warning system and Lundy ALE-28 chaff and flare dispensers.

So much for SAC's order of battle and its range of equipment. At this time, the future of its manned bomber fleet hinged on the B-1 strategic bomber then intended to replace the entire B-52 fleet. The Rockwell Company had won the competition to build the supersonic swing-wing airplane, designed to penetrate to targets flying either at low altitude at just under Mach 1, or at high altitude at Mach 1.6.[5]

To reach its targets the B-1 would need to rely heavily on its defensive avionics systems, which marked a considerable advance on anything previously built. Airborne Instruments Laboratory (AIL) won the competition to build the system, the ALQ-161. From his office at Wright-Patterson AFB, a civilian employee on the program, George Nicholas, watched the system come together:

> "The ALQ-161 was designed to counter the 1972 threat, and in my view there is no question it was a good system to do that. The architecture was advanced, it used channelized receivers to measure the radars' frequencies and set on the jammers. The jammers generated various kinds of countermeasures signals at very high effective radiated powers. The system employed power management, though we did not call it that at the time. The heart of the system was a 128 k digital computer—in those days we considered that a lot of memory."[6]

The ALQ-161 provided automatic cueing for the ejection of chaff, flares or both. It had steerable jamming antennas buried in the aircraft's structure covering each band, to focus the jamming at threat radars. The prototype B-1 was scheduled to fly in 1974 and we shall therefore return it in a later chapter.

The QRC-160-1 jamming pod had changed the course of the air war over North Vietnam, yet as a Quick Reaction Capability equipment it had not passed though the normal procurement process. The pod required skilled maintenance to keep it running, yet there was a dearth of trained service maintenance personnel and the provision of spare parts was haphazard. Had it not been for the GEC civilian contingent at the bases in Thailand, the jamming formation tactic might have failed for the want of operable pods.

At this time the Systems Engineering Group at Wright-Patterson AFB worked to improve the reliability and capability of jamming pods. One program was to rework the QRC-160 variants to fit them into the regular procurement process. The QRC-160-1 went into production as the ALQ-71, the more powerful QRC-160-8 went into production as the ALQ-87.[7]

A further program was aimed at producing a pod to defeat new generation Soviet SAM systems, which were certain to be encountered sooner or later. Captain Bob Seh, a member of the group, commented:

"A lot of folks thought a Soviet equivalent of the Hawk [the US Army's surface-to-air missile system] might be the next threat out there. Hawk was very difficult to jam. It had so many ECCM techniques in it, it was a very good system. Westinghouse had built the QRC-249 jamming pod to counter Hawk. People said 'Take the QRC-249, change it around a bit and you will have a system to go against the SA-2 [and a Soviet equivalent of Hawk].' That system became the QRC-335."[8]

Intended to counter current threat systems as well as predicted new ones, the QRC-335 included a built-in receiver and was the first podded system to radiate both noise jamming and deceptive countermeasures. Travelling wave tubes provided the power, and in its initial form the pod operated in the 2.6 to 5.2 GHz band.[9]

The production version of the QRC-335, the ALQ-101, entered service in 1970. The (V)4, the first major production model, covered the frequency range 2 to 20 GHz.[10] An interesting variant of the ALQ-101 was the ALQ-105 fitted to F-105F Wild Weasel planes. In effect this was an ALQ-101 pod cut in half longitudinally, with the innards repositioned inside two blister fairings mounted on either side of an F-105 fuselage.[11] When fitted with this and other modifications, the F-105F was redesignated the F-105G.

Even before the ALQ-101 entered full production Westinghouse was working on its replacement, the ALQ-119. This incorporated lessons from the Vietnam conflict and it would be built in large numbers. Like its predecessor it was a dual mode system, combining noise jamming and deception programs, and was controlled by its own receiver.[12]

Meanwhile, the requirement for large numbers of APR-25 and APR-26 warning receivers placed great pressure on Applied Technology Inc. Dr John Grigsby remembered:

"By late 1966 we were part of the way through delivering the first order for five hundred receivers, building them at a rate of about ten a week. Then Dr Bill Ayre learned from General Dempster that the Air Force wanted to put radar warning receivers into a lot of other aircraft types. Dempster made it clear that he had no authority to place an order, it was not any kind of directive. He just told Bill what he thought was likely to happen."[13]

On the strength of that statement, and without any Air Force contract, Ayre placed orders with his suppliers for parts for one thousand additional systems. Fortunately for his company, the Air Force's contract for the additional receivers arrived before the bill for the parts.

Considering their novelty and the haste in which they entered service, the APR-25 and the APR-26 had performed remarkably well. Both underwent incremental modifications to make them more effective and more reliable. Finally the changes became so numerous the receivers were redesignated, respectively, as the APR-36 and the APR-37 which replaced the earlier systems.[14]

The next evolutionary step, the ALR-46 warning receiver, was essentially an APR-36 with a Dalmo Victor Corporation digital signal processor. This was the first radar-warning receiver in service featuring reprogrammable software.[15]

In the Navy and the Marine Corps, the equivalent reprogrammable warning system was the ALR-45 built by Applied Technology (by now a division of the Itek Corporation). The missile-warning receiver complementing it was the ALR-50.[16]

Once construction of the CIA's batch of A-12 supersonic reconnaissance planes was well advanced, Lockheed offered the Air Force a more-capable variant to serve in the post-strike intelligence collection role. The Air Force placed an order and the plane went into service as the SR-71 Blackbird. Compared with the A-12, the SR-71 carried a larger intelligence collection payload and an additional crewmember to operate the systems. In June 1966 the 9th Strategic Reconnaissance Wing began forming an operational unit at Beale AFB to operate the SR-71.[17]

Once the SR-71 was operational, the Bureau of the Budget questioned the need for the parallel A-12 program, and the latter was terminated early in 1968. SR-71s replaced the A-12s at Kadena, and that March the Blackbird flew its first operational missions over North Vietnam. It would be a frequent visitor during the years to follow.[18]

Until the early 1960s virtually the only chaff material in use was aluminum foil cut into strips of the appropriate length and width. Then Bjorksten Research Laboratories (BRL) in Madison, Wisconsin, developed a novel method of applying a metal coating to glass fibers. The molten glass was drawn from its container at 2,600 degrees Fahrenheit, then passed through a meniscus of molten metal to produce a thin but even coating over the surface of the fiber.[19]

Metallic-coated glass fiber promised several advantages over aluminum foil as a chaff material. Although they were thinner, the glass fiber dipoles were stiffer and more resilient. More than four times as many fiber dipoles could be carried for a given volume of material. Since the radar echo is proportional to the number of dipoles present, the new material was considerably more effective than its predecessor. Also, since a glass fiber dipole had a round cross-section (instead of the oblong cross-section of aluminum foil dipoles), there was a smaller contact area between adjacent dipoles. That reduced the risk of "birdsnesting," dipoles clumping together uselessly in a tight mass.[20]

The introduction of glass fiber chaff coincided with an important development in dispensing. Until the early 1960s the size and weight of chaff dispensers limited their internal carriage to large aircraft. Smaller planes carried the dispensers in pods mounted on the external weapons stations. An alternative was to carry chaff in packets inside the plane's airbrake wells, and release it by blipping open the airbrakes; that method could be used only once during a sortie, however, and its effectiveness was questionable.

As radar-controlled gun and missile systems became more numerous, there was a pressing need for a chaff dispenser for small tactical aircraft. Yet for mission effectiveness it was important that it did not occupy a weapons station. Also, as tactical fighters became faster, forcible ejection of the chaff became necessary or the dipoles blossomed too far behind the plane to break a radar lock-on.

The story of forced ejection of chaff began at the end of the 1950s when Vic Kutsch, a civil servant at the Naval Research Laboratory (NRL), investigated ways of achieving faster blooming of chaff. He loaded a 37 mm signal pistol with chaff-filled cartridges, with a gunpowder charge to eject the payload. Tests with the modified signal pistol showed it was a viable method for dispensing chaff.[21]

Kutsch's first tactical cartridge chaff dispenser was an in-line ten-hole dispenser, the barrels having the same dimensions as the modified signal pistol. For testing it was mounted in a small pod under the wing of a piston-engined Beechcraft aircraft. The early percussion cap method of firing was unsatisfactory, and an electrically fired system replaced it. The next step was to increase the number of cartridges in the dispenser to twenty-four, firing the glass fiber chaff at right angles to the plane's direction of flight.[22]

Having seen the advantages of glass fiber dipoles, Lundy Electronics & Systems purchased the rights to the manufacturing process and set up the first metallized glass chaff manufacturing facility at Pompano Beach, Florida.[23]

As we observed earlier, radar-controlled AAA caused a large proportion of the US losses over North Vietnam. To counter this the Navy issued a requirement for a chaff dispensing system for tactical fighters. Lloyd Schoppe at Goodyear proposed a system based on Vic Kutsch's twenty-four hole design, but with thirty barrels arranged in six rows of five. With a few changes this became the ALE-29, which went into production using the same 37 mm diameter circular-section cartridges as Kutsch's original design. The ALE-29 was installed in Navy tactical fighters on a scale of two dispensers per aircraft. The ALE-29A, which replaced it in production, had incremental improvements.[24]

In 1966, Tracor beat Goodyear in a competitive bid for the ALE-29B dispenser to launch both infra-red decoy flares and chaff. Tracor built that system for the Navy in large numbers.

At the end of 1965 several Douglas A-3 aircraft were being modified for the standoff jamming and tanker roles. That plane's jamming capability was designed to counter the Vietnamese land-based threat, however, and its manually tuned noise jammers had limited capability.

A better system was needed and the Navy had issued a requirement for a dedicated standoff jamming plane with a state-of-the-art countermeasures suite. The original intention was to modify Grumman A-6 airframes for the role, but the Navy opted for a four-seater which meant a major redesign of the forward fuselage.[25] The four-seat jamming aircraft was designated the EA-6B, later named the Prowler. Airborne Instrument Laboratories built the receivers and other parts of the ALQ-99 high powered tactical jamming system. Raytheon built the main jamming transmitters. Douglas supplied the pods to carry the transmitters, with ram air turbines to provide electrical power. The first EA-6B, one of three A-6A conversions, made its maiden flight in May 1968.[26]

On the afternoon of 21 October 1967 the Egyptian Navy delivered a message that shook navies around the world. That day Soviet-supplied *Komar* ("Mosquito") patrol boats, sitting in the harbor at Port Said, launched three SSN-N-2 Styx active homing missiles at the Israeli destroyer *Eilat* patrolling off the coast. Fired from a range of about 15 miles, all three missiles scored hits on the *Eilat* and she sank with heavy loss of life. For the first time, guided missiles launched from warships had caused the destruction of one of their kind.[27]

Since its appearance at the beginning of the decade, the 70-ton *Komar* missile patrol boat had been a naval curiosity. It had a maximum speed of around 40 knots in calm seas and the two Styx missiles, credited with a maximum range of 23 miles, sat in canisters mounted on the after deck. A Square Tie surveillance radar provided target acquisition. Once launched on the target's azimuth, the missile's active radar homing system picked up the target and guided the Styx to impact.[28]

The *Komar*'s poor habitability confined it to coastal waters and the extra weight topsides made it unstable in high sea states. Yet it could be a nasty opponent. It was as small and hard to find, and as nimble and hard to hit, as the traditional PT boat. It could launch missiles from beyond the range of the guns of a much larger warship. These boats were cheap to build, they employed relatively simple technology and crews did not require long training to become effective. The Soviet government had supplied these craft to several clients including Cuba, North Korea, Egypt and Syria.[29]

The most significant thing about the *Komar*, however, was that it was the least effective of the family of missile-equipped patrol boats and warships in service with the Soviet Navy and its allies. The larger and better-equipped *Osa* ("Wasp") patrol boat, 165 tons, carried four modified Styx (SSN-11) missiles of greater lethality. Several Soviet warships carried the big SS-N-3 Shaddock anti-ship missile, credited with an effective range of more than one hundred miles.[30] There was also a family of Soviet air-launched anti-ship missiles: the AS-1 Kennel, AS-2 Kipper, AS-3 Kangaroo, AS-4 Kitchen and AS-5 Kelt. Some of these weapons had been adapted for firing from land sites.

The sinking of *Eilat* gave a wake-up call to naval thinking comparable with that administered by the submarine earlier in the century. Once more a small and relatively poor nation could afford a craft able to engage major warships with a reasonable prospect of success.

US Navy warships frequently moved close to the coast of North Vietnam to bombard targets ashore. Occasionally coastal artillery batteries replied, though their fire was too inaccurate to pose a serious threat. If Soviet anti-ship missiles appeared in the theater, the US Navy might suffer a loss similar to that inflicted on the Israeli Navy.

The countermeasures systems fitted to US warships were largely ineffective against the missile threat. The warning receiver carried, the WLR-1, was a 1950s vintage manually-tuned narrow-band receiver with little chance of intercepting signals of short duration like those from incoming missiles.

The main jamming system was the ULQ-6, an I-band repeater with a very directional antenna. Jim Sullivan, a civil servant at the Bureau of Ships (BuShips), described its limitations:

> "The ULQ-6 had been designed specifically to counter the Soviet AS-1 anti-ship missile system. As it stood, it was not effective against their later systems. Moreover, if the Soviets had ever launched a missile attack on one of our Navy battle groups, you could be sure they would not have sent in missiles one at a time. There would be ten or fifteen missiles, at least, coming in simultaneously and they would have gone after the carrier.
>
> A major problem with the ULQ-6 was that if it picked up signals from multiple radars it took them all in, combined them, detected them, put inverse gain on them and sent them out. It sent back all the signals with the same modulation. Against two or three missile radars that might have worked. But if there were five or six signals, all carrying the combined modulation, probably the jammer would not have affected any of them."[31]

BuShips ran several programs to improve the ULQ-6's ability to counter the newer Soviet anti-ship missiles. Transmitter power was increased and a range gate pull-off (RGPO) feature was added. The ULQ-6 with RGPO went into service in the mid-1960s, fitted in several warships. Its power output was increased from 1 kW in the original system to 20 kW in the new one. These improvements were incorporated in later variants of the ULQ-6, namely the SLQ-22, the SLQ-23 and the SLQ-24.[32] Yet it was clear that these could not provide effective protection against the range of Soviet anti-ship missiles being deployed. Something altogether better was needed.

Late in the 1960s ITT won the competition to design and build the SLQ-27 Short Stop system to protect warships. Short Stop used advanced techniques to provide intercept, analysis and identification of signals and its high powered jamming transmitters covered all known threat bands. It was designed to respond automatically to threats by radiating jamming or deception signals, by launching chaff or by a combination of these measures.[33]

The system employed digital computer-controlled jamming, feeding automatically steered antennas. The jamming power was switched between antennas, depending on the direction of the threats. To deal with sea-skimming missiles, the jamming antennas were stabilized in elevation so that when the ship rolled the jamming beam maintained position relative to the horizon.

Short Stop's central computer had a puny memory of around 100 kilobytes, and its limitations did not end there. Stan Alterman, director of electronic warfare at ITT's Avionics Division, commented:

"The computer was used for keeping the threat lists, running the displays and the identification function. But our computer was not easily re-programmable like a modern system. The signal sorting, to separate multiple signals in the same channel, was done using hardware. The program was built into the design of the computer. So, if we wanted to change the program, we had to change the hardware."[34]

The SLQ-27 took about three years to develop, and fitted in the guided missile destroyer USS *Biddle* (DLG 34) it performed well during sea tests. Yet its price tag, around $10 million per copy, was too much for general deployment. Jim Sullivan commented.

"What had started out as a $15 million Research and Development effort, ended up at a hundred and some million when they factored in the costs of support and testing. They were going to put it on carriers, cruisers, and important large ships like oilers, about a hundred ships in all. We priced it out for 15 years and we were talking about hundreds of millions of dollars. It would have taken literally the entire Navy budget for EW procurement. Every program that costs money makes enemies, and in this case the missile and gun people worked hard to kill it. They said 'Why bother fooling with the bad guys, just shoot 'em down!'"[35]

In 1972 Short Stop was cancelled, leaving the US Navy with no fleet-wide jamming system to counter the later Soviet anti-ship missiles. To fill that void, a number of Quick Reaction Capability programs were set in train. One such was the SLQ-19, a hut-mounted system containing ULQ-6 repeaters, threat warning receivers with an automatic control system and multi-beam antennas (Navy QRC equipments carried regular service designations). The hut was carried on the fantails of large ships, starting with the re-commissioned battleship USS *New Jersey*. If required, the hut could be lifted between ships by helicopter, to maintain that capability in the firing line. The SLQ-19 was replaced by the SLQ-26, a revised system fitted internally.[36]

With the exception of the USS *Biddle* and the few large ships carrying SLQ-19 or SLQ-26, for most warships the ULQ-6 was the first line of defense against anti-ship missiles. Yet with its low probability of detecting signals, the WLR-1 radar warning receiver was unlikely to provide the notice of impending attack. It was an unsatisfactory situation that could not be allowed to continue.

If the electronic jamming failed to divert incoming anti-ship missiles, the second line of defense would come from chaff. The development of chaff and systems to deploy it by rocket or mortar ran in parallel with the development of electronic jamming systems.

There were three ways chaff could protect a ship from missiles with active radar homing. The Distraction Mode was employed when a missile attack was imminent or in progress. Chaff was launched to create a pattern of clouds each with a radar cross section similar to a warship. When an incoming missile began searching for a target, it saw several. There was a good chance the missile would lock on to a chaff cloud and be diverted clear of the ship.[37]

If an incoming missile locked its radar on the warship, the latter could deploy chaff in the Seduction Mode. A large amount of chaff was put into the sky above the ship, to produce a target with a very large radar cross-section. The aim was to get the missile's seeker head to lock on to the combined return from the ship and the chaff. Then the warship moved away from the chaff cloud at maximum speed, heading to one side, and hopefully the missile held lock on the chaff cloud.[38]

The Dump Mode was employed when an electronic jammer had broken the missile's radar lock-on. A large chaff cloud was positioned to one side of the ship, so that when the missile resumed its search for a target there was false one readily available.[39]

The original Mark 76 Chaffroc (chaff Rocket), deployed on Navy warships during the late 1960s, was a Zuni air-to-ground rocket modified to carry a chaff payload. The rocket was fired from fixed launchers on the deck of the warship. It was a relatively unsophisticated system, but it was cheap and easy to install.

During the 1960s the Army fielded the GLQ-3 ground based communications jammer, a high powered system with an output of between 1.5 and 2 kW. The jammer covered the VHF and UHF bands from 20 to 230 MHz and fitted in a 1¼ ton truck, with a trailer carrying the related communications equipment and generator. A 12-meter high mast supported the rotatable directional antenna.

Using a directional antenna to increase the effective radiated power from a ground communications jammer raised a problem during operations, however. It is a simple matter to take a bearing on an enemy transmitter, but that bearing is not necessarily the best direction in which to aim the jamming. Jamming has no effect on transmitters, it affects only receivers. And in the nature of things, the receiver picking up a message is usually some distance from the transmitter. Thus before initiating jamming, it is necessary to survey the enemy communications net to plot the positions of transmitters and the likely positions of receivers. Since the two are usually co-located this is not difficult, but it takes time.[40]

During the 1970s Fairchild Camera refurbished the GLQ-3 systems and fitted solid state electronics, converting them to GLQ-3As. The new and more capable jammer had automatic control and, later, computer control.

No description of the development of electronic warfare systems is complete without mention of parallel development in EW test and simulation systems. The Air Force Electronic Warfare Evaluation Simulator (AFEWES) at Fort Worth, and the Dynamic Electromagnetic Environment Simulator (DEES) at the Wright Air Development Center continued in use over several decades. Both systems underwent numerous modifications to keep pace with technological developments and changes in the threat.

George Nicholas worked for a time at the Wright ADC Modeling and Simulation Laboratory:

"DEES pioneered the technology of simulating multi-threat electronic warfare environments at radio frequency, in real time, in the laboratory. It has proved to be an extremely valuable simulation tool for doing exploratory research. It could be set to show maybe a hundred radar threats that had been positioned on a map. A plane would then 'fly' through that environment. DEES would show the signals the aircraft would hear at each point, as it flew through that environment. The plane's antenna patterns had to be modeled in three dimensions, and we had to do the same with the radars' antenna patterns including their side lobes. DEES was able to generate a million or more pulses per second, and do that very accurately. Every pulse had to come up at the right frequency and at the right time, it was a very intricate business"[41]

During the late 1960s DEES and AFEWES were joined by a third major electronic warfare simulator, the Red Capability (REDCAP) system built by Calspan. After leaving the Air Force, Glen Miller worked with REDCAP for nearly two decades:

"In electronic warfare the big question is: how much usable information can an enemy put together, in spite of jamming. If he has a thirty-second look here, and a two-minute look there, does he have enough to draw a track for the aircraft? REDCAP enabled us to see how effective our jammers were, in preventing the various types of radar following the plane's movements."[42]

Simulation systems were useful for other purposes. Until the late 1960s the standard method of ground testing a radar-warning receiver was with a signal generator, which produced a stream of pristine pulses on the selected frequency. The signal generators then available did not replicate the rise and fall in the signal from a scanning radar, nor the background signal clutter that occurs in a real electronic environment.

It was clear there was a market for two further types of threat simulator. One would provide a realistic environment for the testing and evaluation of EW equipments. The second would provide realistic training for radar operators. In 1968, Antekna Inc at Mountain View, California, began producing both types.[43]

In the next chapter we shall return to Southeast Asia to see the effect of some of these systems on the widening conflict there.

References to Chapter 6

1. Polmar, Norman, *Strategic Air Command*, Nautical and Aviation Publishing Company of America Inc, Annapolis, Maryland, 1979, p 105
2. Gershanoff, Hal, "Peace is our profession", *Journal of Electronic Defense*, February 1985
3. Polmar, *Ibid*
4. *Ibid* p 127
5. *Ibid* p 179
6. Interview George Nicholas
7. Interview Bob Seh
8. *Ibid*
9. Wilson, Michael (ed), *Jane's Avionics Systems 1983–4*, Janes, London, p 152
10. *Ibid*
11. *Ibid*
12. *Ibid*
13. Interview John Grigsby
14. Interview Art Hepler
15. *Ibid*
16. *Ibid*
17. Crickmore, Paul, *Lockheed SR-71*, Reed Books London, 1993. p 26 *et seq*
18. *Ibid*
19. Correspondence Robert Annen
20. Correspondence Jim Henning
21. Gebhard, Louis, *Evolution of Naval Radio-Electronics and Contributions of the Naval Research Laboratory*, Naval Research Laboratory, Washington DC, 1976, pp 339, 340.
22. Henning

23. Annen
24. *Ibid*
25. Page, Godfrey, "All Weather Tacticians," *Air International*, January 1976
26. Miska, Kurt, *Grumman A-6A Intruder; EA-6A, EA-6B Prowler*, Aircraft Profile No 252, Profile Publications, Windsor, UK
27. Herzog, Chaim, *The Arab-Israeli Wars*, Arms and Armour Press, London, 1982, p 198
28. Moore, Captain John, *The Soviet Navy Today*, Macdonald and Jane's, London, 1975, p 136
29. *Ibid*
30. *Ibid*
31. Interview Jim Sullivan
32. *Ibid*
33. Interview Jim Talley
34. Interview Stan Alterman
35. Sullivan
36. *Ibid*
37. Hyman, Joseph, and DuBose, Layne, "Expendable Decoys in Naval Warfare," *Journal of Electronic Defense*, December 1983
38. *Ibid*
39. *Ibid*
40. Interview Frank Ernandes
41. Nicholas
42. Interview Glen Miller
43. Interview Joe Digiovanni

Chapter 7

THE LONGEST WAR CONTINUES

November 1967 to July 1969

"Nothing in life is so exhilarating as to be shot at without result."

Winston Churchill

By the late fall of 1967 the initial US knee-jerk reactions to improvements to the North Vietnamese air defense system—fighters, guns and missiles—had settled to a more considered response. The counter-systems—the jammers, the Wild Weasels, the jamming escort aircraft, the ELINT and SIGINT planes—had bedded down in their respective roles. Yet the North Vietnamese had sprung some unpleasant surprises earlier and nobody doubted their capacity to do so in the future.

A major worry for US Air Force and Navy intelligence officers was that the newer Soviet air defense missile systems might appear in North Vietnam at any time. The SA-2E and the SA-3, already deployed in the Soviet Union and Eastern Europe, could easily defeat the jamming pod formation. It seemed their arrival in North Vietnam was only a matter of time, and the intelligence community maintained a careful watch for signs of their appearance.

During November 1967 it seemed those fears might have been realized. In a disastrous three-day period, 17 to 19 November, the Air Force lost eight planes to SAMs.[1] In the previous four-month period, July through October, Air Force losses to SAMs over North Vietnam had averaged only two per month.

An investigation at PACAF Headquarters at the end of November examined the evidence. The planes lost were an F-105F on a Wild Weasel mission, two RF-4Cs on reconnaissance missions and five F-105Ds on attack missions. In contrast, the Navy and Marines lost no planes to missiles that month. The Wild Weasel F-105F and the RF-4C methods of operation precluded the use of the jamming pod formation and they had always been vulnerable to SAM attack.[2] Their losses were not abnormal.

Of the F-105Ds, one was lost while attacking Bac Mai airfield near Hanoi on the 17th, two while attacking Phuc Yen airfield on the 18th, and two more were lost while attacking the Thuy Phoung barge yard on the 19th.[3] Each of these attacks had been carried out under direction from a bombing system employing a TSQ-81 ground radar located on high ground at Phou Pha Thi in northern Laos. To exploit the system's accuracy to the full, pilots had been briefed to close formation when they commenced the bomb run. By abandoning the safety of the well-spaced jamming pod formation, the planes had been made vulnerable to SAM attack.[4] Following the investigation, the practice of flying in close formation over defended areas ceased.

The change restored the loss rates to their previous position. In December 1967 no Air Force plane was lost to a SAM though, such is the perversity of the law of averages, the Navy lost three.[5]

In the fall of 1967 Colonel "Marty" Selmanovitz became Assistant to the Commander for Electronic Warfare at Headquarters Seventh Air Force. A few weeks after he arrived in Vietnam, the Foreign Technology Division at Wright-Patterson AFB sent him a cable with new intelligence on the SA-2 system. Selmanovitz learned that the beacon receiver fitted to Fan Song, which picked up return signals from the transponder beacon carried in the Guideline missile, had a bandwidth of only 20 MHz. Moreover, all beacon receivers operated in that same band. Selmanovitz thought it might be possible to use that channel as another conduit to inject jamming into the system.[6]

During 1967 about four hundred ALQ-71 and QRC-160-8 pods arrived in the theater, as had about fifty refurbished QRC-160A-1 pods.[7] Now there were sufficient pods for almost every Thailand-based tactical fighter to carry two. Initially both jammers were set to cover the same range of frequencies. In the light of the new information, however, Selmanovitz suggested that the second pod should be used to attack the beacon channel.

In the SA-2 system, a transmitter in the Fan Song van triggered the transponder beacon carried in the Guideline missile. The latter responded with a coded reply signal, the so-called downlink, which enabled the Fan Song computer to track each missile in flight. The guidance computer then calculated steering signals to fly the missile from its current position to the calculated impact point ahead of the target. If the downlink signal was effectively jammed, the Fan Song computer could no longer track the missile in flight and the latter received no further corrections to its trajectory.

If jamming of the beacon channel was possible, there was no doubt it would reduce losses from SAMs. Yet the desirability of the outcome did not make it any easier to achieve. The one-way radio transmission required a far greater density of jamming power than was needed to jam a feeble radar echo signal. "Marty" Selmanovitz reviewed the questions that needed to be answered:

"We had to get the jamming into the beacon receiver, that was the weak spot. But did we have enough jamming power in our pods to do that? Could we afford to dedicate a pod just for that purpose? What would it do to the rest of the formation? We got some of the people who were really good on pods to look at this. We went out to Systems Command, to the Air Staff. Power density was the problem. All the beacons operated in same 20 MHz wide band, so we could narrow the jamming to that particular band of frequencies. So, we set one pod on each plane to the beacon frequency, with all four [magnetrons] running on the same center frequency. The other jamming pod we left tuned to the Fan Song and Fire Can radars, because we weren't that sure the beacon jamming would work."[8]

Whether or not beacon jamming would work, there was agreement that it would do no harm to test the scheme in action. After all, each plane also carried one pod with the regular jamming settings.

Selmanovitz's proposal was accepted and from December 1967 attack fighters with two jamming pods had two different settings. One was the regular setting to jam the Fan Song and the gun control radars. The other, a so-called "Special Pod", was tuned to the Guideline beacon channel. Following the change there was a marked drop in losses to missiles. During the whole of 1967 on average one aircraft had been lost for every fifty missiles launched. During the period from 14 December 1967 to 31 March 1968, 495 missile firings were reported. These destroyed three Air Force planes, of which one was an F-105F Wild Weasel aircraft not fitted with a beacon-configured pod. Thus, during the latter period, planes employing beacon jamming suffered one loss per 247 missiles fired.

It is possible that other factors might also have contributed to that reduced loss rate, however. Following the November investigation, pilots were more careful to adhere to proper spacing when flying in jamming pod formation. More jamming pods were available in the theater than ever before and their operability was much improved. Also, there were more jamming support and Iron Hand aircraft in action than previously.[9]

In 1968 the Lockheed EC-121 Coronet Solo aircraft arrived at Korat and began operating over Southeast Asia to jam enemy communications. For high frequency transmissions the installation included a trailing antenna some five thousand feet long housed on a large drum. The antenna terminated in a 35-pound streamlined concrete weight. Three Coronet Solo aircraft came to Thailand from the 93rd Tactical Electronic Warfare Group, an Air National Guard unit.[10] With National Security Agency approval the Coronet Solo aircraft flew numerous missions, jamming enemy high frequency tactical communications associated with ground operations.[11]

Over Southeast Asia the Coronet Solo aircraft operated only in the communications jamming role. However, the plane was also equipped to operate as an airborne radio or television transmitting station. Broadcasts could be made live from the plane or, in the case of radio, with pre-recorded tapes.

A further EC-121 variant active in Southeast Asia, the R Model, deserves mention at this point. During 1968, under the Igloo White program, Army and Air Force planes dropped hundreds of acoustic, seismic and other sensors in areas where enemy troops and supply vehicles were likely to pass. The main target was the Ho Chi Minh Trail running through Laos and Cambodia, the supply artery for Viet Cong guerrillas fighting in South Vietnam. When a sensor hit the ground it buried its body, leaving just the camouflaged antenna exposed. It then broadcast the sounds or seismic vibrations of enemy troop or vehicle movements.[12]

EC-121R "Bat Cat" aircraft of the 553rd Reconnaissance Wing flew 12-hour missions from Korat, monitoring the sensors. Each plane carried eight listening positions, and when the crew detected enemy movement, they passed the information by data link to the Igloo White ground station at Nakhon Phanom in Thailand. Controllers at the ground station then directed attack planes to engage.

The EC-121R was itself vulnerable to attack from missiles and fighters, so it carried an electronic warfare suite and an EWO to operate it. Captain "Tofie" Owen, who had previously flown as EWO in B-52s, recalled:

"The EW suite in the EC-121 was similar to that carried by the B-52, and the equipments were just the same: APR-25 and ALR-20 receivers and ALT-28 and ALT-32 jammers. Often we picked up signals from enemy SAM and early warning radars, and I turned on my jammers a few times.

Although there was a SAM threat, our bigger worry was the MiGs. There we were over hostile territory at 15,000 feet in a big prop-driven airplane, flying the same orbits for hours on end. We had ground radars and College Eye EC-121 radar surveillance planes keeping watch for approaching threats. On several occasions we received MiG alerts but fortunately there were no attacks."[13]

The Igloo White operation continued until the US military commitment in Southeast Asia ended.

We have observed the shortcomings of the Shrike missile as a counter to SA-2. Its range was insufficient to engage the Fan Song control radar from outside the SAM engagement envelope. Also, if the target radar ceased transmitting while a Shrike was in flight, the missile lost all sense of direction. ·

In March 1968 a new anti-radiation missile appeared in action, the AGM-78 Standard ARM. This weapon had a maximum range of about 70 miles, it carried a more destructive 219-pound warhead and was a great improvement over Shrike. It also had a memory to allow it to continue on an established heading for a time, even if the enemy radar ceased transmitting. Those attributes made it a big and expensive missile, however. The Standard was half as long again as Shrike, more than three times as heavy and several times more expensive.[14] The Standard would see considerable use by defense suppression planes during the remainder of the conflict.

In the spring of 1968 the USS *America* arrived on Yankee Station with A-7A Corsairs and F-4J Phantoms equipped with the newest Navy electronic deception system, the Sanders ALQ-100. This combined the capabilities of the earlier ALQ-49 (G/H bands) and the ALQ-51A (D through F bands), but in the same 2.3 cubic foot volume as either one of them. To squeeze the additional capability into the same volume Sanders engineers used several novel techniques. There were fears that if an intact ALQ-100 fell into enemy hands some important technology would be compromised. To prevent that, the equipment included an igniter to destroy key parts if the plane crashed or if an ejection seat fired.[15]

In service the igniter's triggering mechanism proved too sensitive, however. It simply could not tell the difference between a genuine crash, and a slightly-heavier-than-usual deck landing. No fewer than seventy-four ALQ-100s were wrecked when igniters went off during deck landings, before the self-destruct system was disarmed.[16]

During 1968 the Douglas EKA-3B TACOS (tanker/counter-measures) aircraft was a frequent participant in air strikes on North Vietnam. The converted attack bomber could refuel other aircraft in flight, and also provide jamming cover for attackers. The jamming suite comprised two Litton ALT-27 D/E-band noise jammers feeding high gain steerable antennas. There was also an ALQ-92 to jam metric-wavelength early warning radars.[17] For self protection it carried Sanders repeaters, a warning receiver and a chaff dispenser.[18]

One or two EKA-3Bs accompanied each maximum-effort strike by a carrier air group. They launched first and provided fuel for the shorter-legged fighters. When the force reached the enemy coast, the EKA-3s moved to their assigned racetrack patterns to provide jamming protection for the force. After an action many a pilot had reason to be grateful for an EKA-3B, as the plane then reverted to its tanker role and provided succor to those needing it. The combination of tanker and standoff jamming aircraft was a hasty improvisation, but a useful one.[19]

The EKA-3B TACOS had been a stopgap pending the arrival into service of the four-seat Grumman EA-6B, but the latter was a long time coming. The earlier two-seat EA-6A jamming escort aircraft for the Marines arrived at Da Nang in November 1966, to replace the aging Douglas EF-10Bs of VMCJ-1. Due to production delays the Douglas-Raytheon ALQ-76 high-powered jamming pods were not available. So the EA-6As first went into action carrying the so-called ALQ-76 "U-Pack", ALQ-76 shells containing elderly ALT-6B noise jammers.[20] In that configuration the EA-6A was little improvement over the EF-10B it replaced.

In 1968 full performance ALQ-76 pods finally arrived, each containing four 400-watt Raytheon transmitters powered by a ram air turbine on their noses. Each EA-6A carried three such pods, normally configured with ten D/E band and two C band transmitters. The jammers fed steerable high-gain antennas in a fairing on the underside of each pod. For setting the jammers on frequency, the aircraft carried an ALQ-86 receiver with antennas in the bullet-shaped fairing on top of the vertical stabilizer. The EA-6A's self-protection suite comprised an ALQ-49 and two ALQ-51 deception equipments, an ALE-18 chaff dispenser and an ALE-32 chaff and flare dispenser.[21]

With the arrival of the new pods, the EA-6A could at last be used to its full potential. Teamed with A-6As and F-4Bs, these planes formed night strike teams attacking targets in the southern part of North Vietnam.[22]

In mid-1966 the Department of Defense had asked the Air Force how its electronic warfare program was running in Southeast Asia. The Air Force responded with assurances that the program was going very well indeed. In a follow-up inquiry, the DoD asked for evidence to substantiate that claim. Embarrassed Air Force officers had then to admit that no hard evidence was available.[23]

There was no shortage of anecdotal evidence on the effectiveness of electronic warfare systems. Crews were enthusiastic about them; they believed that the systems saved aircraft and lives. Yet aircrew observations made in the heat of battle were often erroneous or misleading. There was no means to quantify the effectiveness of individual systems and tactics.

In a quest for more reliable information, the Air Force Special Communications Center (later the Air Force Electronic Warfare Center) conducted a comprehensive evaluation of electronic warfare systems in the theater. The analysts had clearance to the most sensitive sources of information. From March 1967 the AFSS began issuing Immediate Reaction Reports, nicknamed "Comfy Coat" and classified Secret, for dissemination to the operational units.[24]

The AFSCC team in Southeast Asia produced several highly detailed analyses of EW systems and tactics. One such report examined the effectiveness of the Shrike anti-radiation missile during Wild Weasel operations in the period 1 March 1967 through 31 March 1968. The report noted that when Fan Song radar operators detected a Shrike launch, they often ceased transmitting to deny the missile a homing signal. Thus, the report argued, a cessation of signals was not proof that a radar had been hit. The evaluators found it difficult to assess damage caused by Shrikes. They did find evidence, however, that many Shrikes had been launched from outside the optimum maneuver envelope. Overall, the investigators concluded that Shrike's kill probability against enemy radars was in the region of 5 percent. Yet although they rarely caused damage to radars, Shrikes frequently forced them to cease transmitting. That saved many planes and permitted others to complete their missions without being engaged.[25]

On several occasions Wild Weasel crews who had expended their Shrikes carried out dummy attacks, flying the lofted launch maneuver to intimidate missile batteries into turning off its radar. Tests with the Fan Song surrogate radars in the US revealed the Shrike's rocket exhaust gave a distinctive radar response as the weapon left the aircraft, however. If the rocket's plume was not seen, the evaluators considered it unlikely that enemy operators would be duped into turning off their radar on a regular basis.[26]

If a Shrike was launched at a radar within its maneuver envelope, and if the radar remained on air, the evaluators assessed the missile's chances of putting the radar out of action at greater than 40 per cent. So radar operators who persistently ignored the Shrike threat would not survive long.[27]

During the period under review Iron Hand aircraft made 931 attacks on SA-2 sites and launched 1,146 Shrikes. Of that total 370 attacks were on missile sites that posed a direct threat to a strike force, termed "defense suppression missions". The evaluators calculated that these 370 attacks probably caused destruction of or severe damage to eighteen Fan Song radars. Two Wild Weasel planes were shot down while engaged in defense suppression missions.[28]

During the same period Wild Weasel units made 561 attacks on SAM sites that did not pose a direct threat to a strike force, termed "hunter/killer attacks". The evidence suggested they destroyed or damaged more than forty radars, but for a loss of thirteen planes.[29]

The evaluation produced three important conclusions. Firstly, the multiple Shrike firings did not markedly increase the chances of "killing"a particular Fan Song radar, since when a radar ceased transmitting that defeated multiple Shrikes as effectively as single missiles. Secondly, no matter how bravely carried out, a protracted action against an alerted missile site was unlikely to destroy the radar; it was unlikely an alerted missile crew would fail to see the missile launch and cease transmissions well before the Shrike arrived. However, the "bottom line" justification for the effort put into the Wild Weasel operation was that, by their presence, these aircraft reduced SAM firing rates considerably and sometimes by as much as 90 percent. [30]

The use in South Vietnam of light aircraft fitted with high frequency direction-finding equipment, to support Army operations, began early in the 1960s. From those small beginnings the SEMA (Special Electronic Mission Aircraft) force expanded steadily. By the late 1960s the 224th Aviation Battalion (Radio Research), the Army unit involved with this work, had a strength of about 1,100 personnel. It operated a fleet of nearly one hundred single-engined RU-6A Beavers and twin-engined RU-8D Seminoles and RU-21s. The 224th Battalion was subordinate to the 509th Radio Research Group, the Army Security Agency unit assigned to the Vietnam.[31]

Initially the planes' role was to intercept and identify the enemy radio transmissions. They would also try to home on the source of the transmissions, to determine their position for follow-up action.

Major Bill Gardner described a typical RU-6 Beaver direction-finding and location mission in the Mekong River Delta near Saigon:

"The Beaver missions were strictly visual, flying at about 1,000 feet above the ground. In the Delta area, the terrain was flat so we did not have to vary altitude much. The co-pilot did the map reading and recorded the flight data. We had to go out and search for the enemy signals—there were days when we picked up none at all.

If the radio operator in the back of the plane picked up an enemy HF [Morse] signal from the aircraft's wing mounted dipole antennas, the pilot would turn toward the source until there was a null, then take a bearing. The plane then made a 90-degree turn and flew for one minute, and took a second bearing on the transmitter. If the cut of the bearings was narrow, that told us the transmitter was some distance away. If the cut of the bearings was wide, it meant the transmitter was close by. The co-pilot would plot the bearings. After a minimum of three bearings, a plot could be made and the intersection noted. We often got the location to within about 250 meters, that was the best we could do. When the radio operator got a null indicating the aircraft was lined up with the signal source, he would say 'Mark!' The pilot then turned the Beaver on its wing, the co-pilot looked down and marked the location on the map."[32]

It normally required a continuous transmission of between three and five minutes to get an approximate location on the transmitter. That required an incompetent or an untrained enemy operator. Often a transmission ceased in the middle of the process, so the effort produced only a line of bearing.

In 1967 the battalion received a powerful boost in capability, with arrival of the 1st Aviation Company equipped with six Lockheed AP-2E Neptune aircraft, converted Navy patrol planes. The detachment, based at Cam Rahn Bay, was nicknamed Crazy Cat. Bill Gardner described the planes and their mission:

"Of the six Neptunes, three carried COMINT receivers and recording equipment plus a powerful radio jammer. Two planes carried COMINT receivers and recording equipment but no jammer. The remaining plane was used only for pilot training and carried no mission equipment. The three Neptunes with the jamming capability were never permitted to use it, because NSA felt it was more productive to listen to the signals than to jam them. The five mission-equipped birds operated strictly in the

COMINT collection role, recording signals which were exploited after the plane landed."[33]

The Neptunes flew night missions lasting ten to twelve hours along the DMZ, usually at altitudes between 5,000 and 8,000 feet. Each Neptune carried three pilots and between five and seven radio operators. Although ground monitoring stations also performed this task, in that hilly terrain signals collection was more effective from the air.[34]

We now depart briefly from the story of electronic warfare, to follow political and military developments in the US and in Southeast Asia. By the beginning of 1968 the US had about 500,000 combatants in Vietnam. With the Air Force units in Thailand and aboard Navy ships off the coast, the total US commitment in the theater topped the 600,000 mark.[35] In addition, there were about 200,000 men in regular South Vietnamese fighting units. Estimates of the strength of North Vietnamese and Viet Cong forces vary, but were thought to have been around 500,000.

On 30 January 1968 Viet Cong units launched a powerful offensive in South Vietnam to coincide with the Tet religious holiday. They entered several cities and a suicide squad even fought its way into US Embassy in Saigon and held out for six hours, before troops retook the complex. The battles raged for ten days, before the surviving insurgents were driven back with heavy casualties.[36]

In the fighting many guerrilla units were cut to pieces, and in strictly military terms the Tet Offensive was a defeat for the Viet Cong. In political terms, however, the offensive was a disaster for the US cause. The ferocity of the Viet Cong attacks came as a shock and strengthened the widespread perception that the war was not winnable. Reacting to the popular mood at home, President Johnson announced that he would seek a negotiated settlement with the Hanoi government. To set the stage, on 31 March 1968 he ordered a halt to the bombing of North Vietnam except for a small area in the extreme south. He also declared there would be no increase in the US forces deployed in Southeast Asia.[37] On 31 October the President extended the bombing halt to the whole of North Vietnam, though reconnaissance flights could continue.

In 1969 Richard Nixon, Lyndon Johnson's successor, took the process further. He stated that the South Vietnamese had to assume a progressively greater share of the ground fighting, although the US would continue to provide assistance. US troops began a phased withdrawal and did progressively less ground fighting. By the end of the year 100,000 troops had departed.[38]

These policy changes had far reaching effects on the application of electronic warfare in Southeast Asia. The focus of the air war shifted to fighting guerrilla units in South Vietnam and interdicting the Ho Chi Minh supply trail through Laos. There the main danger was optically aimed AAA, and no electronic warfare system available in the theater would affect that.

References to Chapter 7

1. USAF and USN Official Loss List
2. *Ibid*
3. Pierson, James, *Electronic Warfare in SEA 1964–1968*, USAF Security Service 1973, p 87
4. *Ibid*
5. Loss List
6. Interview Hyman "Marty" Selmanovitz
7. Interview Pierre Levy
8. Selmanovitz
9. Pierson, p 121
10. Interview Tony Brees
11. *Ibid*
12. Interview "Tofie" Owen
13. *Ibid*
14. Pierson, p 113 *et seq*
15. Ward, Ed, Cdr US Navy, "History of Airborne ECM," Sanders Associates paper
16. *Ibid*
17. Pierson, p 133
18. Interview J.P. Sheehan
19. *Ibid*
20. Ward
21. *Ibid*
22. *Ibid*
23. Pierson, p 137 *et seq*
24. *Ibid*
25. *Ibid*
26. *Ibid*
27. *Ibid*
28. *Ibid*
29. *Ibid*
30. *Ibid*
31. Interview William Gardner
32. *Ibid*
33. *Ibid*
34. *Ibid*
35. Bowman, John S, ed., *Vietnam War*, World Almanac, New York, 1985, p 192
36. *Ibid*, p 194
37. *Ibid*, p 200
38. *Ibid*, p 233

Chapter 8

THE INTELLIGENCE ATTACK: 2

1966 to 1973

"Information's pretty thin stuff, unless mixed with experience."

Clarence Day

Throughout the 1960s the various US intelligence agencies poured vast effort into assembling an accurate picture of technical developments in the Soviet Union and her allies. They tapped every possible source in their quest to expand the pool of information.

During the late 1960s the Air Force fielded its long awaited new ELINT aircraft, the Boeing RC-135C employing the same airframe as the Boeing 707 airliner. The strategic collection system comprised the ASD-1 airborne element and the GSQ-17 "Finder" ground processing facility located at SAC Headquarters at Offutt AFB, Nebraska.

The development of the USD-7 ELINT system used the talents of several US companies. The prime contractor, Airborne Instruments Laboratory, built the automatic receivers. Sylvania built the digital computers, Raytheon produced the analysis receivers and Sperry built the automatic checkout system. Ling-Temco-Vought modified the KC-135 airframes to carry ASD-1.[1]

The antenna array mounted on either side of the forward fuselage comprised several flat spiral antennas mounted close together, extending over an area about 18 feet long and 6 feet deep. Using amplitude and phase comparison, the system established the direction of arrival of the incoming radar signals.

Signals emerging from the antennas were fed into two separate banks of automatic receivers. The larger bank comprised a number of "wide open" crystal video receivers which monitored the entire frequency band covered by ASD-1. This method gave a high probability of intercepting signals, but the receivers had low sensitivity and they picked up signals only from the radar's main beam.[2]

The other receiver bank consisted of ten narrow band superheterodyne receivers, which together covered the entire band of ASD-1 and swept through their assigned portions at 20-second intervals. The narrow-band receivers had very high sensitivity, but they did not match the high-probability-of-intercept of the crystal video receivers as they might miss signals during the interval between successive scanning sweeps. With their far greater sensitivity, however, these receivers picked up feeble side-lobe or back-lobe signals even when the radar's main beam did not point at the plane. That feature was particularly valuable for collecting signals from the narrow-scanning missile- and gun-control radars, the most sought-after types.[3]

As each radar pulse emerged from the two separate receiver chains it was fed into the computer. The latter converted the pulse into a series of digital electronic "tags" giving its time and direction of arrival, its radio frequency, its pulse width and amplitude. The "tags" then went to electronic "sorting bins" within the computer for collation and identification. The system assumed that a train of pulses with the same frequency, pulse width and amplitude, all from approximately the same direction, came from the same radar. The computer collated this information to determine the radar's pulse repetition frequency (PRF). Once the system assembled a radar's parameters, a series of direction-of-arrival "tags" provided a running fix on its position. The millions of electronic "tags" collected during each mission were stored on magnetic recording tape.[4]

The digital computer for ASD-1 was the largest installed in an airplane up to that time, and it was highly sensitive to excessive heating or cooling. The computer generated about 30 kW of heat and required a substantial air conditioning system to carry away that heat. It was important to protect the computer from overheating—not to mention the crew!

In any ELINT operation, the majority of signals collected are from known radars of little interest. The sought-after signals were those that did not conform to known parameters, or those designated of special interest. When the system picked up these signals, the operator could call them up on the screen, and examine and record them.[5] After the RC-135C landed, the ASD-1 output, held on about half a dozen large spools of recording tape, went to the GSQ-17 ground facility at Omaha for analysis.[6]

The prototype ASD-1 had began flight testing aboard an RC-135 in 1961. There were major problems to overcome with the groundbreaking system, and not until January 1967 did the first RC-135C with a production ASD-1 arrive at the 55th Strategic Reconnaissance Wing at Offutt AFB.[7]

The RC-135C flew its first operational mission in April 1967. Its missions were similar to those of the RB-47Hs it replaced, but much longer. Typically an RC-135C would take off from Offutt and undertake a collection flight along the Soviet Arctic coast, then continue on and land at Mildenhall in England. After a day or two the aircraft returned, flying the same route in the opposite direction. The regular flight crew consisted of two pilots and two navigators. The electronic reconnaissance team consisted of an EW director, an EW operator, an EW specialist and two in-flight maintenance technicians.[8]

During December 1967 the tenth and last RC-135C arrived at the 55th SRW. Even as the RC-135C entered service, many in the reconnaissance community thought it had arrived too late to have a useful life. There was a widespread perception that satellites were about to take over the entire ELINT task. That proved to be an incorrect assumption, however. Once it became clear that satellites could not do everything, the ELINT aircraft came back into favor.[9]

Specialized variants of the RC-135 replaced other types of aircraft engaged in SIGINT collection tasks. During the late 1960s two RC-135S Cobra Ball (later renamed Rivet Ball) aircraft entered service to replace the B-47Es used for TELINT collection. These planes went to the 6th Strategic Wing at Eielson AFB, Alaska, and one of their tasks was to monitor test firings of Soviet ICBMs into the Pacific.

As well as telemetry signals, the RC-135S collected infrared signatures from incoming missile warheads. In recent years this type of intelligence, separate from ELINT, COMINT and TELINT, has become known as MASINT (Measurement SIgnals INTelligence).[10]

The origin of the so-called PPMS (Power and Pattern Measurement Systems, later renamed Precision Power Measurement Systems) was described in Chapter 1. During 1970 General Dynamics modified three RC-135Cs into RC-135U Combat Sent aircraft to replace the aging C-97s. Captain Bill Strandberg flew Combat Sent missions with the 55th Strategic Reconnaissance Wing. He remembered:

"Combat Sent was a fun mission to fly. We had a laundry list of requirements whenever we deployed. We would go out and look for signals from one specific system, rather than sweep the horizon to provide the full operational picture.

We deployed overseas, usually to Mildenhall in England, or occasionally to Kadena in Okinawa, for six-week detachments during which we flew about fifteen missions. The normal mission, refueled, was between twelve and fourteen hours. We had nine Ravens [EW operators] on board together with a small contingent, between six and eight guys, from the Electronic Security Command [now the Air Intelligence Agency]."[11]

In 1967 the RC-135M Combat Apple variant appeared, to provide COMINT collection to support air operations in Southeast Asia. Ling-Temco-Vought modified six aircraft for the role with a lengthened "hog nose" radome on the forward fuselage. For most of the conflict the Combat Apple aircraft flew eighteen-hour missions with the 4252nd Strategic Wing from Kadena, Okinawa. In the spring of 1970 these aircraft were absorbed into the 376th Strategic Wing.[12]

Technically the most ambitious RC-135 variant was the E model, only one of which was built. Code-named "Lisa Ann," the aircraft carried a phased array radar with a peak power output of 7.5 megawatts. It is believed that radar was the largest, the most powerful and (in real dollar terms) the most expensive ever fitted in an aircraft. It occupied much of the fuselage, with a large antenna array looking out to starboard. The radar and computer system required more electrical power than the RC-135's regular alternators could generate. To make up the shortfall, the aircraft carried a fifth engine, a Lycoming T-55 gas turbine in an external pod mounted under the port wing, to drive a 350-kVA alternator.[13]

The phased array antenna employed numerous separate radiating elements arranged close together in a matrix. The phasing of the output from each source was controlled electronically, allowing the number and shape of the radar's beams to be altered rapidly and at will. Thus, for example, in the search mode the radar would radiate one or more wide or fan-shaped beams as it sought out targets. Once a target was detected, the radar could generate pencil beams to lock on to and track that target. At the same time it continued to radiate wide beams to search for other targets and, once these were located, they too were tracked. Today the technology of phased array radars is well understood, but in the mid-1960s it was close to the limit of the technologically possible.

In October 1966 Lisa Ann joined the 4157th Strategic Wing at Eielson AFB, and began flying operational missions to monitor Soviet anti-ballistic missile (ABM) tests off the coast of Siberia. The mode of operation was as follows. As the Soviets brought their range to readiness, Lisa Ann took off and flew to an assigned patrol line over the North Pacific. When the target ICBM lifted off from Tyuratam, US monitoring stations in Iran and aircraft in that area observed its climb-out. That information was relayed to Lisa Ann, and as the missile came over the radar horizon the RC-135E would be flying on the required heading with her starboard-looking radar aligned in that direction.[14]

Lisa Ann's radar would then track the ICBM passing high over Siberia. As the nosecone separated, one set of pencil beams locked on to it. At the same time the radar swept the Kamchatka launch site with wide search beams, looking for the upcoming ABM-1 Galosh anti-ballistic missile. Once the ABM was in flight, the radar tracked it as it closed rapidly on the ICBM warhead. Reportedly the phased array radar could measure the miss distance between the two objects to an accuracy of within 28 feet.[15]

At the same time RC-135S Rivet Ball aircraft eavesdropped on Soviet telemetry transmissions. By combining information from these and other sources, the US intelligence agencies were able to assess how well the Soviet anti-ballistic missile system had performed.

In January 1967 the RC-135E's code-name changed from Lisa Ann to Rivet Amber. The program came to an abrupt end on 5 June 1969, when the RC-135E and its crew of nineteen disappeared during a transit flight from Shemya to Eielson AFB. No wreckage was ever found and the cause of the loss has not been ascertained, though the accepted view is that it was accidental.[16]

During this period US monitoring stations along the southern border of the Soviet Union also collected a wealth of data on radar and missile tests. The Air Force Security Service site at Samsun, on the Black Sea coast of Turkey, kept particular watch on the Soviet radar development facility near Sevastapol. Air Force Staff Sergeant Ted Brown described the site:

"The Samsun site was about 200 feet high. From the viewpoint of signals collection, the nice thing about it was that there was nothing between us and the Crimea except sea. We monitored ELINT activity within our field of view. We picked up signals from the low frequency Soviet ground radars like Flat Face, Spoon Rest and Tall King. We also monitored signals from radars under development, new airborne intercept equipment."[17]

The other two major US listening sites on the south shore of the Black Sea, at Sinop and Trabzon, were primarily engaged in TELINT collection. Much of this work was routine, though there were moments of high drama. One such was on 23 April 1967, while Army Staff Sergeant Gil Bouffard at Sinop tracked signals from the manned *Soyuz I* vehicle as it orbited the earth. It quickly became clear that the craft was in trouble:

"Normally when telemetry signals from a spacecraft came into our field of view, they got stronger and stronger and remained strong until the vehicle passed below the radio horizon. Then they faded. But the amplitude of the signals from *Soyuz I* rose and fell continually.

Then we got a call from the States, saying the Soviet cosmonaut had some sort of problem. We looked at his voice signals on our scope, and saw they were fluctuating also. We deduced that the modulation on the signals was probably due to rotation of the capsule, then we learned that the ground station intended to bring the satellite down earlier than intended. We brought in our Russian language expert to listen to the voice traffic. After a bit he said 'The guy is using the correct call signs, but obviously he can't be the cosmonaut.' I said 'Why not?' He said 'This man he is swearing and cursing.' I replied 'If I was in the position he is in, I would probably be cursing too!'"[18]

The transmissions continued until the craft dropped below the radio horizon from Sinop, then they ceased. That evening Soviet radio announced that

Cosmonaut Vladimir Komarov had met his death bravely in an accident while returning to earth.

Only much later did the Soviets release details of the mishap. The craft had suffered a failure of its stabilization jets, and when it started rotating this could not be corrected. When the capsule began its descent, the heat shield was not in place to protect the craft from the blistering temperatures incurred during re-entry. It suffered severe damage and it is likely that Komarov lost his life at that stage, though after re-entry the capsule's parachutes also failed to open and the craft plunged into the ground.[19]

At the opposite side of the Soviet Union other US military personnel were similarly engaged in collecting intelligence. Major Creed Morgan served as Operations Officer at the Army Field Station at Chitose in Japan:

"Our primary mission was to collect information from Soviet space or missile shots. We could tell when the Soviets were getting ready for a launch. If their space and instrumentation ships set sail, we had a good idea that something was going to come up pretty soon. If they went out in a straight line, we knew there was going to be an orbital launch. If they went into a circle, a square or a box, that usually meant a ballistic missile that was going to impact in that part of the sea and the ships were there to check on its accuracy."[20]

Another listening station in Japan, at Misawa on the northern tip of Honshu, monitored communications from North Korea and China. On the night of 15 April 1969 a North Korean fighter took off, intercepted an EC-121 ELINT collection aircraft of VQ-1 over international waters, and shot it down. Air Force Lieutenant Pat Scott was on duty at the time:

"That night one of the analysts saw a North Korean plane take off from an airfield that we thought was unoccupied; normally there were no planes based there. There was some North Korean air activity but nobody knew what it was. Normally they did not fly over the sea, particularly at night. Off the coast near the Chinese-Soviet border, we got sporadic aircraft tracking. Then we learned that the EC-121 had gone down.

After the incident we looked at our tracking information from the two previous days, and saw the fighter go into that airfield two days before. Just the one plane. That had to be a set up, and that pilot had to be one of their best guys. The EC-121s flew regular tracks off the coast. The North Koreans would have seen them do it over and over again. Probably they said 'He'll be coming again in the next day or two, and we're going to get him.' And they did."[21]

Following Israel's victory in the Mideast war of June 1967 huge amounts of Soviet manufactured equipment was captured, including radars in working condition. At that time Israel was not a close ally of the US, so horse trading took place to secure required systems. In exchange for the Bar Lock (P-50) early warning/GCI radar, the Israelis received a working Westinghouse TPS-43 surveillance radar. Among other radars secured were examples of Knife Rest and Spoon Rest surveillance equipments and a Firecan gun control radar.[22]

Barnie Parker, a GS-12 civilian technician at Eglin, was exploitation manager for the Bar Lock set up at Cape San Blas, Florida:

> "Compared with its US equivalent it was very ruggedly built. It used old style World War II circuitry, with boards and individual components. But it was very reliable, designed to be maintained by people with a little technical knowledge. The magnetrons, I remember, were easy to change. The permanent magnet stayed in place and you pulled the magnetron out. You could even change the magnetron while wearing gloves, which I suppose was important if you had to do it in the depths of the Siberian winter."[23]

Once tests started there were fears that irreplaceable vacuum tubes and magnetrons might burn out before the exploitation was complete. This proved less of a problem than anticipated, however. Many Soviet vacuum tubes were copies of US tubes, and interchangeable with them. When a magnetron burned out, Parker fitted one from a US MPS-19 radar and that worked.[24]

There was one important omission from the inventory of Soviet radar types captured by Israel: a Fan Song missile control radar. There would be more horse trading, before the US government's long running efforts to secure an example bore fruit. Late in the 1960s a working Fan Song Model B arrived from Indonesia.[25]

Early in the 1970s the National Security Agency took over the CIA's ELINT collection activities. The CIA had one last intelligence coup to deliver in this area, however.

During 1972 the Melody station at Beshar in Iran (*see Chapter 1*) still collected useful information on new Soviet radars, by picking up signals reflected off Soviet ICBMs during test firings. In that year, as part of the Strategic Arms Limitation Talks, the US and Soviet governments agreed to limit the number of anti-ballistic missiles (ABMs) each side could deploy. The two nations also agreed not to upgrade existing anti-aircraft systems to give them an ABM capability.

Within the US intelligence community there were fears that the Soviets could be trusted to observe the treaty. The easiest way to cheat would be to modify an existing anti-aircraft missile system, like the long-range SA-5

(S-200), to have an ABM capability. Getting evidence of cheating would be difficult, but Gene Poteat saw a way:

"I suggested that we assume that the Soviets, based on their history, should be expected to cheat on the treaty by testing their SA-5 against one of their own ballistic missiles, and we should try to find a way to catch them at it... Melody had been quickly modified by adding a special ELINT receiver tuned to the SA-5's ground-based target-tracking radar frequency."[26]

Now the Beshar site watched the activities of SA-5 batteries positioned around the Sary Shagan launching complex, and within a short time the observers found what they were looking for. When large missiles launched, Melody observed the SA-5s' Square Pair missile-control radars tracking the rockets. That could be construed as bad faith on the part of the Soviets, and Gene Poteat described the follow-up:

"During one of the ensuing Geneva negotiating sessions Secretary of State Kissinger, using intelligence derived from the Melody intercepts, looked his Soviet counterpart in the eye and read him the dates and times the Soviets had cheated on the treaty."[27]

Taken aback, the Soviet representatives argued that the treaty did not prohibit the use of non-ABM radars for range instrumentation. Nevertheless, that use of the Square Pair radar ceased within three weeks of the complaint.[28] And, the neatest thing of all, the KGB began a none-too-gentle search for the mole who tipped off the Americans.[29] The CIA had reason to feel satisfied with its final venture into the field of electronic intelligence.

References to Chapter 8

1. Hopkins, Robert, *Boeing KC-135 Stratotanker, More than Just a Tanker*, Speciality Press, North Branch, MN, 1997, p 133 *et seq*
2. Interview Joe Kearney
3. *Ibid*
4. *Ibid*
5. *Ibid*
6. *Ibid*
7. Hopkins, *op cit*
8. *Ibid*
9. Interview Rich Haver
10. Interview Bill Strandberg
11. *Ibid*
12. Hopkins
13. *Ibid*
14. *Ibid*

15. *Ibid*
16. *Ibid*
17. Interview Ted Brown
18. Interview Gil Boufard
19. Peebles, Curtis, *Guardians*, Ian Allan, Shepperton, UK, 1987, p 164
20. Interview Creed Morgan
21. Interview Pat Scott
22. Interview Barnie Parker
23. *Ibid*
24. *Ibid*
25. Interview Jerry Sowell
26. Poteat, Gene, "Stealth, Countermeasures,and ELINT, 1960–1975," unclassified article in classified US intelligence journal
27. *Ibid*
28. Prados, John, *The Soviet Estimate*, Princeton University Press, 1986, p 238
29. Poteat

Chapter 9

TEST OF STRENGTH

July 1969 to November 1972

"In war something must be allowed to chance and
fortune, seeing that it is in its nature hazardous and
an option of difficulties. The greatness of an object
should come under consideration as opposed to the
impediments that lie in the way."
Major General James Wolfe

From the summer of 1969 the deployment of US ground forces in South
Vietnam reduced steadily, as South Vietnamese forces assumed a greater share
of the fighting. By the beginning of 1971 US involvement in offensive land
operations was restricted to the provision of air and naval support.

Following the bombing halt, only reconnaissance planes and their
escorting fighters were sent into North Vietnamese airspace. Lockheed SR-71
Blackbirds of the 9th Strategic Wing operating from Okinawa conducted a
large part of this effort. Making Mach 3 dashes over targets at altitudes around
80,000 feet, they were virtually invulnerable to fighter or missile attack.[1]
Unmanned drones assisted in the reconnaissance effort.

The policy of "Vietnamization" of the ground war faced its first major test in
February 1971, with Operation Lam Son 719. This large scale South
Vietnamese incursion into Laos was intended to seize a supply depot near
Tchepone and sever the Ho Chi Minh trail carrying supplies to South
Vietnam. Although the offensive had little electronic warfare involvement, it
would have far-reaching effects on US Army thinking in this area.

More than seven hundred US helicopters supported the operation, for the
most part UH-1 Hueys, CH-47 Chinooks and CH-53Ds. After a spell of
good weather, cloud closed in, forcing the helicopters to fly predictable paths
along the valleys at low altitude. Many were shot down by small arms fire,
others were destroyed when landing grounds came under fire. Then North
Vietnamese regular forces joined the action, bringing 23 mm, 37 mm and 57
mm AAA weapons and also the new shoulder launched SA-7 Grail IR
missile.[2]

When Lam Son 719 ended on 25 March, the US Army had lost 107 helicopters. A large proportion of the surviving machines had battle damage. Aircrew casualties were 55 killed, 178 wounded and 34 missing.[3] The operation established limits to what Army combat helicopters, as then equipped, could achieve when facing regular troops with their organic air defense units.

To counter the SA-7 shoulder-launched missile, Army aviation engineers developed a metal diffuser to fit around the helicopters' engine exhausts. This deflected the hot gasses into the rotor downwash, reducing the helicopter's IR signature. Because of its shape the diffuser was immediately nicknamed "The Toilet Bowl."[4] This was only a stopgap, however. To survive in the battle area in the future, it was clear that combat helicopters needed electronic warfare protection. We shall observe its progress in later chapters.

As we have seen, a major objective of Lam Son 719 had been to cut the Ho Chi Minh Trail, which was difficult to attack in other ways. To avoid air attack, vehicles on the trail ran at night or below an overcast. When the skies cleared they hid at designated stopping places in densely foliated areas. To make life hazardous for trucks at night, a number of Lockheed AC-130 Spectre gunships arrived in the theater. These aircraft carried night vision systems to locate their prey. When the crew located an enemy vehicle, the pilot headed to a point to one side of the target, then he pulled the plane into a steep turn centered on the target and aimed the sideways-firing weapons using an IR sight. In the plane's cargo compartment a team of gunners kept the weapons—20 mm, 37 mm and later even 105 mm guns—supplied with ammunition. The AC-130 was highly successful at engaging vehicles at night, and later several Fairchild C-119 Flying Boxcars were also modified for this role.[5]

Initially there were few anti-aircraft weapons in the area, and the gunships hunted with impunity. Then, as the gunships' depredations became more serious, that immunity evaporated. In March 1971 two AC-130s were engaged by SA-2 missiles, without success. There were two more engagements in April but again no plane was lost.[6] It was a clear pointer to the future, however, and there were urgent requests for self-protection electronic countermeasures systems for the AC-130s. The gunships accordingly began flying with four ALQ-87 jamming pods, two under each wing, as well as chaff and flare dispensers.[7]

December 1971 saw a significant development in the air-to-air conflict over North Vietnam. Eight F-4D Phantom fighters arrived at Udorn fitted with the APX-80 Combat Tree addition to the fighter's airborne intercept radar. Combat Tree received and displayed signals from the MiGs' IFF equipment, in a manner similar to the QRC-248 system carried in College Eye EC-121 aircraft. Provided a radar surveillance aircraft confirmed that no friendly plane was in their area, Combat Tree Phantoms could launch their long-range AIM-7 Sparrow missiles at any plane emitting Soviet-type IFF signals without having to identify it visually.[8]

This was a relatively quiet period in the air war, however, with little US activity over North Vietnam. Combat Tree first saw action on 21 February, when Major Robert Lodge of the 432nd TFW led a pair of F-4Ds on a MIGCAP over northeast Laos. The radar surveillance ship in the Gulf of Tonkin reported MiGs approaching and Lodge turned to meet the enemy planes head-on. Soon afterwards his back-seater, Lieutenant Roger Locher, observed a contact on Combat Tree and saw the planes were hostile. Lodge reported:

"The target was at zero azimuth and closing, with the combined velocity of both aircraft in excess of 900 knots. I fired three AIM-7Es, the first at approximately 11 nautical miles, the second at 8 nautical miles and the third at 6 nautical miles. The first missile appeared to guide and track level, and detonated in a small explosion. The second missile guided in a similar manner and detonated with another small explosion, followed immediately by a large explosion in the same area. This secondary explosion was of a different nature than the two missile detonations and appeared like a large POL explosion with a fireball."[9]

In the weeks to follow Combat Tree would assist other US pilots to score victories.

During this period the North Vietnamese introduced a counter-countermeasures modification to some Fan Song B radars, an optical tracking system. The modified radar received the NATO designation Fan Song F. A large box mounted on the radar's horizontal scanner housed the optical tracking operator with a high-magnification telescope.[10] By means of a servo system he could align the scanners accurately on the target aircraft, without emitting signals that might provoke Wild Weasel retaliation. Optical tracking was ineffective at night or in overcast conditions, but the system proved useful. Once the missile was in flight, of course, the usual uplink, downlink and missile guidance transmissions still had to be radiated.

At the end of March 1972 North Vietnamese regular troops launched a full-scale invasion into South Vietnam, synchronized with an upsurge of guerrilla activity. By now US troops still in South Vietnam had orders not to fight unless they came under direct attack. Those rules did not apply to air and naval units, however, and Air Force, Navy and Marine planes flew numerous missions to bolster the defending forces.

The regular North Vietnamese Army divisions moving south brought their organic anti-aircraft units, including SA-2 and SA-7 missile systems. On 29 March an AC-130 was shot down over Laos by an SA-2.[11] On the night of

5 May an AC-130 came under attack from no fewer than five SA-7s near An Loc. One missile struck the plane's tail and inflicted damage, but the Spectre landed safely.[12]

AC-130s now flew with their cargo ramps partially open, with a crewmen with a Very pistol lying on the ramp scanning the area below the plane. If he saw an SA-7 coming his way he fired a series of flares. There is anecdotal evidence that the improvised countermeasure was successful on occasions.[13] Later, AC-130s had shrouds fitted to the engine exhausts to reduce their IR emissions.[14]

As the North Vietnamese thrusts became more threatening, the prohibition of air attacks on targets in North Vietnam was lifted by stages. On 6 April there was a further escalation of the conflict when B-52s attacked the Vinh petroleum storage area. It was the first time these heavy bombers had operated over North Vietnam, and in the days to follow they struck at other targets there.

Also at this time, the Navy sent surface ships to bombard coastal targets. On 16 April this led to an instance of "anti-radiation missile fratricide." The 7,800-ton guided-missile destroyer USS *Worden* (DLG-18), operating off North Vietnam, was accidentally targeted by an air-launched Shrike missile. The weapon homed on the vessel and exploded about 100 feet above it.[15] Hot fragments peppered *Worden*'s topsides, killing one sailor and wounding nine. The ship lost electrical power in many areas, and for the next half-hour she was almost helpless, until damage control teams restored basic systems. It would take a long period of repairs in a shipyard to restore *Worden*'s full operational capability.[16]

The *Worden* incident produced an important lesson: the danger of launching self-homing weapons in the vicinity of friendly forces. Then Shrike was an "equal opportunity hazard," a menace to friend or foe alike.

The acceleration in fighting in South Vietnam led the US to launch Operation Linebacker on 9 May. To slow the movement of supplies and equipment into South Vietnam, US planes mined North Vietnamese ports and struck at transportation targets and storage areas.

On the following day, 10 May, the main Air Force effort was a set-piece attack by sixteen F-4s on the Paul Doumer Bridge near Hanoi. For the first time, electro-optically guided bombs (EOGBs) and laser guided bombs (LGBs) were to be used against a defended target in North Vietnam. In a further attack, sixteen F-4s were to attack the Yen Vien rail yard with regular bombs.[17]

The 8th TFW at Ubon sent ten flights of F-4D/E Phantoms, a total of forty aircraft, to form the main attack force. The 432nd TFW at Udorn sent six flights with twenty-four F-4s to provide escort cover. The 388th TFW at

Korat sent four Douglas EB-66E jamming escort planes, and three flights with twelve F-105G Wild Weasel aircraft.[18]

As the raiding force advanced over Laos, two flights of F-4s established barrier patrols northwest of Hanoi. Oyster flight patrolled at 2,000 feet, Balter flight patrolled some distance behind at 22,000 feet. MiGs moving in to engage Balter flight, or the main attack force, would pass over Oyster flight waiting in ambush.[19]

Soon afterwards the fighter controller aboard the cruiser *Chicago* reported enemy fighters approaching from the north-west.[20] Thus warned, Major Bob Lodge swung Oyster flight around to meet the MiGs nearly head-on. The North Vietnamese fighters, a pair of MiG-21s, ran obliquely past their adversaries at 15,000 feet with a combined closing speed of more than 900 knots. At a range of 15 miles the enemy planes appeared on the Phantoms' radars and shortly afterwards Combat Tree gave a positive hostile identification.[21]

Between them the Phantoms launched five AIM-7 Sparrow missiles at the enemy fighters. Three were duds, but the remaining two continued on. Suddenly a MiG-21 exploded and went down shedding pieces.

Both sides could play the decoy game, however. From the North Vietnamese account of the action it is clear the two MiG-21s in front of Oyster flight had also been decoys.[22] The intention was to draw the Phantoms into position for a snap attack by four MiG-19s approaching at high speed from low altitude. These entered zoom climbs and pounced on Oyster flight from below.[23] Bob Lodge's Phantom was hit by cannon fire and went down in flames, only back seater Roger Locher escaped. In the ensuing mêlée a MiG-19 was shot down and the remaining MiG-21 suffered damage, before the survivors of Oyster flight broke off the action and sped for home.

Meanwhile, the main attack force was closing rapidly on Hanoi. Four EB-66Es orbited at 30,000 feet just outside the Hanoi SAM zone and began jamming missile acquistion radars.[24] At the same time four Wild Weasel F-105Gs, each carrying two Shrikes and a Standard ARM, slipped into the defended area at low altitude and began searching for active SA-2 sites.

Eight Phantom chaff bombers led the main charge into the Hanoi SAM zone, flying at 23,000 feet. Each plane carried nine M-129 leaflet bombs loaded with chaff, and released these at intervals along the run-in to the target. After a short fall the bombs split open to disgorge the metallized strips, producing a series of chaff clouds to shield the bomb-laden planes following.

Close behind the chaff bombers came the Paul Doumer Bridge attack force flying at 540 knots at 13,000 feet. Each Phantom carried an ALQ-71 jamming pod covering the Fan Song and gun control radar frequencies, and a "special" ALQ-87 pod covering the SA-2 beacon frequencies. Colonel Carl Miller, leading the bridge attack force, recalled:

"Visibility was good and you could see the SAMs for miles. That is the main thing I remember about that mission, the vast number of SAMs going over us, under us, in front of us, behind us. It was quite a sight to behold. If you had one go by you fairly close, it was pretty exciting... "[25]

In Jingle flight, bringing up the rear of the formation, Captain Mike Van Wagenan described the indications on his APR-36 radar warning receiver as a SAM battery prepared to engage:

"The length of the strobe on the screen of the radar warning gear told how close you were to the missile radar. You didn't pay much attention to one-ringers or two-ringers. But a three-ringer, the longest strongest signal, that one said 'Hey! he's tracking you, better start looking out...'"[26]

A missile closed on the Flight from the ten o'clock position and the leader, Colonel Rick Hilton, calmly ordered his pilots to descend a couple of thousand feet to move out of its way. Van Wagenan continued:

"With our spacing, you could tell which airplane the SAM was tracking, and this one was tracking Rick. As we went down the SAM started to come down with us. It came down for a few seconds looking as if it was tracking, then it went ballistic [ceased to guide]. It was as if our electronic countermeasures were getting into it."[27]

The missile roared over the Phantoms and exploded a mile or so down range. In succession, the four-plane flights of F-4s then delivered their dive-attacks on the Paul Doumer bridge.

Mike Van Wagenen, in the last Phantom through the target, described his attack:

"There was so much going on it was impossible to comprehend everything. The human mind cannot take that many inputs, so it rules out a lot of them. The radio seemed to go quiet, the radar warning gear went quiet, everything appeared to go quiet as I tracked the Doumer Bridge underneath my sighting pipper. We just stopped thinking about the other things going on around us. My back-seater was calling off the altitudes... The pipper was tracking up the bridge, I had the parameters like I wanted to see them and released both bombs."[28]

As the bombs fell clear Van Wagenen hauled on his stick and the G forces pushed him into his seat:

"As we came off the target it was like plugging in the stereo—slowly one's senses came back and one could hear the radar warning gear, the radio transmissions, everything else. The human computer was working again. I jinked hard left and right, picked up Mike [Captain Mike Messett, his element leader] and joined up on him. Then I rolled back to the right to see where my bombs had gone. It appeared that all four, Mike's and mine, had hit the first span on the east side of the river."[29]

The bridge had taken several hits and two spans broke apart, making it impassable to wheeled traffic. As the attackers pulled away, the sixteen F-4s headed for the Yen Vien rail yard and delivered their attack. A few minutes later, for the second time that day, MiG-19s delivered a deadly zoom-climb attack on a flight of escorting Phantoms. One F-4 was shot down.

During the 10 May attack the various electronic warfare systems had worked to perfection. Combat Tree, exploiting the enemy IFF transmissions, provided positive hostile identification of the MiGs. That allowed Phantoms to launch Sparrow missiles in the beyond-visual-range mode without fear of hitting friendly aircraft.

The SA-2 batteries launched numerous missiles but failed to down a single US plane. Credit for this must go to the synergistic effect of the radar and downlink jamming from Phantoms, their disciplined jamming pod formation, the chaff trail, the stand-off jamming from the EB-66s and the presence of the Wild Weasel F-105Gs. Both F-4s lost had fallen to optically aimed cannon fire from MiG-19s, and no available electronic countermeasures system could have prevented that.

The electronic warfare tactics employed on 10 May would serve as a template for attacks during the months to follow.

June 1972 saw two further electronic warfare developments in the theater. In the first, the USS *America* arrived carrying four Grumman EA-6B Prowler aircraft of VAQ-132. The new planes flew their first combat support mission on 11 July.[30] In terms of jamming effectiveness the EA-6B was a major improvement over the EKA-3B. The Prowler carried the ALQ-99 tactical jamming system, with the high-powered jamming transmitters and directional antennas mounted in five pods mounted under the wings and fuselage.

The second development at this time was the introduction of the ALE-38 bulk chaff dispenser, manufactured by MB Associates for the Air Force. The F-4 carried two such dispensers under its wings, each holding 300 pounds of dipoles. The ALE-38 could dispense chaff in a continuous stream or in a series of pulses, and was a marked improvement over the chaff bombs used earlier. Now, eight planes each carrying two ALE-38s could lay out a continuous chaff corridor up to 105 miles long.[31]

During the summer of 1972 the Air Force established an integrated intelligence center at Nakhon Phanom AB, code-named Teaball. Teaball received and processed information from all sources, including radar surveillance aircraft and ships carrying the QRC-248 to track MiGs on their IFF signals. This information was combined with COMINT from the Rivet Top EC-121 aircraft. Radio relay aircraft provided secure communications links between Teaball and other parts of the system, and relayed attack information to the fighters on patrol.[32] In spite of high hopes for it, Teaball failed to bring any rise in the kill rate against MiGs. Teething troubles, in particular with the secure communications links, dogged the system until the end of the conflict.[33]

Meanwhile, however, Combat Tree continued to notch up victories. In September 1972 the electronic warfare staff at the 432nd TRW reviewed the unit's achievements with the device:

> "Approximately 17 out of our last 20 MiG kills were made possible either directly or indirectly by the use of Combat Tree equipped aircraft. We are certain that NVN is aware of our ability... This has been reflected in a change in their tactics from constantly squawking [transmitting with IFF]... to use of their IFF only during critical phases of the GCI intercept and recovery."[34]

During September 1972 Seventh Air Force received a powerful reinforcement, with the arrival at Takhli of the 474th Tactical Fighter Wing with forty-eight F-111A swing-wing strike aircraft. The plane's primary role was to deliver low altitude precision strikes at night, flying single-ship penetration missions. For a tactical aircraft the F-111A was well endowed with electronic warfare systems. The aircraft carried a Loral ALR-41 linked with a Dalmo Victor APS-109A to provide radar warning. The primary countermeasures system was the Sanders ALQ-94, an internal system with a number of deception techniques, supplemented with an ALQ-87 noise-jamming pod. To complete the suite the F-111A carried an ALE-28 chaff and flare dispenser and an AAR-34 infrared tail warning system.[35]

An official analysis of the early operations provides an insight into the tactics employed by F-111As:

> "During the limited Linebacker I exposure [28 September to 22 October 1972] there were 70 incidents of the F-111 being illuminated and tracked by SAM batteries. Although 16 SAMs were launched in about eight encounters, only one aircraft was damaged. The low level anti-SAM tactic employed by the F-111 involved active ECM at missile launch, chaff – accompanied by turning into the missile, and rapidly climbing 1,000 to 1,500 feet (vertical 'jink' maneuver) followed by a TFR [terrain following radar] descent to the lowest practical clearance above the terrain. Repeated vertical jinking and dispensing of chaff was required for successive SAM launches."[36]

Most AAA detonations occurred behind the aircraft, and crews believed the enemy gunners had fired at the sound of the aircraft. No MiG engagement was reported. Two F-111s were lost but it appears that neither was caused by enemy action. One plane flew into the ground, the cause of the other loss was not established.[37]

During this period Lieutenant Colonel Elbert Harbour was SAC Project Officer at Eglin AFB, running the Giant Stride program aimed at developing penetration tactics for B-52s attacking missile-defended targets from high altitude. Under Harbour's direction, B-52s on training sorties flew frequent jamming runs against the SADS-1 radar at Eglin. The tests revealed that against a B-52 radiating jamming, the Fan Song surrogate achieved "burn-through" when the bomber came within a 13-mile slant range. Inside that distance the radar operators could track the bomber's skin echo through the jamming.[38] That burn-through range applied only to a B-52 with the latest Phase V ECM suite and with all E/F band jammers radiating full power, however. For those bombers carrying the earlier Phase III ECM suite, or with some jammers not developing full power, the burn-through range was somewhat greater. Harbour commented:

"We tried out all kinds of jamming modulations. But, when push came to shove, if you were in the Fan Song's beams you were in the Fan Song's beams. That radar was an extremely effective system against a B-52 flying by itself and jamming. At that time the BWOs [backward wave oscillators fitted to the jammers] were more holy than righteous, they didn't always put out uniform power over the selected bandwidth. You sometimes got holes in the jamming in the wrong place."[39]

During October 1972 there was a new round of peace talks and President Nixon re-imposed restrictions on the bombing of North Vietnam, though attacks continued on targets in the southern part of the country. During one of these actions, on 20 November, a MiG 21 made a determined attempt to engage a cell of B-52s and launched AA-2 Atoll missiles at one of the bombers. The latter's IR decoy flares lured the missile clear, however.[40]

Freed from the need to defend targets further north, several SA-2 firing units redeployed to the area now under attack. On the night of 22 November, eighteen B-52Ds struck at supply depots west of Vinh. Four F-4s laid a chaff corridor through the target area while three EB-66s provided standoff jamming. A pair of F-105G Wild Weasels provided defense suppression and five F-4s flew as escorts.[41]

Shortly before one of the B-52s reached its bomb release point, two Guideline missiles detonated nearby. Rear gunner Staff Sergeant Ronald Sellers observed the damage inflicted on the bomber:

"The number 2 engine was burning... The first thing I noticed was a large amount of fuel coming out of the wings, all along the wings... I would estimate that 2½ feet of the left tip tank had gone; also noticed a 2 foot hole in the horizontal stabilizer... I did not see anything that was notable until the right wing caught fire... the whole inter-surface of the wing was burning. We had many, many explosions... "[42]

Losing altitude, Captain Norbert Ostrozny nursed the crippled bomber to the Thai border where he and his crew ejected to safety. Seven years after the B-52 entered combat in Southeast Asia, the first of these heavy bombers had fallen to enemy action.[43]

Following the end of Operation Linebacker, the withdrawal of US forces from Southeast Asia resumed. Yet, although a peace settlement seemed near, formidable obstacles remained.

References to Chapter 9

1. Crickmore, Paul, *Lockheed SR-71*, Reed Books, London, 1993
2. Everett-Heath, John, *Helicopters in Combat*, Sterling Publishing Co Inc, New York, 1992, p 101 *et seq*
3. *Ibid*
4. Interview Tom Reinkober
5. Ballard, Jack, *Development and Employment of Fixed-Wing Gunships 1962–1972*, Office of Air Force History, Washington DC, 1982, p 171
6. Davis, Larry, *Gunships*, Squadron/Signal Publications, Carrolton, Texas, 1982, pp 35–5
7. Ballard, p 246.
8. Michel, Marshall, *Clashes*, Naval Institute Press, Annapolis, Maryland, 1997, p 181
9. Futrell, R. Frank *et al*, *Aces and Aerial Victories*, Office of Air Force History, 1976, p 85
10. Interview Bill Cannon
11. Ballard p 231
12. *Ibid*
13. Davis p 34
14. Cannon
15. Lake, Rear Admiral Julian, "Warship Vulnerability," *International Defense Review*, 6/1981
16. *Ibid*
17. For a detailed account of that day's air fighting see Ethell, Jeff and this author, *One Day in a Long War,* Random House, New York, 1988. The description of the action given here is based on the research for that book.
18. USAF pilot's briefing sheet for the operation, copy in possession of the author
19. *Ibid*
20. *Ibid*
21. Interviews of Chuck DeBellevue and Steve Ritchie
22. Correspondence with Zoltán Buza
23. *Ibid*
24. USAF Briefing sheet
25. Interview Carl Miller
26. Interview Mike Van Wagenan

27. *Ibid*
28. *Ibid*
29. *Ibid*
30. Polmar, pp 202–3
31. Unnamed Authors, *Description of the AN/ALE-38 Chaff Dispenser*, MB Associates, San Ramon, CA, 1973
32. Michel, p 251
33. *Ibid*
34. Johnson, Major Calvin, *Linebacker Operations September–December 1972*, Project CHECO, Office of History, HQ PACAF, p 50
35. Checo report "F-111 in SEA," quoted in Johnson, *Linebacker Operations*
36. *Ibid*
37. *Ibid*
38. Interview Maj Gen Bert Harbour
39. *Ibid*
40. *Ibid*
41. *Ibid*
42. Michel, p 193
43. Johnson, p 32

Chapter 10

OPERATION LINEBACKER II

December 1972

"History never looks like history when you are living through it. It always looks confusing and messy, and it always feels uncomfortable."

John Gardner

On 14 December 1972, following yet another breakdown in the peace talks with the North Vietnamese government, President Richard Nixon approved the launching of Operation Linebacker II. This was to be a far more violent affair than its predecessor and involved the use of all types of aircraft, including B-52s, to hit targets in the Hanoi and Haiphong areas.

B-52 crews on temporary duty on Guam or in Thailand had no inkling of the latest shift in the international situation. Captain Andy Vittoria, a B-52D EWO with the 307th Strategic Wing at U-Tapao, Thailand, was summoned to base from a brief spell of leave.

"After we had assembled in the briefing room they told us 'Gentlemen the target tonight is Hanoi!' There was an audible gasp, you could have heard a pin drop. Then the slides came up with our targets, right in the middle of Hanoi. The thing I remember was the big red circles on the map, the SAM rings. I thought 'Oh, man, we're going inside that?' At Vinh there had just been small circles indicating the SAM rings. But now there was this big solid irregular blob covering the whole area around Hanoi and Haiphong."[1]

During the pre-raid planning for Linebacker II, MiG-21s were thought to pose a greater threat to the heavy bombers than the SAM batteries. For that reason the B-52s were to fly in file to their targets, to ease the task of the F-4 escorts protecting their flanks. The attack was to take place at night, in three separate waves with about four hours between waves.

115

Two B-52 variants were to take part, D and G Models. The older D Model aircraft had all been through the Phase V ECM retrofit program. Only about half of the G Model bombers assigned to the operation had been so modified, the rest carried the less effective Phase III suite.[2] Details of the Phase V suite were given in Chapter 6, but it is appropriate to repeat them here.

B-52 Phase III ECM Suite
Fitted to about half the B-52Gs assigned to Linebacker II.

Sensors	Jammers	Dispensers
• APR-9	• Five ALT-6B	**Chaff**
• APR-14	• Two ALT-13	• Eight ALE-24
• APS-54	• Two ALT-15H	**Flares**
• ALR-18	• One ALT-15L	• Six ALE-20
	• One ALT-16	

B-52 Phase V ECM Suite
Fitted to all B-52Ds and about half the B-52Gs assigned to Linebacker II.

Sensors	Jammers	Dispensers
• ALR-20	• Four ALT-6B	**Chaff**
• APR-25	• Six ALT-28	• Eight ALE-24
• ALR-18	• Two ALT-32H	• Two ALE-25
	• One ALT-32L	**Flares**
	• Two ALT-16	• Six ALE-20

During Linebacker II the most important jammers were those covering the Fan Song radar and the missile downlink channels, the E/F-band ALT-6B, ALT-13 and ALT-28. The Phase III aircraft carried seven such jammers, the Phase V aircraft carried ten. The newer ALT-28 jammers generated greater power than the ALT-6Bs and ALT-13s, increasing the advantage of the Phase V suite.

As mentioned in the previous chapter, a Fan Song missile control radar achieved burn-through against a B-52 radiating jamming when the bomber was within a slant range of 13 miles. Inside that distance the radar operators could track the bomber through the jamming. It must be stressed, however, that this burn-through range applied only to a B-52 with the Phase V ECM suite with all the E/F band jammers radiating at full specified power. B-52s putting out less power could be tracked through jamming at somewhat greater distances.

During the afternoon of 18 December forty-eight B-52s thundered off the ground at Andersen AFB, Guam and U-Tapao. The first wave was on its way. In the hours to follow the two succeeding waves, comprising respectively thirty and fifty-one bombers, also got airborne.[3] The bombers' targets were the airfields at Hoa Lac, Kep and Phuc Yen, the vehicle repair facility at Kinh No, the Yen Vien railroad yard, the Hanoi railroad repair facility and the Radio Hanoi broadcasting station.

More than one hundred fighters and attack fighters supported the B-52s. Fourteen F-111s delivered low altitude attacks on a spread of targets, including five fighter airfields. Sixty-three F-4 Phantoms provided the fighter escort. Seventeen F-105G Wild Weasels and about a dozen Navy A-6Bs and A-7s operated against missile batteries.[4] A-6As attacked known missile sites.

Twenty-two F-4s, carrying either ALE-38 bulk chaff dispensers or M-129 chaff bombs, flew through the defended areas at 45,000 feet to lay chaff lanes. The F-4s flew in four-plane jamming pod formations, to establish chaff corridors 3 miles wide and 50 miles long to protect the B-52s coming behind.[5]

Also supporting the heavy bombers were thirty-one dedicated jamming aircraft: nine EB-66Es, eight EKA-3Bs, nine EA-6As and five EA-6Bs. Six SIGINT aircraft monitored the electronic spectrum: an RC-135, two EA-3Bs, two EP-3Bs and an RA-5C.[6]

Wave One of the raiding force, with forty-eight B-52s, commenced its attack at 1945 hours (times are given in time zone G, Hanoi local time). The heavy bombers flew in three-plane cells in trail one mile apart, with a small lateral separation to spread the trains of bombs across the target. Succeeding aircraft in each cell flew 500 feet higher than the one in front. Cells followed each other at four-minute intervals.

As the bombers entered the defended area, EWOs gave undivided attention to the ALR-20 receiver. The screen displayed the radio spectrum from 20 MHz to 20 GHz, split between seven horizontal traces stacked one on top of the other. Andy Vittoria, in a B-52D, described the disconcerting picture as he neared the target:

"On Trace Four showing the E/F band [that covering the Fan Song radar transmissions] was this huge wide wedge containing a mix of radar signals and jamming. There was so much power, the top of the wedge broke through into the trace above.

I used my manual dot to scan from 2800 to 3100 MHz, back and forth, looking for Fan Song radar signals. When I found them I put them up on my expanded trace and marked the point with grease pencil. Then I narrowed down the bandwidth of four E/F-band transmitters [ALT-6Bs and ALT-28s], and set two on the Fan Song azimuth beam and two on the elevation beam. Then, as instructed, we were to jam the missile downlink signal in the blind. So I estimated where they would be and put a grease pencil mark there. Then I brought on my remaining E/F band transmitters and set them on to that mark.

I picked up A-band signals from a Spoon Rest acquisition radar, and put a jammer [the ALT-32L] on it. Once the jammers were transmitting, I monitored them the whole time, to see if the radars were still painting me. And always, out the corner of my eye, I kept watch on Trace Two in case there was a SAM uplink signal [on 850–875 MHz]."[7]

The North Vietnamese batteries fought back hard, launching Guideline missiles in salvoes of two or three at the raiders. Some well-placed missile sites under the bombers' tracks achieved "burn through," allowing clear shots at individual bombers passing overhead. B-52D Lilac Three, flying at 38,000 feet, took a hit as it was about to release its bombs on the Kinh No vehicle repair facility. The missile inflicted serious damage, but the crew released the bombs on the target and made a normal landing at U-Tapao.[8]

Eleven minutes later B-52G Charcoal One, flying at 34,000 feet, was engaged in similar circumstances. The heavy bomber went down and only three of the six crew ejected to safety.[9]

Wave Two of the raiding force, comprising thirty B-52s, commenced its attack at midnight on the same targets. Peach Two, a B-52G, had released its bombs from 38,500 feet on the Kinh No complex and commenced its post-release turn when a missile exploded off the port wing. The explosion tore away the external fuel tank and parts of the wing tip and wrecked the two outer engines. Fuel gushing out the wing tank caught fire and the blaze worked its way along the wing. Despite the desperate situation, Major Cliff Ashley and his copilot held the crippled plane in the air long enough to reach Thailand where all seven crewmembers ejected safely.[10]

Wave Three of the raiding force comprised fifty-one B-52s attacking the Radio Hanoi buildings and the nearby rail repair yard. Rose One, a B-52D leading the final cell, released its bombs on the radio station and entered its post-target turn. Shortly afterwards a missile detonated beneath the left side of the bomber. A fire took hold and four of the six crewmen ejected before the bomber plunged into the ground.[11]

Rainbow One, a B-52D, was flying at 34,000 feet on its bomb run for the railroad repair yard when a missile exploded nearby. Despite moderate damage, the bomber remained flyable and made a normal landing at U-Tapao.

During the first night of Operation Linebacker II, it is estimated that the North Vietnamese batteries launched 164 Guideline missiles. The seventeen Wild Weasel F-105Gs and about a dozen Navy A-6B and A-7 Iron Hand sorties launched twelve Standard ARM and forty-seven Shrike missiles. Two missiles, a Standard ARM and a Shrike, were credited with inflicting damage to missile sites. Defense suppression (when the target emitter ceased transmitting following launch of an ARM) was assessed as occurring on nineteen occasions.[12] Of the 129 B-52s, three were shot down and two suffered moderate to severe damage, in each case from missiles. A Navy A-7 on an Iron Hand mission also fell victim to a missile and an F-111 was lost to unknown causes.[13]

That night chaff afforded the heavy bombers uneven protection, as strong winds at high altitude quickly blew the dipoles out of position. Later it was calculated that the chaff remained in position to screen the B-52s for only eight minutes at most.[14] There is, however, anecdotal evidence that while chaff was in position it sometimes triggered the proximity fuses of Guideline missiles, so they detonated harmlessly clear of the bombers.

Acting in synergy, the various countermeasures exerted a powerful suppressive effect on the North Vietnamese air defenses. The accompanying table lists the aircraft types, excluding tankers, supporting the first-night's operation.

First Night of Operation Linebacker II, 18 December

Wave 1

Heavy bomber force	48	B-52s
SAM suppression force	5	F-105Gs
SAM site attack force	4	F-4s
Chaff dropping force	4	F-4s
Combat air patrol/Escort force	20	F-4s

Wave 2

Heavy bomber force	30	B-52s
SAM suppression force	8	F-105Gs
Chaff dropping force	10	F-4s
Combat air patrol/Escort force	20	F-4s

Wave 3

Heavy bomber force	51	B-52s
Chaff dropping force	8	F-4s
Combat air patrol/Escort force	23	F-4s

Electronic Warfare Jamming Aircraft	9	EB-66E
	8	EKA-3B
	9	EA-6A
	5	EA-6B
Electronic Warfare Support Aircraft	1	RC-135
	2	EA-3B
	2	EP-3B
	1	RA-5C
Airfield attack force	14	F-111s
Radio transmitter station attack	1	F-111
Navy aircraft	34	A-6s
	9	A-7s
Number of heavy bombers	129	
Number of supporting aircraft (excluding tankers)	197	
Total Sorties Flown (excluding tankers)	326	

For the second night of Linebacker II, 19/20 December, the targets for the ninety-three B-52s included the Kinh No vehicle repair facility, the Radio Hanoi station and the Yen Vien railroad yard raided earlier. In addition there were two new targets, the Bac Giang transshipment point and Thai Nguyen thermal power plant. Again the B-52s attacked in three waves. A total of 169 planes flew in support.[15]

The night's action was a clear success for the attackers. Ninety-three B-52s attacked five defended targets. There were no losses, though three bombers returned with minor damage.[16]

For the third night of the operation, 20/21 December, there were ninety-nine B-52s and the routes and tactics were similar to those of the previous evening. The support force comprised 111 Air Force planes plus a contingent from the Navy.

Wave One, with thirty-three heavy bombers, attacked the Hanoi railroad repair facility. The first two cells through the target area reported only four missile launches and no plane suffered damage. Then the action began in earnest. The next nine cells of bombers, attacking the Yen Vien railroad yard and the nearby Ai Mo warehouse complex, came under attack from an estimated 130 missiles.[17] Three B-52s were shot down.

Wave Two comprised twenty-seven B-52s heading for the Hanoi rail yard, the Bac Giang transshipment point and the Thai Nguyen thermal power plant. These bombers struck their assigned targets without loss.[18] Wave Three, comprising thirty-nine B-52s bound for the Hanoi rail yard and the Kinh No vehicle repair complex, was hit worst of all, with three heavy bombers shot down and one suffering moderate damage.

The action on 20/21 December would be the most costly during Linebacker II, with six B-52s shot down and one damaged. The Navy lost an A-6A. Afterwards it was estimated that more than two hundred and twenty Guideline missiles had been launched.

During the first three nights of Linebacker II, B-52s flew just over three hundred sorties against targets in the Hanoi area. An estimated 567 missiles had been launched, causing the destruction of nine heavy bombers. Analysis of these actions revealed the shortcomings of the B-52G for this type of mission, and pointed out a weakness in the heavy bombers' tactics.

Seven of the nine B-52s lost had been B-52G aircraft. That variant was more vulnerable than the B-52D for two major reasons. Five of the seven B-52Gs lost had not been through the Phase V modification program.[19] The unmodified bombers radiated significantly less jamming power in the all-important E/F band. The other major vulnerability of the B-52G was the presence of six large integral fuel tanks in its wings. If hot missile fragments pierced a tank, it caught fire. Only one B-52G returned with battle damage and that had been relatively minor.

Of the nine heavy bombers lost so far, no fewer than six had been engaged in their post-target turns at the time they were hit.[20] As in the case of the F-105, the B-52's E/F-band jammers radiated a pattern shaped like a huge inverted saucer fixed rigidly to the underside of the aircraft. When a B-52 applied bank, its "footprint" of jamming on the ground shifted to the outside of the turn. Thus a SAM site situated on the inside of the turn might have an unjammed shot at the bomber. An unmodified B-52G when making a post-target turn within range of a missile site faced the greatest risk of all.

To the surprise of SAC planners, there had been little MiG activity. B-52 crews reported seeing enemy fighters in their vicinity on several occasions, but later analysis revealed that most of these "MiGs" were escorting F-4s.[21]

Following the first three maximum effort attacks, Linebacker II entered its second phase. From night four, 21/22 December, attack forces were smaller and they employed different tactics. Bomber streams were more concentrated than previously, with the interval between cells reduced to two minutes (compared with four minutes). Thus, a raiding force would pass through the target in about 15 minutes (compared with 30 to 40 minutes during earlier strikes). After releasing their bombs, on many planned tracks the B-52s now maintained their heading until they were outside the missile defended area. That took bombers deeper into the defended area, but it was less of a hazard than entering a banked turn while there. In a further move to reduce losses, the vulnerable B-52Gs were excluded from attacks on North Vietnam for the time being.[22]

On night four the attack force comprised thirty B-52Ds from U-Tapao. The targets were Quang Te airfield (six B-52s), Bac Mia storage area (twelve) and the Van Dien supply depot (twelve B-52s), all in the vicinity of Hanoi. The supporting force comprised 121 planes of all types.[23]

The attacks on Quang Te and Van Dien took place without loss. At Bac Mia, however, the defenders were more aggressive and missiles brought down two B-52s. For a time it seemed that Andy Vittoria's heavy bomber might share their fate. He kept a wary eye on Trace Two of his ALR-20 receiver, watching for a SAM uplink signal on 875 MHz indicating a missile coming his way. He found that when the SAM uplink signal did appear, it was impossible to ignore it![24]

> "It was a big long single strobe, so big it broke through into Trace Three above. What got your attention was the way it walked across Trace Two. You could not miss it, it was so big and so bright. Then you knew a missile was coming for you!"[25]

He set his jammers on the Fan Song to jam the azimuth and elevation beams, and the missile downlink channel:

> "I moved my audio dot over the [uplink] signal to listen to it, a high pitched warbling note. It sounded real scary. The gunner reported a

missile coming up and told the pilot to break right. We did a 45 degree bank—which felt like 90 degrees—and dropped about 3,000 feet. The missile continued on; the gunner watched it go past our left side and explode above us."[26]

The bomber emerged from the encounter unscathed, and followed the other two planes in the cell through the target.

Other people had other scares that night. As the B-52s began their bomb runs, four F-111As of the 474th TFW delivered low altitude attacks on the fighter airfields at Hoa Lac, Kep, Phuc Yen and Yen Bai. Captain "Pepper" Thomas, navigator in one of the swing-wing bombers, takes up the story:

"We were coming off the target, on what up till then had been a nondescript mission. Then I heard that note on the radar homing and warning gear: 'Der – dit dit dit dit... Der – dit dit dit dit'. That was the sound we expected to hear when a MiG's radar was operating in the scan mode. We were down at 200 feet doing 500 knots and this thing was following us 'Der – dit dit dit dit... Der – dit dit dit dit.'

I said 'Les [Major Les Holland, the pilot] that sounds like an airborne intercept radar.' I looked at the radar warning gear and there in our 6 o'clock position was a little dot on the third ring. That meant an I band radar, probably on an enemy fighter. I said 'Holy S★★t, Les, there's a MiG chasing us!' I turned the ALQ-94 [deception system] to transmit, but it made no difference. The signals just kept coming, 'Der – dit dit dit dit... Der – dit dit dit dit.'

By now I guess my voice was rising, because Les was getting concerned. The next thing I knew, he had accelerated and was weaving the airplane from side to side, at the same time punching out chaff. He said 'I'm going to get this SOB off of us.' Well, that made no difference either. The 'signal' remained on our RWR gear all the way across Laos and up to the approach to Takhli: 'Der – dit dit dit dit... Der – dit dit dit dit.' Afterwards we found that the cause was a malfunction in our plane. The signal we heard was from our TACAN transmissions, which had bled into the RWR gear."[27]

Let that incident represent the scores of false alarms put out by radar warning receivers during Linebacker II, causing needless fear in aircraft cockpits.

As well as the two B-52s lost to missiles that night, a Navy A-6A was shot down by AAA while delivering a low level attack on Kien An airfield.

On night five, 22/23 December, the targets were the petroleum storage area and railroad yard at the port of Haiphong. The defenses were less formidable than those around the capital. Moreover, the raiders' ingress and egress routes were over the sea, beyond reach of the missile batteries for most of the way. As on the previous night the attack force consisted of thirty B-52Ds, this time with 90 supporters. Although an estimated 43 missiles were launched, for the first time during the Linebacker II no heavy bomber suffered damage. One F-111 failed to return, however.[28]

Night six, 23/24 December, saw thirty B-52Ds sent against the Lang Dang rail yard and three SAM sites north of Haiphong; eighty-two other planes provided support. The defensive reaction was weak and there were no losses.[29]

On night seven, 24/25 December, the now-usual 30-plane B-52D attack force struck at rail yards at Kep and Thai Nguyen well clear of the capital; eighty-one planes supported the heavy bombers.[30] Yet again no aircraft was lost. A B-52D came under fire from a 100 mm AAA battery, whose shells burst some distance from it. During the post-flight inspection, however, the ground crew discovered several small holes and dents in the plane's skin. It was the only time a B-52 took AAA damage during the entire conflict.[31]

Following a respite on Christmas Day, Linebacker II resumed at full strength on night eight, 26/27 December. Thus the third phase opened, with a further maximum effort raid involving 120 B-52s. Seventy-five B-52Ds attacked targets in the Hanoi area: the Hanoi, Doc Noi and Giap Nhi rail yards, the Kinh No storage complex, the Van Dien vehicle repair shops, the Hanoi petroleum storage area and a troublesome SAM site.

Simultaneously forty-five B-52Gs attacked targets in less-well defended areas clear of the capital. Fifteen made for the Thai Nguyen rail yards and a similar number went against the electrical transformer station and rail yard at Haiphong.[32] Over one hundred tactical aircraft supported the raiders.

By now the SAC planners had digested the lessons from the previous attacks. Instead of dividing the heavy bombers between widely spaced waves as in previous large scale attacks, a single massed assault would hit all the target complexes simultaneously. The leading cell at each target commenced its attack on zero hour, and the last bomber would complete its attack within fifteen minutes. The seven waves of bombers attacking targets around Hanoi ran in from four different directions, relying on altitude separation to prevent collisions.[33]

Ebony cell, down to two B-52Ds after one plane aborted, was running in to attack the Giap Nhi rail yard at 36,500 feet when it came under fire. The EWO in the lead aircraft picked up Fan Song and uplink signals and, with jammers set on the radar frequencies and the uplink channel, the plane continued its bomb run. Nearly thirty missiles had been aimed at the cell when, shortly after bomb release, Ebony Two took a hit and went down. Four of the crew ejected.[34]

Three minutes later Ash cell, at the same altitude and also down to two B-52Ds after one aborted, was running in to attack the Kinh No vehicle complex. Ash Two picked up three uplink signals. With one E/F-band jammer out of action, the EWO put two jammers against the downlink and the rest against the Fan Song beams. The jamming configuration of Ash One is not known, but shortly before bomb release a missile detonated beneath it. The plane suffered serious damage but the crew succeeded in bringing it back to Thailand. During the attempt to land at U-Tapao, however, the bomber crashed. Only two crewmen survived.[35] Two other heavy bombers returned with minor damage from missile fragments.

For night nine, on 27/28 December, sixty heavy bombers attacked the rail yards at Lang Dang, Duc Noi and Trung Quant, the Van Dien supply center and three missile sites. Again more than one hundred tactical aircraft provided support. Again the defenders mounted a spirited opposition, shooting down two B-52s.[36] The MiG-21 force was also active and was credited with shooting down both F-4E escorts lost that night.[37]

Night ten, 28/29th December, sixty bombers attacked the Lang Dang rail yard, the Duc Noi missile support facility and two missile sites. Except for Lang Dang, the targets were all in the Hanoi area and the heavy bombers received the usual support.[38] The large number of missiles fired on previous nights, coupled with the attacks on missile storage sites and the depredations of Wild Weasel and Iron Hand units, now had their cumulative effect. Raiding crews noted far fewer missiles launches than on earlier nights, and engagements were not being pressed home with the same vigor. No bomber took damage during this attack.[39]

On night eleven, 29/30 December, the action was similar to that of the previous night. Sixty bombers, with strong support, attacked the Lang Dang rail yard again, and also the missile support facilities at Phuc Yen and Trai Ca. Again the defensive reaction was weak and no bomber took damage[40]

Following the action on the night of 29/30 December, the North Vietnamese government agreed to resume negotiations. President Nixon ordered yet another halt to the attacks on the enemy homeland. On 27 January 1973, almost exactly four weeks after the final Linebacker II strike, the Peace Accord was signed in Paris. For the US the war in Vietnam was over.

During Linebacker II, B-52s flew 741 sorties. Of those 523 (about 70 percent) were against targets in the defended area around Hanoi. The remaining 218 sorties were against less heavily defended targets elsewhere in North Vietnam.

Thanks to the large supporting forces and the massive use of electronic countermeasures, the heavy bombers did not suffer excessive loss. Air Force and Navy defense suppression aircraft launched 421 AGM-45 Shrike and 49 AGM-78 Standard ARM weapons.[41] Nearly half of the Shrikes were fired preemptively in the target area, before Fan Song signals had been picked up. There is evidence that only two Standard ARMs and one Shrike inflicted damage to the control radars at missile sites during the operation. Defense suppression, when the emitter ceased transmitting after launch of an anti-radiation missile, occurred on 160 occasions.[42] Chaff-dropping F-4Es flew 207 sorties. Dedicated jamming aircraft, B-66Es, EKA-3Bs, EA-6As and EA-6Bs, flew 256 sorties to support the heavy bombers.[43]

In the course of the operation the defenders launched an estimated 850 missiles, three-quarters of them aimed at heavy bombers. Fifteen B-52s were destroyed, four suffered moderate or severe damage and four suffered minor damage. Except for the one case of minor damage from AAA, Guideline missiles caused all the losses and damage to B-52s.[44]

When the US involvement in the Vietnam War ended, the SA-2 missile system had seen action there for more than eight years. US aircrews encountered only one type of missile control radar on a regular basis, the Fan Song Model B (the Model F featured an optical tracking system, but the radar was the same). That greatly simplified the jamming problem.

Things could have been a great deal worse. The Soviets had deployed widely the newer C through E models of the Fan Song radar and the later SA-3 (S-125) missile system. Compared with Fan Song B, the newer radars operated on shorter wavelengths and had a better target resolution capabilities. To employ the jamming formation against the I-band SA-3 system, for example, planes flying in adjacent resolution cells would have to have been about 75 feet apart. That would have placed two or more planes within the lethal range of an exploding SA-3 warhead, making the tactic futile. Had the newer systems appeared in quantity in North Vietnam, US attack fighter crews would have found themselves "living in interesting times."

After the Cold War, Soviet advisors who served at SAM batteries in North Vietnam revealed why the newer missile systems had not appeared there. During the late 1960s relations between the USSR and China had deteriorated sharply.[45] The Soviet government feared that if the later SAM systems went to North Vietnam, the Chinese would obtain examples and mass produce copies. To prevent any risk of that, the Soviet government refused to supply these systems to North Vietnam.[46]

The Vietnam conflict had begun more than a decade before the first US troops arrived, and it would go on for more than two years after the last of them left. However, the US forces' eight-year involvement made this the nation's longest war and it cost more than 57,000 American lives.

With the end of the fighting came the end of the long running electronic warfare battle in Southeast Asia. There were many lessons to be learned, and in the next chapter we shall look at the ways in which they were applied.

References to Chapter 10

1. Interview Andy Vittoria
2. Various Authors, USAF Southeast Asia Monograph Series published by the US Govt. Printing Office: *Linebacker II: A View from the Rock*, 1979, p 41 *et seq*

3. Boyne, Walter J, "Linebacker II," *Air Force*, November 1997
4. Comfy Coat Evaluation, "Linebacker II Electronic Warfare Effectiveness", declassified official document
5. *Ibid*
6. *Ibid*
7. Vittoria
8. Information from the Linebacker II account on the Internet at http://members.aol.com/dpoole1272/home/lbdays.htm. This was written by David Poole as a memorial to his father, CMSgt Charlie S. Poole, gunner in B-52D *Rose One* who was killed in action during the first day of the operation.
9. *Ibid*
10. *Ibid*
11. *Ibid*
12. Comfy Coat Evaluation
13. *Ibid*
14. Interview Rudi Smart
15. Comfy Coat Evaluation
16. *Ibid*
17. Boyne
18. Linebacker II Internet
19. *Ibid*
20. *Ibid*
21. Interview Dave Sjolund
22. Comfy Coat Evaluation
23. Linebacker II Internet
24. Vittoria
25. *Ibid*
26. *Ibid*
27. Interview Pepper Thomas
28. Linebacker II Internet
29. *Ibid*
30. *Ibid*
31. *Ibid*
32. *Ibid*
33. *Ibid*
34. *Ibid*
35. *Ibid*
36. "A View from the Rock," p 145
37. USAF and USN Official Loss List
38. Comfy Coat Evaluation
39. *Ibid*
40. *Ibid*
41. *Ibid*
42. *Ibid*
43. *Ibid*
44. *Ibid*
45. Isaacs, Jeremy, and Taylor, Dowling, "The Cold War," CNN TV Program
46. *Ibid*

Chapter 11

IMPACT OF THE NEW TECHNOLOGY: 1

1972 to 1980

"The important thing is not to stop questioning. Curiosity has its own reason for existing. One cannot help but be in awe when he contemplates the mysteries of eternity, of life, of the marvelous structure of reality. It is enough if one tries merely to comprehend a little of this mystery every day."

Albert Einstein

Following the end of the war in Vietnam, electronic warfare experts in the armed services, industry and government sought to digest and apply the lessons learned during that conflict. At the same time, significant advances in microelectronics made their impact.

In the summer of 1976 the 1st Tactical Fighter Wing based at Langley AFB, Virginia, became operational with the new McDonnell Douglas F-15 Eagle fighter. The event marked a significant milestone in the history of US electronic warfare, for the F-15 was the first air superiority fighter to enter service with space assigned at the design stage for an internal countermeasures suite.[1] A decade and a half earlier that would have been unthinkable, and it demonstrated that Tactical Air Command had taken to heart the lessons from its past.

The F-15 carried a Northrop ALQ-135 E/F band power-managed noise jamming system, a Tracor ALE-45 chaff and flare dispenser, a Loral ALR-56 radar warning receiver and a Magnavox ALQ-128 airborne interrogation system.[2]

Although underpowered and vulnerable, the Douglas EB-66 had established its value as a jamming escort plane over North Vietnam but the last EB-66 passed out of service in 1973, leaving the Air Force without a replacement. The General Dynamics F-111A, carrying a variant of the ALQ-99 jamming system fitted to the EA-6B, was selected for the role. It had the performance to penetrate into enemy territory with strike forces, and as a two-seater it could accommodate an EWO to operate the jammers. Forty-two A Models were being phased out of front-line service as attack fighters, replaced by the later D, E and F Models. In September 1971 the Secretary of the Air Force approved a design study to modify the F-111A for the jamming escort role, as the EF-111A.[3]

For reasons unrelated to the merits of the EF-111A, the program then languished for nearly four years. Tactical Air Command was re-equipping with F-15s and F-16s and the Air Force had pressing demands on its funds. Not until January 1975 did Grumman Aerospace receive a contract to modify two F-111As as EF-111A development prototypes. The first, carrying an aerodynamic mock-up of the 16-foot-long "canoe" beneath the fuselage to house part of the jamming system, flew in December 1975. The second aircraft, carrying the full electronic warfare suite, made its maiden flight in March 1977. After testing, the Defense System Acquisition Review Council approved funding to convert forty F-111As to the electronic warfare role and bring the two prototypes to production standard. The EF-111A received the official name "Raven."[4]

In November 1981 the 388th Electronic Combat Squadron at Mountain Home AFB, Idaho, took delivery of its first EF-111A and others followed at five-week intervals. A year later, before it had its full complement of planes, the 388th ECS deactivated and its assets went to the 390th ECS at the same base. In July 1983 the 42nd ECS activated at Mountain Home and in the following February it transferred to Upper Heyford in England.[5]

During the early 1970s, Major "Tofie" Owen worked at the Research and Development Acquisition Logistics Support section at Warner Robbins AFB, Georgia. He described the areas of interest in electronic warfare at that time:

"In my estimation there were four significant EW programs that started at Warner Robbins during the 1972 to 1974 time frame. The first was the move from the analog radar warning receiver to the digital RWR. That led to the ALR-46, which started out as a Warner Robbins project before Dalmo Victor put it into production.

The second major program concerned programming software to control digital RWRs. At Warner Robbins we created the EW integrated reprogramming concept, and set up the facility for software reprogramming which still exists today.

The third program was sparked off by the 1973 war in the Middle East, which led to the question 'What do we do to counter the SA-6?' That resulted in a project which I consider myself one of the fathers of, the ALR-69 receiver that provided warning of continuous-wave missile illumination threats. That system also came out of Warner Robbins.

Top: The high powered Tall King (P-14) long range early warning radar. The supporting tower was more than 100 feet high, and the huge openwork scanner was 112 feet across. The small buildings give scale to the structure. The task of accurately plotting the coverage of this radar was the subject of the imaginative Palladium operation by the CIA. *via CIA*

Above: Bar Lock (P-35) Early Warning/Ground Controlled Intercept (EW/GCI) radar, used to direct MiG fighters into action.

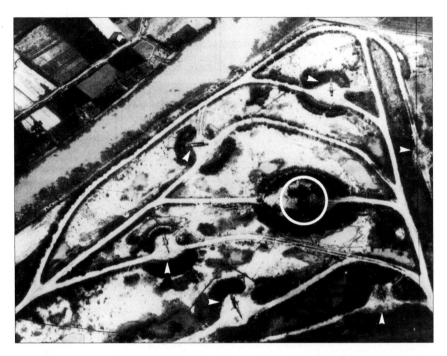

Above: Aerial view of a typical SA-2 site in North Vietnam, showing the six missiles on their launchers (arrowed) around the Fan Song control radar (circled). *USAF*

Below: SA-2 Guideline two-stage surface-to-air missile on its launcher.

Above: Interior of the operating cabin of the Fan Song B radar. *via Toperczer*

Below left: Fan Song E radar van. This radar differed from the earlier B model used in North Vietnam, in that it had two additional circular dishes mounted above the horizontal scanner. *Kinski*

Below right: The introduction of the shoulder-launched SA-7 infrared missile system in 1971 made low altitude operations more hazardous for slow flying US planes in Vietnam. *via Toperczer*

Above: Douglas EB-66E jamming escort aircraft, fitted with 28 assorted jamming transmitters on racks mounted in what had been the bomb bay. *USAF*

Below: General Electric QRC-160-1, the first jamming pod employed over North Vietnam, mounted under the wing of an F-105 attack fighter. Used by planes flying the special four-plane jamming pod formation, the jammer proved highly effective. *via Haugen*

Above: The Republic F-105G was the Air Force's primary Wild Weasel aircraft during the latter part of the Vietnam War. On this aircraft a Shrike anti-radiation missile is visible on the starboard outer wing pylon. *Kilgus*

Right: The energetic General K.C. Dempster, standing, pictured during a gathering at the Officers' Club at Nellis in 1966. Dempster played a pivotal role in the introduction of electronic warfare counters to the SA-2 missile system. To the left of Dempster is Bill Ayres, President of Applied Technology. To the right of Dempster are General William Chairsell, who commanded the 388th TFW when the jamming pods and special formation were introduced into combat. To the right of Chairsell is Major Garry Williard who led the first-ever Wild Weasel mission over North Vietnam in December 1965. *Levy*

Left: The RC-135 entered regular service in the ELINT collection role with the 55th Strategic Reconnaissance Wing in 1967, and has served with the unit ever since. The RC-135V Rivet Joint, depicted, is one of the latest versions equipped to perform the full SIGINT collection task. *USAF*

Below left: The Grumman EA-6B Prowler first went into action over North Vietnam in July 1972. *USN*

Bottom left: The EF-111A Raven, a conversion of the F-111A attack fighter to the jamming escort role, entered service in 1981. The aircraft gave excellent service during Operation Desert Storm a decade later, but due to budgetary cutbacks it was phased out of service in 1996. *USAF*

Above right: Bill Bahret, a civilian working in the Avionics Laboratory at Wright-Patterson AFB, was a leading proponent of low observables technologies during the 1960s and 1970s. *Bahret*

Below: The F-117A low observables attack fighter. The photo shows well the facetted appearance of this first-generation stealth plane, necessitated by the limited computer analysis power available at the time it was designed. *Lockheed, via Spick*

Above: The RP-2E "Crazy Cat" aircraft, a modified Navy P-2 patrol plane, served with the Army as a long endurance SIGINT collector flying close to the border with North Vietnam. *via Buley*

Below: Interior of the RP-2E, showing the control units for the radio receivers and the recording equipment. *INSCOM*

Above: Beechcraft RC-12N aircraft carrying Guardrail Common Sensor equipment. Operating in three-aircraft units, these aircraft can pinpoint the location of a radio or radar transmitter to within a few tens of yards. *TRW*

Right: Army Torii SIGINT Collection Tower at Wobeck, overlooking the border with East Germany. *INSCOM*

Right: Straight Flush missile control radar for the SA-6. The circular scanner for tracking targets was mounted at the top, with the horizontal scanner for the target acquisition radar underneath it.

Below: The highly mobile SA-6 (Kub) missile system came as a nasty shock for the Israeli Air Force, when it first saw action in the Mid-East War of 1973. This tracked vehicle served as both missile transporter and launcher.

Above: SA-3 Goa (S-125) missile site in Poland. This system was credited with the destruction of the F-117A Nighthawk stealth fighter over Yugoslavia in March 1999. On the left is the missile launcher. The radar in the center is the Spoon Rest B (P-18) acquisition radar which operates in the 85 MHz band and is reportedly able to plot the movements of low observables aircraft. On the right is the Low Blow missile-control radar. *Klinski*

Below: The SA-8 Gekko missile system performed impressively during tests before Western Intelligence officers in Germany, and later at Eglin AFB. The system is self contained on its amphibious transporting vehicle.

Above: EC-130H Compass Call communications jamming aircraft of the 43rd Electronic Combat Squadron. The blisters protruding from the rear fuselage contain jamming antennas, and the directional Yagi VHF jamming antenna array can be seen strung between the horizontal and vertical stabilizers and supporting posts under the rear fuselage. During its mission the plane flies a racetrack pattern, directing jamming to port or to starboard as needed. *Bakke*

Below: Crew positions for the jamming team, in the fuselage of the EC-130H. *Bakke*

Right: John Corder, seen here with the rank of Brigadier General, held a number of posts in which he influenced developments in electronic warfare during the 1980s and early 1990s. Early in the 1980s he commanded the 65th Air Division in Europe, which controlled the operations by EF-111A Raven, F-4 Wild Weasel and EC-130H Compass Call units. Later in the decade he commanded the Tactical Air Warfare Center at Eglin. As a Major General during Desert Storm, he served as General Horner's senior operations officer. *Corder*

Above: AH-64 Apache attack helicopter at a forward refueling point. The radiating head for the ALQ-144A active infrared countermeasures system is visible immediately to the rear of the rotor shaft. Also evident are the large infrared emission suppressor fitted around the starboard engine, and the flat-sided canopy glass to reduce optical and IR glint. *US Army*

 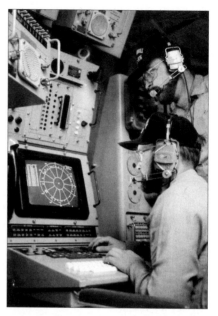

Above left: Antennas of the Raytheon SLQ-32 (V)3 fitted to a US Navy cruiser. The upper group of antennas were for the reception of signals, the lower group of antennas transmitted the jamming. Each ship carried two such antenna groups, one on each side of the hull. *Raytheon*

Above right: The SLQ-32 operator's console in a warship's Combat Information Center. *Raytheon*

Right: Firing a Nulka active decoy rocket from the USS *Peterson* (DD-969) in 1998. *NRL*

Below left: Seaman loading the Mark 36 Super RBOC Decoy launching system aboard a US Navy destroyer, *circa* 1984. This system employed 130 mm caliber mortars to launch the chaff rounds into position above the the ship. *NRL*

Below: SLQ-49 ("Rubber Duck") inflatable radar reflectors, designed to decoy enemy missiles clear of warships. Developed by the British Royal Navy after its experiences in the Falklands Conflict, this system also went into service with the US Navy. *NRL*

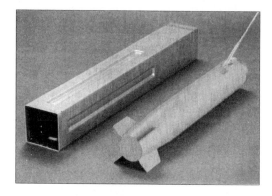

Left: Star electronic warfare system of the Kosovo conflict was Raytheon's ALE-50 towed decoy, carried by the F-16 Fighting Falcon and the B-1B Lancer. The decoy's body is 16¼-in long, it has a diameter of 2¾-in and it weighs just under 6½ pounds. *Raytheon*

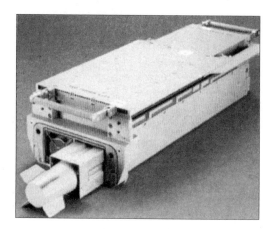

Left: Two-decoy installation fitted to the F-16, one of two such carried under the fighter's wings. *Raytheon*

Below: Four-decoy installation fitted to the B-1B, one of two such mounted on the rear fuselage. *Raytheon*

The fourth of those Warner Robbins programs provided a capability for which I coined the term 'power management.' Called Compass Tie, it provided for an ALR-69 to control the jamming from a suitably modified ALQ-119 pod."[6]

The idea of using an automatic receiver, to tune a jammer to the victim radar's frequency and then switch it to transmit, was not new. Previous systems designed to perform that task had not functioned well in combat, however. They often ignored the real threats, but frequently reacted to false alarms.

A new-generation radar receiver could tune in a new-generation jammer, and also narrow the jammer's bandwidth to concentrate the available power precisely on the victim radar's frequency. With a directional antenna, it could also focus the jamming power in the direction of the victim radar. Taken together' these moves promised to give a massive increase in the jammer's *effective* radiated power—the amount fed into the victim radar's antenna. The state-of-the-art receiver could also identify the victim radar and select the appropriate jamming modulation to defeat it. If more than one radar was present, such a system could select the highest priority threat and jam that.[7] With time those far-sighted ideals would be achievable, but it would take some years to bring them into service.

In the 1970s the idea of reprogrammable software caught the imagination of the EW community. If used to full potential, it promised major advances in capability. No longer would it be necessary to make wiring and other changes to a countermeasures system or a radar-warning receiver to meet each new threat. Maintenance crews could feed in the software changes electronically during the turn-around between flights, without having to remove boxes from the aircraft. Those managing the reprogramming process soon learned there were several obstacles to overcome before they reached that desirable goal, however.

Each organization connected with reprogramming maintained its own database on threat radar systems, and no two databases were in full agreement. Moreover, the information was usually incomplete and in the wrong format for reprogramming purposes. A new organization was necessary, and under the revised system the Electronic Warfare Center at San Antonio assembled the Air Force's electronic warfare reprogramming database. The Logistics Center at Warner Robbins AFB performed reprogramming changes to the radar warning receivers and jamming systems. The Tactical Electronic Warfare Center at Eglin AFB, Florida, made mission data software changes. The Communications Agency at Scott AFB, Texas, established secure communications channels to deliver new software to units in the field.[8] Such organizational moves do not make riveting reading, but in modern wars this is the stuff that decides battles.

Originally established in the mid-1970s, that software-reprogramming organization has remained in use with few changes into the new millennium.

Development of the Westinghouse ALQ-131, the Air Force's follow-on jamming pod from the ALQ-119, began early in the 1970s. The new pod had a greater frequency coverage than its predecessor, and included a power management module to control the jammer. It also featured digital reprogrammable software.[9]

The Air Force's new Dalmo Victor ALR-46 radar warning receiver also featured digital reprogrammable software to assist in identifying threat signals. The system had seen combat during the closing stages of the Vietnam War, where it functioned effectively.

Angle-deception countermeasures techniques had served the Navy and Marines well over North Vietnam in the ALQ-51 and ALQ-100 equipments, and they also featured in the newest Air Force jamming pods. By the early 1970s, however, there were signs their usefulness would soon be at an end. The latest Soviet airborne and missile-control radars employed monopulse angle tracking, which was invulnerable to angle-deception countermeasures.

The alternative deception technique, the range gate stealer, suffered from a fundamental limitation: because of time delays, the skin echo from the aircraft always reached the radar a little ahead of the repeater signal. Thus a good operator could tell the false target from the real one. That remained the case until Al Evans at the Navy's Electronic Warfare Development Branch at Point Mugu, California, came up with a clever Ranrap [Random Range Program] to overcome the problem. Tony Grieco, who worked with him, outlined the method of operation:

> "Ranrap had a pulse tracking system, to track the PRF of the enemy radar. In that way, it anticipated when each next pulse would arrive at the aircraft. Then it radiated deception pulses, some of which reached the radar just ahead of each of the skin echo pulses. In that way it presented the radar operator with seven or eight realistic targets. He had to try to figure out which was the real one. The idea was a major breakthrough, it has allowed us to use deceptive countermeasures up to the present day."[10]

Ranrap became available just in time to meet the changing threat. It required a new architecture in each countermeasures system, however, so it could not be retrofitted to earlier systems. Ranrap was incorporated in the Sanders ALQ-126 deception system (D through I band) which entered service at the end of 1972, and in several later jammers.[11]

In 1978 General Bill Creech, Assistant to the Vice Chief of Staff of the Air Force, issued a priority requirement for a more effective communications jamming capability. To get it quickly he wanted it produced "in house." Tony Brees, by then a colonel in the Air Staff, recalled:

"He said he wanted me to lead an effort to take the jamming equipment off the three EC-121 Coronet Solo aircraft, and put it into C-130s. He said 'I don't want any bells and whistles added, I just want a straight equipment transfer.' It was not going to go through the usual acquisitions requirements cycle, it was just a flat done deal that we were going to put this stuff on the airplane. Eventually he would want nineteen C-130s fitted out in this way."[12]

Early on it was decided to omit the trailing antenna from the C-130 installation. There was no great difficulty in installing the jamming equipment in the larger fuselage of the new plane, though there were problems with positioning the antennas to achieve good results. The prototype EC-130, designated "Compass Call," flew for the first time in the spring of 1979.[13]

Before conversion began on the remaining planes, there were pivotal decisions regarding the Compass Call program. First, these aircraft would not be required to make propaganda broadcasts, that role would go to a separate variant of the C-130. Secondly, the planes would carry new high-powered communications jamming transmitters instead of the earlier ones. It took about a year to complete the conversion of the eighteen planes and the re-convert the prototype to the new standard.[14]

Just too late for service in Vietnam the Tracor Company produced the ALE-40, the first chaff dispenser designed for carriage by the smaller Air Force tactical aircraft. The F-4E carried four such dispensers, holding a total of 120 units of chaff, mounted on either side of the inboard weapons pylons. The chaff was housed in square-section cartridges and, as in the case of the Navy's ALE-29 dispenser, it achieved rapid deployment of the material by using a pyrotechnic squib. A later variant of the ALE-40 would also dispense IR decoy flares.[15]

Also during this period Goodyear produced the ALE-39 dispenser to replace the ALE-29, the ALE-29A and the ALE-29B in Navy and Marine aircraft. The new dispenser employed an improved programmer/sequencer, and could dispense both chaff and flares. The usual fit was two dispensers carrying a total of sixty units. The payloads could be loaded in any combination, in multiples of ten, and the system could dispense the different types independently or concurrently.[16]

In May 1972 the Greenville plant of E-Systems Inc (previously LTV Greenville) began converting seven RC-135Cs to the V Model Rivet Joint configuration. Using state-of-the art electronics, the V Model combined the capabilities of the earlier C and M Models and permitted simultaneous collection of ELINT and COMINT information. At the end of the decade the six M Model Combat Apple aircraft underwent conversion to the W Model, which carried the same operational equipment as the V Model and performed the same Rivet Joint mission.[17]

In Rivet Joint the EWOs and the COMINT operators worked together, to produce a detailed assessment of the enemy threat systems in the area and their status. This vital information was then passed in near real time to the relevant combat commander.

An important lesson from the Vietnam War had been that many crews were lost during their first five combat missions. Those that passed that hurdle had a very good chance of completing the hundred-mission tour of operations. The obvious answer was to give crews realistic training before they went into action, to help them survive their difficult early missions. During the 1970s the Air Force established three important new combat training programs with electronic warfare inputs, to achieve that aim.[18]

The first new course, "Red Flag," was instituted in 1976. Based at Nellis AFB, Nevada, and flown over the Nevada desert, it ran realistic war-type exercises against US aggressor fighter units using Soviet tactics.[19]

"Blue Flag," instituted in 1979 at Hurlbert Field near Eglin, involved only "paper" aircraft and was for command and control staffs. It resembled a video game with the air battle displayed on the screens at the command center. Staff officers gathered information on the air battle, integrated it, and then directed simulated defensive and offensive air units into action.[20]

"Green Flag" complemented Red Flag. Also centered on Nellis AFB, it brought in the ground portions of a Soviet-style integrated air defense system. Ground transmitters radiated emissions like those from the SA-2, the SA-3, the SA-4, the SA-6 and other Soviet missile- and gun-control radars. Raiding forces employed their regular tactics and jamming, and aimed live ordnance at mock targets. Wild Weasel and jamming support aircraft also took part in the exercises.[21]

During the 1970s the Navy's electronic warfare test range at China Lake, California, and its EW training ranges at Pinecastle, Florida, and Fallon, Nevada, were used to evaluate new equipment and tactics. Full air wings deployed to these sites for co-ordinated training in air strike tactics. By the 1980s Fallon had evolved into a Strike University. China Lake concentrated on seaborne threats and the range at Nellis concentrated on land based threats.[22]

Still in the field of training, the idea of the computer-generated "virtual battlefield" started to take hold in the 1970s. Today such simulators are common in amusement arcades, but in those days they were at the cutting edge of display technology. Antekna secured a contract to build EW training simulators that linked in with the regular flight simulators for B-52 pilots and navigators. Crews had the pattern of threats laid out as they would see them during their actual war mission. The crew had to activate jammers, drop chaff and take other measures to counter the various threats. Thus a B-52 crew could fight its war, including the electronic warfare aspects, without leaving the ground.[23]

Antekna Inc continued to expand into the simulations market until 1979, when it was acquired by ITEK.

Following the termination of the Navy's SLQ-27 Short Stop program, in 1973 Chief of Naval Operations Admiral Elmo Zumwalt asked manufacturers to submit proposals for design-to-price EW systems for warships. High value warships would receive high value countermeasures protection, other vessels would receive less protection.

The Navy required three variants. The basic model, the (V)1 priced at $300,000, was a receiver-only suite that detected and analyzed a limited range of radar threat emissions and determined their bearings. If required it could cue the launching of chaff. The (V)1 would go in small auxiliary and amphibious warfare ships.[24]

The intermediate model, the (V)2 priced at $500,000, consisted of a (V)1 with additional receiver subsystems to extend the frequency coverage. This would go in frigates and destroyers.[25]

The top-of-the-range (V)3, priced at $1.4 million, consisted of a (V)2 receiver linked to an active countermeasures suite which included high-powered jammers. This would be fitted in cruisers, large auxiliary ships and amphibious warfare ships.[26]

The companies competing to build the new shipborne system were quickly whittled down to two, Hughes and Raytheon. Hughes built the SLQ-31 which employed much current technology. Raytheon built the SLQ-32 which exploited its new Rotman Lens technology. The latter produced a high effective radiated jamming power in the required direction, by combining the outputs from a number of low powered travelling wave tubes. Both systems employed high probability of intercept receivers to provide warning of threats and control of the (V)3's active countermeasures systems.[27]

The Raytheon SLQ-32 won the competition, and in 1977 the company received a contract to produce the system in quantity. The first production SLQ-32s went to sea in 1979, and in the years that followed it deployed throughout the fleet. In terms of number built and their longevity in service, the SLQ-32 is the US Navy's most successful shipborne countermeasures system ever. Carried in more than four hundred US warships, it would remain in production for two decades with the last one coming off the production line in 1997.

The Mark 76 Chaffroc system, intended to protect warships from radar-homing missiles, did not produce a chaff cloud quickly enough to give a good chance of deflecting the newer types of missile.[28] The replacing Mark 84 Chaffroc system appeared early in the 1970s and carried the chaff in sub-units in the body of the rocket, like the munitions in a cluster bomb. When the rocket reached its prescribed altitude, an explosive charge blew the sub-units clear of the casing. Then, after a short delay, an explosive charge in each sub-unit deployed the chaff. The use of explosive multi-point dispersal produced a chaff cloud far faster than was possible with the Mark 76.[29]

The Mark 84 was a big improvement over its predecessor, though it retained some shortcomings. Rockets launched in a war situation, perhaps without warning, could be a major hazard to personnel or equipment in the vicinity. Moreover, the latest anti-ship missiles required yet larger quantities of chaff to decoy them clear of a warship.[30]

To overcome these deficiencies the Mark 33 RBOC (Rapid Blooming Offboard chaff) system entered service in the mid-1970s. Instead of a rocket, the Mark 33 employed a 112 mm mortar. Four clusters of mortars, each cluster having six barrels, were carried aboard each ship.[31] Later in the decade, the Mark 36 SuperRBOC (SRBOC) system began to replace the Mark 33 RBOC aboard the larger Navy ships. The new system employed larger, 130 mm caliber, mortars.[32]

Stung by its calamitous helicopter losses during the Lam Son 719 operation in the previous year, in 1972 the Army set down a list of demanding requirements for its future battlefield helicopter. The goal of improved survivability was pursued along four main avenues. During Lam Son 719 small arms fire had caused many helicopter losses. To reduce that threat, the new helicopter would carry lightweight armor to protect the crew and vulnerable parts. It would need equipment to navigate accurately at night or in bad weather, and to engage targets at night. Its offensive weaponry would need to out-range most weapons an enemy might use against it. Those avenues of development fall outside the purview of this account. The fourth avenue for improvement is highly relevant to this account, however: the installation of an electronic warfare suite to counter missile- and gun-control radars and IR homing missiles. Also, passive measures would reduce the helicopter's infrared emissions.[33]

When it came to building EW systems for helicopters, weight and cost considerations ruled out the use of modified versions of systems designed for high performance fixed-wing planes. Bob Silmenn, then at Dalmo Victor, outlined the problem:

> "You could not carry a regular radar warning receiver in a small helicopter, because it was too heavy and it would have reduced the payload that could be carried. Another consideration was price. In those days our ALR-69 cost about $250,000. That was almost as much as a Huey helicopter."[34]

The Melpar/E Systems APR-39, the first radar warning receiver fitted into Army helicopters, was a simple analog system introduced during the late 1960s. At the end of that decade, digital software reprogramming became available. Helicopter pilots flying the combat zone had high workloads; they could spend little time watching their warning receiver scopes. To overcome that problem Dalmo Victor's APR-39A, which replaced it, had a then-novel speech synthesizer which announced each threat audibly.[35]

The Army also issued requirements for a tailor-made range of active countermeasures systems, to defeat both radar guided and IR weapons. It remained to be seen whether these cheap and lightweight systems could provide a useful increase in helicopters' survivability in time of war.

Early in the 1970s the ESL Company at Sunnyvale, California, began work on a state-of-the-art SIGINT collection system for the NSA. The architecture was both novel and imaginative. A Beechcraft U-21, a twin-engined plane based on the King Air 90, carried a battery of receivers to pick up the enemy signals and relay them via data link to a ground station. Its crew of two pilots flew and navigated the machine, but they played no direct part in the intelligence collection process. Operators at the ground station controlled the plane's receivers via a data up-link, and processed and analyzed the information passed via the downlink from the aircraft. The great advantage of the new architecture was that the labor-intensive business of signal analysis could take place in real time on the ground. The system received the code-name Guardrail.[36]

In 1972 Guardrail II appeared, with provision to take bearings on enemy transmissions. To exploit this capability Guardrail II aircraft operated in two-plane teams flying separate patterns, to provide a base line for triangulating bearings. Each aircraft passed its bearing information by data link to the ground station, enabling the latter to obtain fixes by triangulating the sources.[37] Guardrail II was a huge improvement over previous airborne direction-finding systems used by the Army. There was no need to fly long, straight legs to take bearings on an enemy transmitter in order to locate it. With Guardrail II a two-plane team could establish the approximate position of the transmitter within about a minute, without needing to venture within one hundred miles of the signal source.[38]

By the end of 1974 Guardrail had passed through two more variants, IIA and IV, each giving improvements in frequency coverage and plotting accuracy. During the mid-1970s the NSA fielded two Guardrail IV systems, one in Germany and one in Korea. Army personnel manned both systems.[39]

In 1978 the Army purchased three Guardrail V systems, complete with twenty-one RU-21H aircraft, for its own use. The new system employed the USD-9V(2) ground and airborne equipment, the latter still carried aloft in the RU-21 aircraft. The system covered the bands 20–75 MHz, 100–150 MHz and 350–450 MHz, with direction finding in the two lower bands.[40] A complete Guardrail system comprised an Army Aviation company with six to eight planes and an associated ground station.

Captain John Thomas commanded one of the first companies to operate Guardrail V, based at Fort Bliss, Texas:

> "The significant difference between Guardrail and the earlier systems was the rapid pass-down of information from the airplane to the ground station. With the other systems, the plane had to land to unload the information. For fast moving tactical operations, Guardrail's real time or near real time analysis capability conferred a great advantage. Lower level enemy tactical formations, like companies or battalions, can move quickly. So if we can't get information on them to our combat commanders quickly enough to assist their decision making process, the information is not all that valuable from the tactical perspective. Take an enemy artillery battery. After engaging our forces, it could be on the move within 20 or 30 minutes. So if our guys can't engage it within 20 or 30 minutes of detection, there will be nothing left there to hit."[41]

In the years to follow Guardrail would undergo further improvements; we shall return to it in later chapters.

During the early 1970s the Army received another important addition to its electronic warfare capability, the RV-1D version of the Grumman OV-1 Mohawk aircraft. Thirty-six Mohawks were modified to carry the ALQ-133 Quick Look II ELINT collection system. The identifying feature of this variant was a slab-sided pod on each outer-wing station, housing electronic equipment and antennas.[42] Provided the aircraft was in line-of-sight range of its associated ground station, Quick Look II could pass back ELINT data in near-real time. Alternatively, if the aircraft was outside the range of the ground station, it could record the data and download it when it later came within range of the ground station.[43] In the decades to follow RV-1Ds would operate alongside OV-1D Mohawks carrying side-looking target radar and Guardrail RU-21s, keeping watch over areas of military tension.

Decoy flares were effective for countering the first-generation IR missiles, but the individual flares were effective for only a relatively short time. So an aircraft spending long in a threat area needed to dispense a large number, and a slow-moving aircraft doing that at low altitude was likely to become a magnet for enemy fire. Something better was needed, and two systems duly appeared.

Apart from their propensity to chase almost any IR source, early IR missiles like the SA-7 suffered from another weakness. The missile's tracking head employed a rotating sensing element. When the head pointed directly at a source of IR energy, say a helicopter's exhaust, it produced a null signal. That condition had to be met before the interlock circuits would allow the missile to launch. Once the missile was in flight the same condition applied; a null signal meant the missile was going in the right direction and required no correction to its trajectory. If the tracking head produced a signal modulated at the same rate as the rotating sensing element, it meant the missile's trajectory required correction. The missile turned in the required direction, and when it was re-aligned on the target the null signal returned.

If the target aircraft radiated an IR signal modulated at or near the same rate as the missile's rotating sensing element, the homing head would never find the all-important null signal. So the missile could not be launched. If the missile was in flight when the IR jamming began, the guidance system commanded a series of violent turns that took the missile well clear of the target aircraft.

During the 1970s Sanders Associates developed two separate active IR jammers. The first, the ALQ-144, employed an electrically heated silicon carbide IR source with a mechanical shutter to produce the required modulation. The system entered production and has since been widely installed in small and medium sized helicopters.[44]

The second Sanders system, the ALQ-147, worked in a slightly different manner. It burned regular jet engine fuel to heat a silicon carbide element, and again a mechanical shutter modulated the IR output. The ALQ-147 also went into large scale production and was installed in Army OV-1 Mohawk and Rockwell RV-10 Bronco fixed-wing planes.[45]

Both types of active IR jammer ran continuously while the aircraft was over a danger area. The ALQ-144 did not radiate in the visual part of the spectrum, while ALQ-147 carried filters to prevent it doing so.[46]

Between 1973 and 1990 US forces fought no major action. Yet they were involved in a number of minor engagements. As a separate matter there were the conflicts involving allies of the US, notably Israel. Where these conflicts led to incidents with electronic warfare interest, these actions are described in the next chapter.

References to Chapter 11

1. *International Countermeasures Handbook 1982*, EW Communications Inc, Palo Alto, California, p 92 *et seq*
2. *Ibid*
3. Interview Glen Miller
4. Thompson, Warren, "Jammers Delight," *Air International*, December 1986
5. *Ibid*
6. Interview "Tofie" Owen
7. *Ibid*
8. *Ibid*
9. *Ibid*

10. Interview Tony Grieco
11. *Ibid*
12. Interview Tony Brees
13. *Ibid*
14. Owen
15. Streetly, Martin, *Airborne Electronic Warfare*, Jane's Publishing, London, 1988, p 18.
16. Letter, Vic Kutsch
17. Interview Bob Seh
18. Brees
19. *Ibid*
20. *Ibid*
21. *Ibid*
22. Interview Rear Admiral Grady Jackson
23. Interview Joe Digiovanni
24. Interview John O'Brien
25. *Ibid*
26. *Ibid*
27. Interview Dick Curtis
28. Hyman, Joseph and DuBose, Layne, "Expendable Decoys in Naval Warfare," *Journal of Electronic Defense*, December 1983
29. *Ibid*
30. *Ibid*
31. *Ibid*
32. *Ibid*
33. Interview Tom Reinkober
34. Interview Bob Silmenn
35. *Ibid*
36. Interview David Adamy
37. *Ibid*
38. *Ibid*
39. *Ibid*
40. *International Countermeasures Handbook 1988*, p 136
41. Interview Maj Gen John Thomas
42. Proctor, Jerry, "Grumman Mohawk," *Warplane* partwork, Orbis Ltd London, p 1926 *et seq*
43. *Ibid*
44. *International Countermeasures Handbook 1988*, p 118
45. *Ibid*
46. *Ibid*

Chapter 12

SHORT WARS, NEAR WARS, OTHER PEOPLE'S WARS

1969 to 1989

"There never was a good war."
Benjamin Franklin

During the period reviewed in this chapter there were innumerable conflicts around the world. Some led to large-scale wars, others never got past the confrontation stage. The account that follows covers only those actions and incidents relevant to the history of US electronic warfare.

On 5 October 1973 a Lockheed EP-3 ELINT aircraft of Fleet Air Reconnaissance Squadron 2, operating from Hellenikon in Greece, flew a routine patrol off the north coast of Egypt. Mission commander Lieutenant Lee Buchanan (later the Assistant Secretary of the Navy for Research, Development and Acquisition) had reason to remember the flight:

"The most distinctive feature of that mission was the utter lack of electronic activity coming from Egypt. There was nothing radiating, absolutely nothing. When we called the squadron after the mission, we remarked on the complete dearth of activity."[1]

With hindsight, that should have set alarm bells ringing. In the world of ELINT, no news can be very bad news.

The following afternoon the Middle East erupted into war yet again, as Arab forces launched large-scale attacks to recover territory seized by Israel six years earlier. Egyptian assault units crossed the Suez Canal and stormed positions on the east bank. Simultaneously, Syrian forces attacked Israeli positions on the Golan Heights.[2]

On the southern front the Israeli Air Force went into action against the bridging and ferry operations along the Suez Canal. The area had strong SAM and AAA defenses, with SA-2 and SA-3 batteries in position to cover the crossings. Highly mobile SA-6 batteries moved to the east bank to give depth to the air defenses. With them the advancing Egyptian Army units brought SA-7 shoulder-launched missiles and self-propelled and towed AAA weapons.[3]

The next EP-3 mission to enter the area, on the afternoon of 6 October, found a situation entirely different from the previous one. Now there was a deluge of radar and other signals, some of them ominously unfamiliar. Again, Lee Buchanan was mission commander:

> "Our patrol took us just to the north of the Suez Canal, so we had a direct line of sight on several surface-to-air missile engagements. We picked up the signals from an SA-6 battery as it shot down one of the first Israeli F-4s to fall. Then we watched other SA-6 actions."[4]

By dawn on 7 October several pontoon bridges were in place across the Suez Canal, and Egyptian infantry and armored units were streaming eastwards. Israeli pilots quickly learned to respect the SA-6, and to avoid it by flying at ultra-low altitude. But then, as over North Vietnam, the raiders suffered losses from AAA.[5]

The SA-6's Straight Flush continuous wave (CW) missile control radar was almost impervious to jamming from the ALQ-101-6 and -8 pods carried by Israeli planes, nor did its signals register on the planes' radar warning receivers. Moreover the small Gainful missile flew on ramjet power, which left little smoke or glow to betray its presence. That made the missile very hard to detect and avoid.[6]

During the first four days of the war the Israeli Air Force lost about fifty aircraft.[7] Badly hurt, the Israelis turned to their US ally for help. At this time Air Force Lieutenant Colonel Dave Brog worked at the Electronic Warfare Division of Air Force Operations in the Pentagon, but had visited Israel several times previously in an official capacity:

> "A few days after the Yom Kippur War began, an Israeli officer came to HQ USAFE [US Air Forces in Europe] in Germany to talk about their problems. I called USAFE and explained what we, the air staff, were trying to do. At the start of the war the Israeli Air Force had only ALQ-101-6 and ALQ-101-8 jamming pods. We got permission to take forty ALQ-119 pods from USAFE and fly them to Israel, together with a Technical Sergeant to help with installation.
>
> Above all the Israelis wanted to know which settings we used to counter the SA-6 system. We gave them what we had, a setting for a velocity gate pull-off signal intended to distract the missile's CW seeker head. But we did not know enough about the missile to know whether that setting would work. The Israelis decided not to use our setting. They

were afraid the jamming pod would act as a beacon and they were unwilling to take the chance. So the Israelis used the ALQ-119s to counter just the SA-2s and SA-3s, but not the SA-6."[8]

By the end of the first week of the conflict the Egyptian and Syrian advances had been halted. That removed the pressure on the Israeli Air Force to attack well-defended targets. Moreover, with good information on the whereabouts of the SA-6 units, air crews could now avoid them. Thereafter the Israeli loss rate fell to a more acceptable level.[9]

It took a few days to fit the ALQ-119 pods to Israeli fighters. By then the initial crisis had passed and Israeli forces were on the offensive on both fronts. The new pods were useful but, as mentioned earlier, no attempt was made to use them against the SA-6s.[10] After eighteen days of heavy fighting, a cease-fire was declared on 24 October,

The most significant result of the 1973 conflict, so far as this account is concerned, was the huge haul of modern Soviet-built weaponry and electronic equipment captured by Israeli forces. This will be discussed in the next chapter.

In the summer of 1982 fighting erupted in the Middle East yet again. Following increasing tension between Israeli Forces and Palestine Liberation Organization guerrillas in Lebanon, on 6 June Israeli forces crossed the border and advanced deep into that country.

Two days later advancing Israeli troops clashed with Syrian forces. The fighting became general, and on 9 June the Israeli Air Force launched a long-planned operation against Syrian air defense missile batteries in the Bekaa region of eastern Lebanon. Several batteries of SA-2, SA-3, SA-6 and SA-8 missiles were deployed in the region and, months earlier, the Israeli Air Force had drawn up a plan to knock out many of them.[11] The resultant operation would serve as model for the US attack on the Iraqi air defense system nearly a decade later, so it deserves to be described in some detail.

As a prelude to the attack there had been a long running intelligence collection effort by Israeli Boeing 707 ELINT/Electronic Warfare aircraft and photographic reconnaissance drones. These gave a detailed picture of the locations, operating frequencies and operating procedures of the missile batteries. The SA-6s were the primary target and, although the system had excellent mobility, those in the Bekaa area had remained static for long periods. That made the attackers' task a lot easier.[12]

On the morning of 9 June IAF Boeing 707 ELINT/Electronic Warfare aircraft made a final check of Syrian air defense radar transmissions to confirm the accuracy of the intelligence picture. Then these planes began jamming Syrian surveillance and missile acquisition radars in the area. At the same time, Israeli long-range gun and rocket batteries bombarded air defense and missile sites within their range.[13]

For the next phase of the operation, the Israeli Air Force ran several high-speed target drones (the air-launched Samson decoy has been mentioned in this context)[14] through the missile-defended area. Each one carried equipment to give it a radar response similar to that from a fighter plane. The drones achieved their purpose and one by one the Syrian missile control radars sprang into life. With the batteries' acquisition radars jammed, the narrow-beam missile control radars had to make lengthy searches to find the drones.[15]

Once several missile batteries had taken the "bait," a signal from the controlling plane initiated the main attack. A number of F-4s commenced low level runs on individual missile batteries, using terrain to screen their approach. Each attack fighter carried an ALQ-119 or an ALQ-131 jamming pod for its protection. After launching their Shrike and Standard anti-radiation missiles at the radars, the F-4s withdrew at low altitude.[16] Following them, other low flying attack fighters launched Maverick TV-guided air-to-surface missiles at non-radiating air defense targets. A few minutes later, to allow time for the smoke to clear, reconnaissance drones photographed the targets and transmitted the pictures for real-time bomb damage assessment. Finally, F-16s delivered follow-up attacks with conventional bombs on missile batteries whose radars were out of action.[17]

From start to finish the attack on the missile sites lasted about fifteen minutes. The Israelis claimed to have put out of action seventeen of the nineteen SA-6 firing units in the area, plus some SA-2 and SA-3 batteries.[18] The action showed what could be achieved by an imaginative approach to this most difficult of air operations. No Israeli plane was lost.

During the attack on the missile batteries, about fifty Syrian MiG-21 and MiG-23 fighters took off to engage the Israeli planes. F-15s and F-16s, airborne in anticipation of such a move, delivered a devastating counter-attack. Directed by E-2C Hawkeye radar surveillance planes, the Israeli fighters claimed the destruction of twenty-two MiGs and damage to seven more. Again, no Israeli plane was lost.[19]

For the Israeli Air Force the Bekaa action was sweet revenge against the SA-6, the missile system that had caused it so much grief nine years earlier.

The next action of significance to this account also occurred in the Middle East, though this time US forces were directly involved. On 5 April 1986 a terrorist bomb exploded in a West Berlin nightclub frequented by US servicemen. Three people were killed and more than two hundred injured, including fifty US military personnel. Intelligence reports linked the outrage to the Libyan dictator Muammar Gadafy, so President Reagan ordered a retaliatory air strike against targets in Libya.[20]

That strike, Operation Eldorado Canyon, was launched on the night of 14/15 April 1986. Eighteen F-111Fs of the 48th TFW based at Lakenheath in England ran in at low altitude to attack targets in and near to the Libyan capital, Tripoli. Nine F-111Fs, each carrying four laser-guided 2,000-pound bombs, were to hit Colonel Gadafy's command post at the Al Azziziyah barracks at Tripoli. Six swing-wing bombers, each with twelve laser guided 500-pounders, were to hit the military airport just outside the city. The remaining three bombers were to go for the Sidi Belal marine training facility, each with four 2,000-pounders.[21]

Each F-111F carried an ALQ-131 pod mounted under the rear fuselage, ALE-28 chaff and flare dispensers and an ALR-41 radar warning receiver. Supporting the Air Force bombers were five EF-111A Ravens from Upper Heyford, making the jamming escort plane's debut in combat.

Shortly before reaching the Libyan coast, one F-111F crashed into the sea. The reason for the loss, the only one during the operation, was never firmly established.[22]

Simultaneously twenty-six A-6s and A-7s from the carriers *America* and *Coral Sea* struck at the Al Junhiriya barracks and the Benina military airfield near Benghazi. Supporting the Navy bombers were F/A-18s and A-7s carrying anti-radiation missiles and EA-6B jamming aircraft. Navy F-14s provided fighter cover for the Air Force and the Navy raiding forces.

The Iran-Iraq war had opened in September 1980, when Iraqi forces launched a land invasion to seize territory in western Iran. With Iran in a state of turmoil following the revolution to depose the Shah, Saddam Hussein expected an easy victory. Not for the only time, he miscalculated badly. Following the invasion the Iranian people put aside their differences and rallied behind Ayatollah Khomeini. The conflict degenerated into a brutal slugging match that would continue for eight years.

The Iran-Iraq war produced little to interest students of US electronic warfare, apart from the inadvertent attack on the frigate USS *Stark* (FFG-31). On the evening of 17 May 1987 the warship was cruising in the Persian Gulf about 85 miles northeast of Bahrain. She was 60 miles outside the Iraqi-imposed maritime exclusion zone around Iranian ports. *Stark* was participating in a two-day exercise with the destroyer *Coontz* (DLG-9), the command ship *La Salle* and a USAF E-3A AWACS aircraft operating from Dhahran in Saudi Arabia.[23]

Like other frigates, *Stark* carried the SLQ-32 (V)2 countermeasures system which provided radar warning but no electronic jamming capability. The warship carried Super RBOC chaff and it was armed with Standard surface-to-air and surface-to-surface missiles, a 76 mm gun and a Phalanx rapid firing gun designed to shoot down incoming missiles.

Also that evening, an Iraqi Air Force Mirage F1EQ aircraft carrying two Exocet anti-ship missiles took off from Shaibah near Basra. At this stage of the conflict Iraqi planes often attacked tankers moving to and from Iran. The E-3A detected the incoming fighter-bomber at about 1955 hours local time, and a joint US-Saudi monitoring station ashore identified it as a Mirage F1.

The E-3A maintained almost continuous plots on the Mirage, which it passed to the three US warships.[24]

The fighter-bomber cruised at about 200 knots at altitudes below 3,000 feet, conducting a radar search for targets. When *Stark* made radar contact with the plane it was about 70 miles west of her. The aircraft was not viewed as a threat and apart from tracking it, the ship's crew took no further action. At the time the most important matter concerning *Stark*'s crew was the naval exercise in progress. The warship was running at Condition 3, with one-third of the crew at battle stations, sensor and weapon stations manned and able to engage at short notice.[25]

At 2100 hours the E-3A crew observed the Mirage turn on to a northeasterly heading and increase speed to 290 knots. Two minutes later the *Stark*'s SLQ-32 operator picked up emissions from the plane's Cyrano attack radar. By now the Mirage was 43 miles from the frigate and closing obliquely at 310 knots.[26] At 2105 the Mirage turned directly towards *Stark*, the range 32 miles and closing. At 2107 the SLQ-32 operator confirmed that a Cyrano radar in the search mode was illuminating the ship and switched the SLQ-32 audio signal to a speaker for a brief period, so everybody in the Combat Information Center could hear it.[27]

The warship put out a call on the 243 MHz international distress frequency asking the plane to identify itself, but received no reply. At the same time a sailor was ordered on deck to arm the two chaff launchers, though the automatic sensing and launching system was not activated. The SLQ-32 detected a Cyrano radar lock-on lasting about 6 seconds[28] then, unknown to those aboard the warship, the Mirage launched both Exocet sea-skimming missiles.

Stark sounded general quarters and the Phalanx close-in weapons system was switched to the anti-air warfare mode and the radar began transmitting in the search mode. Had it found an incoming missile the radar would have locked-on automatically, though the Gatling gun would not have fired without a further switch selection. The warship's Mark 92 fire control system, which directed the 76 mm gun and Standard missiles, also attempted to acquire the aircraft. Neither radar found the Iraqi plane or the incoming missiles, however, because these were close off the port bow and blocked from view by part of the ship's superstructure.[29] Surprisingly, nobody ordered the ship to turn through the narrow angle necessary to clear the firing arcs of her defensive weapons.

When an Exocet homing head began transmitting, the SLQ-32 should have provided both audio and visual alerts. It failed to give either. There was no audio warning because the operator had turned off that part of the system so it did not distract him from other duties and if the SLQ-32 gave a visual alert it appears to have gone unnoticed. Those in *Stark*'s Combat Information Center received no electronic warning of the approaching missiles.[30]

At 2109 hours a port side lookout on *Stark* noticed a small blue light close to the horizon, almost stationary and bobbing up and down. Only at the last moment did he recognize its significance and yell "Inbound missile!" By then it was far too late for any countermeasure to take effect. The missile was about 12 degrees off the port bow, in the blind zone of the ship's Phalanx radar.[31]

Five seconds later an Exocet slammed into *Stark*'s hull. It passed through a sleeping area on the second deck and continued through the ship's post office and barber's shop before coming to rest against the hull on the starboard side. The warhead failed to detonate, but as the missile broke up it released about 300 pounds of flammable propellant. A few seconds later the second missile impacted in the same general area and detonated about five feet inside the hull. The explosion blew a hole 15 feet in diameter in the side of the ship and ignited the unburned propellant from the first missile. A huge blaze started, which required several hours to bring under control. Thirty-seven seamen were killed and eleven seriously wounded. Assisted by a salvage tug, *Stark* limped into the port in Bahrain.[32]

The *Stark* incident is a sad story of misadventure on all sides. The Iraqi pilot had not intended to attack a US warship, he was after one of the tankers trading with Iran. And, until the very last moment, *Stark*'s officers never considered the possibility that their ship might be in danger.[33] Much has been written about "the fog of war" but here we see the effect of "the mist of peace." The most difficult situation a service officer can be called upon to handle is the sudden and unexpected transition from peace to war. It is a no-win situation from which few reputations emerge intact.

Had her crew appreciated the danger in time, *Stark* could certainly have mounted a vigorous defense. Merely by locking-on to the Mirage with her Mark 92 fire control system, the ship would have shown she was not a tanker. The launch of a Standard missile, whether aimed or not, would have reinforced the point. Properly handled, the SLQ-32 should have provided over one minute's warning of the approach of the Exocets. That was long enough to turn the ship so her weapons could engage the threat, launch SRBOC chaff and set the Phalanx system to engage the incoming missiles. As we have seen, none of those things was done.

The *Stark* incident underlines the point that even the best equipment is useless, if it is not turned on at the critical time or is improperly handled. Following the incident there was a rigorous inquiry. Among other measures, there were improved operational procedures in potential combat areas. Also, the SLQ-32 was modified to provide an improved capability against Exocet.

Throughout the Cold War the US Army had focused its activities on Europe, and in particular the border separating East from West Germany. In 1982 Colonel Paul Menoher was assigned as the Senior Intelligence Officer of VII Corps there. The Military Intelligence Brigade supporting the Corps included a battalion with Improved Guardrail V aircraft, and Mohawks with side-looking radar and the Quick Look ELINT system. He outlined the role of this unit:

"VII Corps held a huge general defensive position, facing portions of East Germany and Czechoslovakia. We had three US divisions and an armored cavalry regiment, plus a German division, so our forces were spread thin. There were four major avenues of approach into our sector, governed by the local topography, where armored forces could advance rapidly. Our task was to identify the main attack so the commander could concentrate forces to meet it.

We were constantly looking for any indication that hostilities might be imminent. That might have come in the form of changed communications patterns, large-scale changes of callsigns, repositioning air defense radars, signs of unusual troop movements, massing of artillery, etc. As any tactical commander will tell you, the biggest concern was the enemy artillery. That was potentially the biggest killer of our guys. We had to win that counter-fire fight. The key thing was to find where the enemy artillery was massing. If the enemy moved forward his battery locating radars [Small Yawn and Pork Trough] and they started radiating, it meant that was where he expected the counter-fire fight to take place. We needed to know that."[34]

The unit's Improved Guardrail V and Mohawk aircraft flew missions almost every day, watching for military activity in East Germany and Czechoslovakia. In addition, the Brigade had ground sites along the border looking to the east. Paul Menoher continued:

"We had some communications jammers, ground based GLQ-3Bs and TLQ-15s in the Corps. The divisions also had ground based and heliborne TLQ-17s. In my opinion, they were not especially effective. In action, the ground-based systems would have jammed only for short periods, one or two minutes at most. The longer they jammed, the more vulnerable and exposed they were to counter-action. The procedure would have been to jam for a short time, then move to a new position before resuming jamming."[35]

The campaign of intelligence surveillance continued until the Berlin Wall came down in November 1989.

The confrontation along the Inner German Border lasted forty-one years, from 1948 until 1989. An even longer-running confrontation involving US forces, that in Korea, began with the cease-fire in 1955 and continues at the time of writing. In 1984 Paul Menoher took command of the 501st Military Intelligence Brigade in Korea:

"The tension was intense all the way along the border, you could cut it with a knife. There was always a possibility of another sudden invasion. Many of the indicators that we normally looked for, to show an imminence of hostilities, were already there. The North Korean troops were forward deployed in positions to launch an attack with little tactical warning. They had four Corps on line, with artillery brigades and exploitation brigades right behind them. They had very little mobile air defense other than towed guns, and few of those were radar controlled. ELINT was not the big player that it would have been in Europe, COMINT was far more important."[36]

The Brigade's 3rd Military Intelligence Battalion operated six Guardrail Vs and eighteen Mohawks, RV-1Ds and OV-1Ds. It also ran a field station with three forward detachments on the border looking into North Korea. Paul Menoher continued:

"We had pairs of Guardrail aircraft up every day, sometimes we flew multiple missions per day. The North Korean communications system was similar to that used by the Soviets, though they had devised some methods of their own. Their troops were focused on communications security, it was hard to get much from them. On the other hand, we knew that if they launched a major attack it would entail a lot of signals traffic, no matter how well they planned it beforehand."[37]

Although Guardrail was a fine intelligence collector, the initial versions were unpopular with the pilots. Major Jerry Proctor, Operations officer of the battalion, explained why:

"The airframes were based on the Beech King Air, we called them 'Pigs in Space.' They were grossly overweight, underpowered and they had no autopilot. We would scrape along close to the stall, trying to maintain the required altitude around 16,000 feet. The pilot had to hold the wings as flat as possible, the less wing-rock the better the signals collection. The Guardrail aircraft flew in pairs, with about 50 miles between them, flying up and down the border. One pilot paid attention to the flying while the other took a break, every 30 minutes they would change over. We would do that for four or five hours. The plane was a flying antenna, with a transmitter to relay the information to the ground. The pilots were just drivers of the antenna system, keeping it up there."[38]

SIGINT collection and transmitter location also had applications in other areas. During the low-intensity conflicts and anti-drug operations in Central and South America, the US provided technical assistance for friendly governments. There, a less-complex version of Guardrail was sufficient. For its "Crazy Horse" program the Army acquired three Beechcraft RC-12G aircraft fitted with the Sanders URR-75 receiving system. Normally the planes flew in pairs to permit signals triangulation. In the preferred mode of operation, signals were passed by data-link to the ground station in regular

Guardrail fashion but in some cases local conditions did not allow a ground station within line-of-sight range of the plane's operating area. Then the data-link equipment was removed from the plane to make room for two radio operators in the fuselage, and the signals were recorded for analysis after landing.[39]

During the early 1980s the Crazy Horse planes went on detachment to Honduras as part of the US effort to assist the El Salvador government to put down an insurrection. From the SIGINT viewpoint this was regarded as a "Radio Shack war," against guerrillas using HF and VHF communications systems purchased on the commercial market. Captain Garry Long flew Crazy Horse missions over El Salvador:

> "To communicate between themselves, the guerrilla units used commercially available equipment, everything from high frequency sets to hand-held walkie-talkies. Generally speaking, these commercial systems used narrow frequency bands.
>
> The guerrillas' communications system was not structured. Most transmissions were in voice and there was not much communications discipline. That made the task of interception easier. On the other hand, the guys knew each others' voices. They would come up on the radio and start talking without using callsigns or announcing who they were. Also they spoke in regional dialects and used lots of slang. That made things more difficult for us."[40]

Over time the US operators learned to recognize the speakers' voices. The Crazy Horse planes collected much useful intelligence on the guerrilla units and on the locations of their transmitters, which was passed to El Salvador government forces.

References to Chapter 12

1. Interview Lee Buchanan
2. Cordesman, Anthony, and Wagner, Abraham, *The Lessons of Modern War*, Volume I: *The Arab-Israeli Conflicts, 1973–1989*, Westview Press, Boulder, CO, 1990 p 73 *et seq*
3. *Ibid*
4. Buchanan
5. Cordesman
6. Interview David Brog
7. Cordesman
8. Brog
9. Cordesman, p 136 *et seq*
10. Brog
11. Cordesman, p 187 *et seq*

12. Clary, Major David, "EW in the Bekaa Valley: A New Look," *Journal of Electronic Defense*, June 1990
13. Cordesman, p 190 *et seq*
14. *Ibid*
15. *Ibid*
16. *Ibid*
17. *Ibid*
18. *Ibid*
19. *Ibid*
20. Venkus, Colonel Robert E, *Raid on Qaddafi*, St Martin's Paperbacks, New York, 1993, p 68 *et seq*
21. *Ibid*
22. Interview Craig Johnson
23. Sharp, Admiral Grant, "Formal Investigation into the Circumstances Surrounding the Attack on the USS *Stark* (FFG-31) on 17 May 1987," quoted in Cordesman, Anthony and Wagner, Abraham, *The Lessons of Modern War*, Volume II: *The Iran-Iraq War*, Westview Press, Boulder, Co, 1990, p 549 *et seq*
24. *Ibid*
25. *Ibid*
26. *Ibid*
27. *Ibid*
28. *Ibid*
29. *Ibid*
30. *Ibid*
31. *Ibid*
32. *Ibid*
33. *Ibid*
34. Interview Lt Gen Paul Menoher
35. *Ibid*
36. *Ibid*
37. *Ibid*
38. Interview Jerry Proctor
39. Interview Garry Long
40. *Ibid*

Chapter 13

THE INTELLIGENCE ATTACK: 3

1973 to 1991

"You shall know the truth, and the truth shall make you free."

Book of John, Chapter 8

After the Vietnam War the various US intelligence agencies continued their close watch on the activities of the Soviet Union and her allies. Ground monitoring stations around the globe played a vital role in the process. With large staffs to collect and analyze information, these conducted around-the-clock operations and produced in-depth analyses. At the same time, however, these facilities were vulnerable to political shifts in the host nations.

The first major upset came in 1974, following the Turkish invasion and occupation of northern Cyprus. When Turkey failed to reverse that move, the US government severed military relations. In retaliation the Turkish government ordered the closure of US monitoring stations on its territory. The disagreement lasted until the fall of 1978, when the US government restored relations and the Turkish government allowed the US monitoring stations to re-open.[1]

The loss of the Turkish stations was serious but not calamitous, because monitoring in that area continued using the ground stations in Iran but, as things turned out, the reinstatement of the stations in Turkey came in the nick of time. In 1979 Ayatollah Khomeini took power in Iran and his government adopted an increasingly anti-American stance. By February 1980 the US monitoring stations in that country had ceased operations, never to resume.[2]

Yet, as one door closed, another unexpectedly opened. In the 1980s the rift between the Soviet Union and the People's Republic of China continued. Observing the ancient dictum, "The enemy of my enemy is my friend," the Chinese government made common cause with the USA. In a move that would have been unimaginable even a few years earlier, the Chinese government allowed the US to establish a missile tracking station in Xinjiang Uighur in Western China. The US government supplied the equipment, the

Chinese government provided the operators and both nations shared the intelligence take.[3]

During the closing stages of the 1973 Arab-Israeli War, Air Force Lieutenant Colonel Dave Brog arrived in Israel with a small party of US service officers to discuss ways they could assist. When the war ended the question changed to "How could the Israelis repay their ally for the help received?"

In the aftermath of the war the US officers were taken to the Egyptian Air Force base at Fayid beside the Suez Canal. The facility contained large numbers of SA-2 Guideline, SA-3 Goa and SA-7 Strella missiles ready for delivery to front-line units, and the US officers were allowed to select examples to send to the US for technical exploitation.[4]

The booty included tantalizingly few pieces of the SA-6 system, however. Dave Brog recalled:

> "I was shown an SA-6 TEL [transporter-erector-launcher vehicle]. The Israelis did not have an SA-6 missile control radar [Straight Flush]. Nor did they have a complete missile [Gainful] though they had pieces of one. The missile had been launched, but the warhead failed to detonate and the missile broke up when it fell to the ground. The remains were taken to Rafael, an Israeli electronics company, where a team of engineers was trying to put together the bits and reassemble the seeker head."[5]

After Israeli engineers had learned all they could from the pieces, Dave Brog passed them to Wright-Patterson AFB for more detailed examination.

Colonel John Marks, Director of Intelligence at Air Force Systems Command, also went to Israel to collect items of interest. That visit to the Holy Land was no holiday:

> "I spent about two weeks in Israel, working from about four in the morning until seven each evening, going from one place to another and making a list of items they had, that I wanted. It was the biggest haul of Soviet radar equipment that we had ever seen. They gave me pretty much whatever I wanted. We bought two C-5 loads of radar and other items back to the US. Some of the stuff was in good condition, some had been beaten up."[6]

The largess included Knife Rest, Spoon Rest and Bar Lock early warning radars, Fansong and Low Blow missile control radars, and ZSU 23-4 tracked AAA systems with the Gun Dish control radar.[7]

As the equipments arrived at the Foreign Technology Division (FTD) workshops at Wright-Patterson AFB, engineers brought the radars to working order. John Marks described the standard evaluation procedure:

> "The first thing was to put on the radar all the instrumentation we could, and then run it. We measured everything that was measurable: frequency, PRF, pulse width, everything. Then we would calibrate the radar and

determine its level of accuracy. We found that some equipments had different operating modes, they could switch from one frequency to another. Usually we did not dismantle the set, unless we saw something that was completely new to us. If that were the case we would get the real experts in, and have them dismantle it very carefully.

One important thing we wanted to know at that stage was if there were major differences between a simulated Soviet radar we had built, and the real system. Although no drastic changes were required to any of our simulated radars, some of the changes were significant."[8]

Examples of each radar were sent to the secret Western Test Range, where their capabilities were evaluated clear of prying eyes and ears. Aircraft flew runs against each set, allowing US operators to learn how to get the best out of it. Then planes flew jamming runs to determine the set's vulnerabilities.

Some intelligence coups result from hard work, others fall into the lap like a windfall apple. Yet, even with the latter, the exploitation process required a lot of effort. On 6 September 1976 a MiG-25 Foxbat interceptor took off on a training exercise from Sakharovka air base near Vladivostok. Shortly afterwards the pilot put out a distress call before the aircraft descended below the radar horizon. The next time anybody saw the plane it was circling the civilian airport at Hakodate, Japan, almost out of fuel. The plane touched down and ran off the end of the short runway.[9]

Apart from some minor damage to the undercarriage, the MiG-25 arrived intact. Its pilot, Lieutenant Viktor Belenko, informed bemused Japanese officials that he sought political asylum and asked to be put in touch with the US Embassy.[10]

Colonel John Marks, by now commander of the Foreign Technology Division at Wright-Patterson AFB, recalled:

"The duty officer put the call through on a classified line, my guy in Japan came on and he was all excited. He said the Japanese Air Force general in charge of intelligence had called him, to say that a defecting Russian pilot had landed in a MiG-25 at an airfield in Japan. The Japanese general had said they would like us to do the intelligence exploitation of the aircraft."[11]

John Marks went to his safe to pull the contingency plan covering this eventuality. He set up a command post to control the response, then called Military Airlift Command to provide a plane to fly the exploitation team to Japan with its equipment. Then he sent recall messages to key FTD specialists in the various areas of the Soviet aircraft design: avionics, radar, engines, airframes, etc. Nobody knew how long the MiG-25 might be available so it was important to begin the examination as soon as possible.

The weeks that followed saw feverish diplomatic activity between Moscow and Tokyo. The MiG-25 was Soviet property and Japan was legally bound to return it. For its part the Japanese government strove to fulfill its international obligations. John Marks explained what this meant in practice:

> "They strung it out by asking the Soviet Government questions, one at a time. 'Should we fly the MiG back to you?' The Soviet Government had to staff through each question to say what they wanted done. Of course, that took time. When the Japanese government got the answer to one question, like 'We will send a ship to collect it,' they would think of another question. And so it went on, week after week"[12]

For each answer, there was another question. The diplomatic game resembled a prolonged rally in tennis. In the end it was agreed that the plane was to be disassembled and crated, and transported to the USSR by ship. Yet, the Japnese insisted, the task of dismantling the complex fighter plane had to be done with care. It would be dreadful if it suffered damage because the work was rushed. That line bought a bit more time.

Meanwhile the FTD teams toiled to learn all they could about the Soviet fighter. Short of flying the aircraft, everything possible was done to measure its capabilities. A US pilot carried out high speed taxiing runs to get the feel of the controls. The engines were run on the ground against thrust gauges. Propulsion experts and metallurgists removed an engine for detailed examination. The Fox Fire (Smertch-A) airborne intercept radar, the IFF and data link systems were run on the ground and their parameters carefully noted.[13]

Finally on 12 November, sixty-seven days after it had put down at Hakodate, the crated MiG was loaded on to a Soviet freighter. The party was over.

The follow-up exploitation of the MiG-25 took several months. John Marks recalled:

> "For me the key question was: how accurate was the FTD's previous assessment of the MiG-25, compared with what we found on the real airplane. I had my guys build charts comparing our previous estimates on the engine, the airframe, the avionics, the radar, the performance etc, with what we found when we examined the fighter. The capability of the Fox Fire radar turned out to be a little better than we had predicted, but overall their technology was way short of ours."[14]

John Marks' handling of the MiG-25 incident did no harm to his career. A few months later he pinned on brigadier general's stars.

During the 1960s US manufacturers had developed and produced a range of coherent pulse, pulse Doppler and continuous wave radars for airborne and surface missile control applications. Historically the Soviets had lagged some years behind the west in the development and introduction of such advanced systems. The Fox Fire radar fitted to Victor Belenko's MiG-25 belonged to an earlier generation and lacked these refinements.

From the mid-1970s the technology gap started to close, however. The J-band pulse-Doppler High Lark (Sapfir) radar conferred on the MiG-23M Flogger a limited ability to engage low flying targets. Early in the 1980s the Flash Dance (Zaslon) I-band pulse Doppler radar appeared aboard the MiG-31 Foxhound. The latter fighter carried new semi-active radar homing missiles which gave it a full look-down shoot-down engagement capability.[15]

A notable advance in land-based systems came with the Flap Lip multifunction, phased-array missile-control radar associated with the formidable SA-10 Grumble (S-300) long range air defense system. Designed to engage high performance aircraft and cruise missiles, the SA-10 deployed around the Soviet Union early in the 1980s to replace the aging SA-5 system.[16]

During the Vietnam War the Army Security Agency (ASA) teams produced a stream of valuable SIGINT information on enemy dispositions and movements. Yet, although most ASA teams came under the operational control of the intelligence unit they lodged with, they did not "belong" to the unit commander. The latter's organic combat intelligence company collected and analyzed every aspect of intelligence, except SIGINT. And a level of security prevented co-operation between the unit and an ASA team located perhaps a few yards away.[17]

After the war there was a widespread feeling that Army intelligence collection and analysis could have been handled better, and Major General James Ursano headed a board to study the military intelligence structure. The resultant report, issued in 1975, criticized the existing state of affairs. Later an official Army historian wrote:

> "A succession of previous Army reviews—in all, eleven had been made since World War II—had upheld the validity of the Army Security Agency's traditional vertical command structure. The Ursano panel dissented vigorously. In the panel's opinion, the ASA pattern of organization had actually impeded the development of an efficient mechanism for carrying out intelligence and electronic warfare."[18]

The report said the organization's monopoly of signals intelligence and electronic warfare had artificially kept signals intelligence out of the general intelligence flow. Also, ASA largely excluded the rest of the Army from involvement in electronic warfare, while at the same time its own preoccupation with cryptology prevented it from keeping up with new trends in the electronic warfare field.[19]

The report made a series of far-reaching recommendations, which the Army Staff accepted. The Army Security Agency was broken up and its school, its research and development activity and its tactical units were integrated into the regular Army command structure. Those parts of ASA left were merged with the US Army Intelligence Agency and a number of intelligence production elements, to become the US Army Intelligence and

Security Command (INSCOM). This organization now performed the task of multi-discipline intelligence collection, security and electronic warfare functions at echelons above corps level.[20]

At the tactical level, ASA units merged with regular military intelligence units to form multi-discipline Combat Electronic Warfare and Intelligence (CEWI) units. Each division had a CEWI battalion, each corps had a CEWI group or brigade.[21]

The end of the Cold War led to further massive readjustments within the US Army intelligence service. In Germany VII Corps was inactivated and INSCOM closed down its three major fixed sites for intelligence gathering in Europe. Soon afterwards the INSCOM brigade in Japan was reduced to group status.[22]

Following the collapse of the Communist regime in East Germany in 1989, elements of the East German Volksarmee were integrated into the German armed forces. The dowry of the enforced marriage brought another mass of Soviet-built equipment. Of particular interest were the various SAM systems now available, complete with trained operating crews.

At the firing range near Ramstein in southern Germany, western technical experts looked on as the radar operators endeavored to track German, British, French and US tactical aircraft flying jamming runs against their systems. Afterwards an eight-man ex-Volksarmee operating team with an SA-8 came to Eglin AFB, to conduct a series of fully instrumented tests there.[23]

Other Soviet missile systems, including the long sought SA-5, were also brought to the US for detailed examination at this time.

The early 1980s saw further far-reaching developments in computer technology and microelectronics. Also, Soviet advances in radar, missiles and electronic systems led to a need for more capable countermeasures systems. These moves will be described in the next chapter.

References to Chapter 13

1. Peebles, Curtis, *Guardians*, Ian Allan, Shepperton, UK, 1987, p 202
2. *Ibid*
3. *Ibid*, p 204
4. Interview Dave Brog
5. *Ibid*
6. Interview Major General John Marks
7. *Ibid*
8. *Ibid*
9. Baron, John, *MiG Pilot*, Avon Books, New York, 1976, p 111 *et seq*
10. *Ibid*
11. Marks

12. *Ibid*
13. *Ibid*
14. *Ibid*
15. Butowski, Piotr, "From Alkali to AAM-L," *Air International*, October and November 1994
16. Unattributed article based on material supplied by the Russian manufacturer, "The S-300 PMU-1," *Military Technology*, November 1993
17. Interview John Black
18. Finnegan, John, *The Military Intelligence Story*, Second Edition, History Office, US Army Intelligence and Security Command, Fort Belvoir, Virginia, p 48 *et seq*
19. *Ibid*
20. *Ibid*
21. *Ibid*
22. *Ibid*
23. Interview Barney Parker

Chapter 14

IMPACT OF THE NEW TECHNOLOGY: 2

1980 to 1992

"My father worked for the same firm for twelve years. They fired him. They replaced him with a tiny gadget this big. It does everything that my father does, only it does it much better. The depressing thing is, my mother ran out and bought one."

Woody Allen

The 1980s saw further far-reaching developments in computer technology and microelectronics. At the same time there were important developments in Soviet radar, missile and electronic systems which required more-capable countermeasures systems to reduce their effectiveness. In this chapter we shall observe the effects of these changes.

Since the mid-1960s Strategic Air Command had relied on a combination of electronic countermeasures and low level penetration tactics to enable its B-52s to reach targets in the Soviet Union. By the early 1980s most B-52s had passed through the Phase VI Defensive Avionics upgrade program. Additions to the bomber's sensor suite included the ALR-20A panoramic receiver and the ALR-46 digital warning receiver. The Westinghouse ALQ-153 tail warning system was a solid state pulse-Doppler radar able to detect aircraft

---

B-52 Phase VI Defensive Avionics Suite[1]

Sensors	Jammers	Dispensers
• ALR-20	• Ten ALQ-155/ALT-28	**Chaff**
• ALR-46	• Two ALT-32H	• Eight ALE-24
• ALQ-117	• One ALT-32L	**Flares**
• ALQ-122	• Two ALT-16	• Twelve ALE-20
• ALQ-153	• One ALQ-122	
	• Four ALQ-117	

173

and incoming missiles and cue the appropriate flare, chaff or countermeasures response. The Northrop ALQ-155 was a power management receiver system linked to ALT-28 E/F/G-band transmitters. The ALQ-117 was an active countermeasures set to counter I-band radars, including fighter AI sets. The ALQ-122 was a false target generator.[2]

With this electronic warfare suite the slow-flying heavy bombers stood little chance against the new generation Soviet fighters and missile systems, however. In January 1980 Major Vern Luke was assigned to the Acquisition Office at SAC Headquarters, as Defensive Electronics Manager. He recalled:

> "The Soviets were making wholesale changes to their fighter radars. The newest fighters carried pulse-Doppler radars with monopulse lock-on, and carried semi-active coherent missiles. These gave the fighters a look-down shoot-down capability. It didn't matter how low the B-52 went, they could pick it out from the clutter. None of the systems we had in the B-52 were capable against that."[3]

Luke had the task of seeing into service the ALQ-172 countermeasures system, manufactured by ITT Avionics, to replace the ALQ-117. The system employed velocity gate stealers and other techniques to confuse pulse-Doppler and continuous-wave radars.

Throughout much of the 1970s it seemed that the future of Strategic Air Command's manned bomber force lay with the planned replacement for the B-52, the Rockwell B-1. The bomber made its maiden flight in 1974, with deliveries scheduled to commence in 1979 against a production order for 240 planes.[4]

By mid-1977 the B-1's test phase was well advanced, with three aircraft flying and a fourth nearing completion. Yet doubts now emerged concerning the bomber's ability to reach targets inside the Soviet Union. At the same time the Advanced Technology Bomber (which later emerged as the Northrop B-2) was in the definition stage and showed great promise. With two very expensive manned bomber programs on the table, the Carter administration chose the newer plane. Accordingly, in June 1977, the B-1 production contract was cancelled.[5]

In October 1981 President Reagan announced his intention to reverse the previous administration's ruling and re-instate the B-1 bomber in production. That decision would lead to the most acrimonious airplane procurement program and also the most acrimonious electronic warfare procurement program, of all time. Stan Alterman, an Assistant Deputy Undersecretary of Defense at the time, outlined the position:

> "The President said 'This is very mature technology, the plane is ready to go. We need it. We will do it for $20.5 billion.' It was a negotiated deal, $20.5 billion for one hundred planes, period."[6]

Despite opposition in Congress, in January 1982 the Air Force received authority to order one hundred examples of the B-1B, essentially a B-1A with some improvements. The President promised Congress that the B-1B would attain initial operational capability in October 1986. Such a tight schedule might have been attainable if the bomber and its most important systems were fully tested and ready to enter production right away. Yet that was assuredly not the case, as many of those involved with the program knew.[7]

In no area was there greater need for change than with the defensive avionics suite. AIL had built the original ALQ-161 system for the B-1A to counter the Soviet air defense system existing in the early 1970s. In 1982 the company signed a $2.5 billion contract to produce the improved ALQ-161A defensive avionics system for the B-1B. The minor change in nomenclature concealed a huge difference in requirements, however.[8]

By 1982 the Soviet air defenses were altogether more formidable than they had been a decade earlier. Stan Alterman again:

"I was concerned about electronic warfare suite for the B-1B. The ALQ-161 had been designed to counter an older set of threats. It did not have a capability against the more modern threats, the architecture was not proper. The ALQ-161A was the largest single electronic warfare program ever funded, and we could see it was going to produce a system that would not work properly. But once you have a contract like that, you don't make changes easily. You can't say 'Let's update the whole of the ECM system.' There was no more money, this was a fixed price multi-year contract. The President had to make that deal to get the program through Congress.

When you have a problem you know can be fixed later, it tends to be deferred… People did not want to point the finger at its limitations, to say that the king [or the President] had no clothes."[9]

Air Force Colonel Monte Correll, serving with the Electronic Combat Directorate at SAC Headquarters in the early 1980s, was also unhappy with the official statements issued on the B-1B program.

"When the B-1 was resurrected one of the questions asked was 'Is the ECM system ready?' The Air Force told Congress that it was ready, that it was completely developed. So, we started off with the façade that this system had been developed and tested.

In the B-1B, a lot of things were required that were never in the baseline ALQ-161 program. For example, the I/J-band jammers had not been in the original program. Prior to resurrecting the program, that capability had not been developed. The idea was that a B-1A running supersonic would outrun the enemy fighters, so it was unnecessary to jam their radars."[10]

In October 1984 the prototype B-1B made its maiden flight, five months ahead of schedule with the program running within budget. In retrospect, that was the high water mark of the new bomber's reputation. From then on things deteriorated, slowly at first, but with a quickening pace.

Monte Correll left the Air Force in the summer of 1986 and took a job with AIL's liaison office at Omaha near to SAC Headquarters. There he gained his first sight of the problems afflicting the ALQ-161A program:

"The company was developing the ALQ-161A, and producing the boxes for it, at the same time. As people learned more, they changed the configuration of this box, of that box. They ended up with three different configurations of equipment in the B-1B, depending on when the boxes had been manufactured."[11]

The B-1B's fall from grace came suddenly and without regard for the feelings of those associated with it. Monte Correll continued:

"When I joined AIL everything had looked good, none of the bad news about the B-1B program had hit the streets. I had three months of being the good guy.

Then the sky fell in and I became the whipping boy. At the Air Force Association Symposium in Washington in the fall of 1986, it all came out. People learned about the ECM troubles, the fuel leaks and the plane's innumerable other problems. These problems became public the day after IOC [the Initial Operational Capability date]. The airplane had been declared operationally capable but, Oh by the way, here is a basketful of problems… "[12]

The media declared open season on the B-1B and every recital of its failings, whether true or not, received wide coverage. Those associated with the plane learned the meaning of the term "pariah status."

During the remainder of the 1980s the various contractors worked hard to cure or reduce the B-1B's shortcomings. Yet, in the cruel political climate that surrounded the bomber, it was impossible to get funds for major changes. The shortcomings of the defensive avionics suite would remain. We shall return to this maligned aircraft in a later chapter.

After the ALQ-161A, the next largest US airborne electronic warfare program of the period was the Airborne Self Protection Jammer (ASPJ). This program, too, ran into severe technical and political problems.

In October 1977 the Navy and the Air Force signed a Memorandum of Agreement to work on the ASPJ as a joint program, with the Navy as lead service.[13] ASPJ was to be a state-of-the-art internally mounted system, with an advanced signal processor to perform threat identification, threat prioritization and selection of the appropriate jamming responses. The jammer would employ the latest techniques in power management and had reprogrammable software to keep abreast of changes in the threat.[14]

The Navy needed the new jammer to replace the aging ALQ-126B in all its tactical fighters, while the Air Force wanted it for the new F-16C multi-purpose fighter.[15] To enable ASPJ to fit in the space vacated by the ALQ-126B, it could not exceed the latter's 2.3 cubic foot volume nor could it weigh more than 250 pounds.

In August 1981 Westinghouse and ITT were declared winners of the competition to build the new jammer, designated the ALQ-165. The first three equipments were due for delivery in the spring of 1983.

Almost immediately the program ran into difficulties. With hindsight it is clear that the services had demanded too much from the available technology, they demanded that it fit into too small a volume and they demanded it to be ready for production too soon.

To take one example, to achieve the required performance within the required volume the designers of the ALQ-165 had to use large numbers of hybrid circuits. These hermetically sealed devices were about 1 inch square and contained up to fifty solid state devices. The hybrid circuits were at the cutting edge of technology, and the jammer contained 224, of 125 different types. Quantity production proved difficult, however, and when several hybrids failed to work properly they had to be re-designed.[16]

When the program failed to achieve its initial (and unrealistic) delivery dates, the Navy imposed a ceiling price for the development contract. That capped the government's liability for the program, and required the contractors to pay for changes to cure the ALQ-165's problems.[17]

In 1985, more than two years behind schedule, the first working ALQ-165s arrived at Naval Air Station Point Mugu for development test and evaluation. Gradually the worst of the jammer's technical problems were cured and August 1987 the companies received the go-ahead to build the first hundred production units.[18]

The first production verification units were delivered in December 1989, and it now seemed the worst of the ALQ-165's troubles might be over. But at that point the Air Force withdrew from the program and cancelled its order, citing higher budgetary priorities and concerns over the jammer's cost and reliability.[19] The Air Force had large numbers of ALQ-119 and ALQ-131 jamming pods available, so it would not suffer greatly from the loss of the ALQ-165. For the Navy it was a different matter. Its aging ALQ-126B system could not deal with the newest threat radars. The only feasible replacement that could fit in its planes was the ALQ-165. The Navy decided to continue with the program on its own.

In July 1991 the Navy placed contacts for the second production lot of thirty-six ALQ-165s. Meanwhile, on Capitol Hill, the ALQ-165 had gained a reputation as yet another defense program that suffered cost overruns and failed to meet requirements. In the Senate, influential politicians started to give the program a difficult time. They made it clear that unless the ALQ-165 met all of its operational and reliability criteria, further funding for the program would cease.[20]

The ALQ-165's operational evaluation process began in August 1991 and continued until the following May. This should have been routine but it was not. The ALQ-165 had to demonstrate that it could achieve two measures of effectiveness. First, that it was at least as effective as the ALQ-126B against the older threat systems. And secondly, that when flown against a range of threat systems it would improve aircraft survivability by at least 30 percent, compared with an aircraft carrying no jamming system.[21]

As expected, the ALQ-165 proved far more effective than the ALQ-126B against the older threat systems. The stumbling block came when it had to show it could improve aircraft survivability by 30 percent, compared with a non-jamming aircraft. During the operational evaluation the aircraft employed "current operational tactics": that is to say they flew at ultra-low level to avoid being engaged by the specified radar-controlled threat weapon systems. These tactics ensured high survivability rates, even without the use of a jammer. The ALQ-165 was in a no-win situation, and failed to meet the requirement for a 30 percent improvement in aircraft survivability.[22]

The evaluation did not test the ALQ-165 against the later threat systems it had been designed to counter, because there were no threat simulators for SA-10 and later Soviet missiles on the open-air ranges. Nor did the evaluation include runs against representative defensive threat systems at medium or high altitude. Certainly the ALQ-165 had problems, but against the latest Soviet systems it was the most effective US jamming system available for tactical aircraft.[23]

When the results of the ALQ-165's operational evaluation became known, in May 1992, those campaigning against the jammer redoubled their efforts to end the program. They succeeded. In December the Undersecretary of Defense for Acquisition announced that apart from the existing contracts, there would be no further funding for the ALQ-165 program. More than fifteen years of effort and more than $1.5 billion would yield only 136 ALQ-165 systems for the Navy.[24]

Following the collapse of the program the Navy was in an unenviable position. Its reason for initiating development of the ASPJ fifteen years earlier still remained: the age and limited capability of the ALQ-126B. During that period the threat had advanced to a dangerous extent.

In the months to follow the manufacturers delivered the ALQ-165s ordered previously, only to see most of them go straight into a Navy storage facility where they were quietly forgotten. In a later chapter we shall examine the jammers' eventual fate.

The introduction of digital computers provided fine-tuned power management for countermeasures systems. Just as a modern personal computer comes with a range of software options, a modern countermeasures system comes with a range of techniques tailored to specific radars. Modern receiver systems can identify victim radars with greater precision than before and select the optimum techniques to counter those radars.

There are more than two hundred theoretical methods of jamming a radar or a communications system (see reference)[25]. Many of those are not practicable, however, while others await advances in technology to make them workable.

The Avionics Laboratory at Wright-Patterson AFB has the task of investigating new and old countermeasures techniques to see which are applicable. One successful technique was "terrain bounce," to protect low flying aircraft from radar-homing missiles approaching from above. The jammer picked up the radar signals, amplified them and beamed the high-powered repeater signals at a point on to the ground ahead of the aircraft. This produced a "puddle" of reflected energy on the ground, to presented a radar target more attractive than the plane. Paul Westcott, one of those working at the Avionics Laboratory, commented:

"Ground bounce is effective in defeating a fighter AI [airborne intercept] radar as well as a homing missile... The idea is to make the enemy fighter's radar look at the ground in front of the aircraft. We found that for much of the time the radar did not resolve the two separate targets, it saw just a single target. But then there came a point where the missile saw two separate targets. The greater the energy coming up from the ground, the more biased was the missile's aiming point in that direction."[26]

During the 1970s the technique was tested at the White Sands missile range, carried aboard an F-106 drone. It was very effective for defeating semi-active or active radar homing missiles, and also against ground-launched missiles that climbed above the target aircraft and dived on it from above. The technique caused missiles to miss by distances much greater than the lethal envelope of the warhead, and is used by more than one type of US aircraft currently in service.[27]

The first-generation Soviet IR missiles had been typified by the air-to-air AA-2 Atoll (R3S) and the shoulder-launched SA-7 Grail (Strella). These carried seeker heads operating in the 1 to 3 micron band, that part of the spectrum where jet exhausts show up most distinctively, and could engage jet aircraft only from the rear sector. Those designing decoys and active IR jammers built their systems to produce their maximum IR output in that part of the spectrum.[28]

In the years to follow the Soviets made major advances in the development of IR missiles. The next generation of seeker heads used indium antimonide detectors working in the 3 to 5 micron band (Band IV). Aircraft flying at high speed generate heat due to skin friction, and produce a sufficiently large IR signature in Band IV for a missile to home on to the plane from any angle.[29]

The new band lay well outside the range of cover of the first-generation IR flares and active IR jammers, yet large numbers of the early missiles remain in service. So new countermeasures systems need to be effective against both old and new generation missiles. Those building IR decoys had to develop new burning compounds to cover the larger band spread, and those building active IR jammers had to extend their coverage to counter the range of IR weapons.[30]

Having employed its Rotman lens technology successfully in the SLQ-32 (V)3 jamming system for warships, Raytheon saw another application for it. The Westinghouse ALQ-119 jamming pod had entered service in the 1970s and employed technology dating from the 1960s. By the mid-1980s more than half the Air Force's inventory of jamming pods comprised ALQ-119s which would have been replaced had funds been available. Raytheon now made a proposal to the Air Force, as Dick Curtis recounted:

"The Air Force had all these ALQ-119 jamming pods that were unreliable and didn't develop enough effective jamming power. We knew it was much easier to get funding to modify an inventory equipment, than to build a completely new one. There is a lot of money in retrofit and repair, that can be used to upgrade things in the inventory. The external structure of the pod did not need to be changed that much, we could use the shell and the cooling system, also the same ground support systems. We said to the Air Force, 'If you give us a contract, we will increase the effective radiated power output of the pod by a factor of ten. And we can increase the mean time between failures from a few tens of hours, to several hundred hours.' They gave us a contract to modify a few ALQ-119s along the lines we had suggested."[31]

Dick Curtis and his team removed about two-thirds of the components from the ALQ-119, but left the E/F-band systems in place. The new threat radars operated in the higher G through J bands, and many of them employed pulse-Doppler and continuous-wave techniques. A new power chain was needed to cover those.

As the work progressed the Raytheon team encountered a worrying problem. When the ALQ-119 had originally been designed, at the end of the 1960s, the primary threat ground radars operated in the E/F bands. The jamming pod was configured to radiate in those bands in front of the aircraft, and radiate to the rear against radars working in the higher bands. For that reason the high band power generation system had been located near the rear of the pod.[32]

Now the primary threat ground radars operated in the G through J bands and it was necessary to engage those ahead of the aircraft. If the jamming had to be carried the length of the pod there would be significant power losses. Yet to re-position most of the major components would negate many of the advantages of modifying an existing system. The difficulty was solved in an imaginative way, as Dick Curtis explained:

"My Chief Scientist, Bob Fusfield, said 'Why not fly the pod backwards?' Everybody laughed, but it turned out to be a good solution. The electronics were laid out better when we turned it around, there were shorter runs. We changed the cooling system and turned around the air intake so it faced in the opposite direction. Also we had to take the pointed radome off what was now the back, and put it on the front of the pod. Fortunately, there was no great change in the center of gravity. Turning around the pod was one of those simple ideas that made a lot of sense."[33]

During 1980 and 1981 the Air Force ran tests with the new pod, designated the ALQ-184. It performed impressively and was considerably more effective and reliable than its predecessor. Raytheon received an order to build five pre-production pods for reliability and flight testing, plus modification kits for seventy more. Later the company received a contract to convert all remaining ALQ-119 pods to the ALQ-184 configuration.[34]

Throughout the 1980s the surface Navy's main electronic warfare program was getting the SLQ-32 countermeasures system into service throughout the fleet. In 1985 Raytheon received a contract to produce a high powered variant of the SLQ-32 (V)3, to replace the SLQ-17 aboard aircraft carriers. That became the SLQ-32 (V)4.

A few months before the Stark incident (*see Chapter 12*) John O'Brien, the Director of Surface EW programs at Raytheon's Santa Barbara facility, received a request to attend a meeting at the Pentagon. Senior Navy officers wished to discuss the possibility of building a variant of SLQ-32 to give frigate-sized warships an active jamming capability. It will be remembered that these smaller warships carried the (V)2 variant, with only the receiving capability. O'Brien recalled:

"The Admiral asked what could we do about putting an active EW system into the frigates? Could we build an ECM system small enough to go in some of those ships, one that would put out enough power to conceal their radar cross section—which is quite a bit smaller than a cruiser's. Then he said, 'And can you do it in three months?' We said we could."[35]

The request came at a particularly favorable time so far as Raytheon was concerned. Its Goleta plant was busily producing SLQ-32 (V)3 equipments which had the active jamming capability, so parts could be diverted for the new jammer. Also, the company had started producing components for the Air Force's ALQ-184 contract. The company had tested a scaled-down Rotman lens directional antenna for the ALQ-184 which would also serve for the small-warship jammer. Moreover, to meet just this eventuality, the SLQ-32 (V)2 console had circuitry incorporated at the design stage to accommodate a jamming capability.

The new jammer, code-named "Sidekick," was shipped to the Navy about three months after that initial meeting.[36] The first Sidekick-equipped frigate arrived in the Persian Gulf within a couple of months of the *Stark* incident. Later, the new system was designated the SLQ-32 (V)5 and Raytheon produced about sixty units for installation in frigates likely to operate in high threat areas.[37]

By the early 1980s the seeker heads fitted to the latest radar homing anti-ship missile were more difficult to counter than their predecessors. Improvements in electronics gave these missiles a greater ability to discriminate between a chaff cloud and a warship.

Methods of chaff manufacture and launching had also improved, however. The newer types of glass fiber chaff produced a larger radar cross section for a given volume than earlier types. Also, a breakthrough in technology made it possible to scatter chaff rapidly and effectively without resort to sub-munitions. That meant a greater proportion of the decoy's volume could be devoted to the carriage of chaff.

The improvements in chaff technology were incorporated in Sea Gnat, the system that replaced Super RBOC. Produced under a multi-national NATO program, Sea Gnat used the same launcher as its predecessor. For the seduction and distraction modes Sea Gnat employed separate types of decoy, however.[38]

The Mark 214 mortar round performed the seduction function for Sea Gnat. When the round reached a height of about 300 feet, the centrally mounted explosive charge detonated to deploy the chaff cloud rapidly.[39] The Mark 216, the distraction round for Sea Gnat, worked in a different way. This carried the chaff payload in three separate sub-munitions. As the enemy missile approached the warship, multiple rockets were fired away from the ship at an elevation angle of about 45 degrees for a distance of about a mile. As each rocket neared its deployment range, a small charge ejected the three chaff packages. These descended by parachute for a short time then, at differing altitudes, further explosive charges pushed out the chaff dipoles.[40]

Also at this time the Navy introduced the SLQ-49 distraction decoy, nicknamed "Rubber Duck," developed by the British Royal Navy following the Falklands War. This decoy consisted of two inflatable multi-faceted floating corner reflectors, each about 20 feet in diameter. A length of rope linked the reflectors to a sea anchor to ensure the two units separated. The decoy was stowed on the ship's deck in a couple of canisters similar to those housing the inflatable life rafts.[41]

At the time of writing the Grumman EA-6B Prowler has been in service for nearly three decades. In the absence of a funded replacement its service life must continue for at least another decade. While the plane's designation has remained unchanged, its jamming systems have undergone numerous changes.

As described earlier, the Prowler entered service early in the 1970s. The basic, or "Standard," model carried only the low risk elements of the ALQ-99 jamming system covering four frequency bands and the Sanders ALQ-92 communications jamming system. Grumman built twenty-three Standard EA-6Bs, in addition to five pre-production aircraft.[42]

The next model of the EA-6B, termed the EXCAP (EXpanded CAPability), first deployed in January 1974. This carried an upgraded ALQ-99 system which could jam eight bands, twice as many as the Standard model. Grumman built twenty-five EXCAP aircraft.[43]

The third major EA-6B variant, the ICAP (Improved CAPability), deployed in April 1977 and gave increased frequency coverage. The fourth major variant, the ICAP II (Improved CAPability II) appeared in July 1984. This was equipped to carry and target the AGM-88 HARM anti-radiation weapon, giving the plane a "hard kill" capability. Grumman modified all surviving EXCAP and ICAP models to the ICAP II configuration.

The next major change came with the Block 86 model EA-6B which appeared in 1988. This featured further improvements to the ALQ-99 system, the installation of an ALQ-126B self-protection system, an improved signals processing unit and new radio equipment.[44]

The Army's Guardrail V airborne SIGINT collection system gave fast and reasonably accurate fixes on communications transmitters, and it had proved reliable in service. Yet as mentioned earlier, the aircraft carrying it was not really equal to the task. Its operational ceiling at 16,000 feet imposed limits on the reception of line-of-sight transmissions.[45]

In 1984 the next variant appeared, Improved Guardrail V. This retained the electronics of Guardrail V but carried these aboard the Beechcraft RU-12D which used more powerful engines. This plane could cruise at altitudes up to 31,000 feet and for crew comfort there was an autopilot and, more importantly, a pressurized cabin.[46]

Late in the 1970s Fairchild Weston (previously Fairchild Camera) received a contact to build a new communications jammer for the Army. This became the TLQ-17A, giving an output of 550 watts, which entered service early in the 1980s. Smaller than the GLQ-3A, this equipment was designed for use in the battle area. The ground version, called "Traffic Jam," and its related communications equipment fitted into two Jeeps. At the time of writing Traffic Jam remains in service, though both elements are now carried in a single light tactical vehicle.

The TLQ-17A also forms part of the "Quick Fix" system carried in the EH-1H Huey and EH-60 Black Hawk helicopters. The jammer covers the 1.5 to 20 MHz HF band and the 20 to 80 MHz VHF band.

In addition to the TLQ-17A, Army Combat Electronic Warfare and Intelligence (CEWI) units received the following systems:

- TSQ-38 Trailblazer VHF collection and DF system. This employed two control stations mounted in 1¼-ton trucks, and three unmanned satellite stations each carried in a ¼-ton truck.

- TRQ-32 Teammate VHF collection and DF system mounted in a HMMWV light vehicle.

- MLQ-34 Tacjam VHF collection and jamming system.[47]

At the end of the 1970s the most difficult problem facing US electronic warfare system designers was that of countering the monopulse tracking radar. One of the first such systems to deploy with Soviet forces was the Land Roll tracking radar used with the SA-8 missile system. The Fire Dome missile guidance and tracking radar, fitted to later versions of the SA-6 and the later SA-11 Gadfly battlefield missile system, appeared at about the same time.[48]

Monopulse tracking was impervious to the anti-conical scan and inverse gain lock-breaking repeating systems then in widespread use. And while there was no shortage of theoretical techniques to counter it, tests of the various onboard systems showed that none of them offered the combination of effectiveness and tactical flexibility necessary for general service use.

That left offboard countermeasures, that is to say those not on the target aircraft. The most common of these was of course chaff, but the latest tracking radars carried circuitry that reduced its effectiveness. Another method was to carry expendable jammers and release these during the final stages of a missile engagement. This type of device reached fruition as the Sanders POET (Primed Oscillator Expendable Transponder), launched from the standard Navy ALE-39 chaff and flare dispenser. The decoy was released when the missile was closing rapidly on the aircraft. It picked up signals from the radar-homing missile, amplified them and re-radiated them. Thus for a short time the decoy's small transmitter produced a radar target that was more attractive than the aircraft. POET went into production for the Navy.[49]

POET was effective only during the very short time it was in flight and within a couple of hundred yards of the airplane. It needed to be released at exactly the right point in the engagement, but the difficulty was knowing when that was. The radar warning receiver was of little help in deciding when to launch, since it gave no indication of the missile's range or its estimated time to impact.

Given those difficulties, the only effective way to use POET decoys was to dispense them at intervals when a missile was thought to be approaching. The plane's two ALE-39 dispensers housed a total of only sixty chaff units, flares and POETs, however, so there were limits to how long a crew could employ that tactic.[50]

Clearly, some better method was needed to counter the monopulse radar, and that led to the consideration of a small decoy that could be towed a hundred yards or so behind the plane. The decoy picked up the radar signals, amplified them and retransmitted them. Early in the 1980s Gene Starbuck, a civil servant at the Naval Research Laboratory, hand-built four towed decoys known initially as Multi-Service Decoys (MSDs). He remembered:

"Those original towed decoys cost around $65,000 each. As my Navy sponsor used to put it, if you lose a decoy there goes your daughter's college education. When I said I wanted to do live firing tests with the decoys, he nearly flipped. He said 'Why would you want to do that? If the missile hits the drone, you could lose the program!' My answer to him was, if the decoy can't protect the drone, what good will it be in combat? So we outfitted an F-100 drone with a pod carrying an MSD."[51]

Major General John Corder, then commanding the Tactical Air Warfare Center at Eglin, supported the towed decoy experiments. He agreed to piggyback the decoy test on a live-firing missile test at Tyndall AFB, when three F-15s would launch AIM-7 missiles at drones. The pilots were not told about the towed decoy test, though. Gene Starbuck again:

"There was this F-100 drone flying straight and level over the Gulf of Mexico, they were going to shoot it down. No problem at all. Three AIM-7s were launched at the drone, and they all missed! The next day the same three F-15 guys went up with three more missiles. Three more shots, again they all missed. Those pilots were being graded on the firings, we had three very unhappy F-15 pilots until they were told what we had done...

We did twenty-five live firing tests with the MSD, and every one was successful. We did lose drones, but not because they were hit by missiles. In one case, an F-100 drone made three passes over the test range, and a ground-launched missile was fired at it during each pass. The decoy defeated all three missiles. Then the drone reeled in the decoy and headed back to Tyndall. But when it was on the landing approach the gyros failed, and the drone nosed into the Gulf of Mexico. As I used to tell people, the operation was one hundred percent successful but the patient died!"[52]

Despite its obvious potential, the very idea of towing such a thing behind them was anathema to many a fighter pilot. The opposition to the decoy was vociferous, if not always well thought out. Gene Starbuck explained:

"A lot of pilots just didn't want the towed decoy. That was the biggest battle we had to fight in the early days. There were pilots around who thought they could outmaneuver a missile—they didn't understand that a modern missile can maneuver at up to 40G. Even pulling 9G, a pilot was not going

to lose it. We were talking about the end game of a missile engagement.
They didn't have a solution of their own to the problem, but they really
didn't like our solution."[53]

By the winter of 1986 Gene Starbuck and his team had proved that the
towed decoy was a viable concept. Now the system was put out to industry,
inviting production bids. Five companies put in bids and in 1998 the
Raytheon/Hughes team secured the contract to build the first production
towed decoy system. It was designated the ALE-50.

The mission of the Army Research Laboratory's Survivability, Lethality
Analysis Directorate (SLAD) at White Sands is to search for radiation
interference, deliberate or accidental, that might threaten the operation of a
particular Army system. There has been a group engaged in this work since
the 1950s, and Tom Reader explained how it functioned:

> "We look at the effects of outside signals on the whole range of Army
> missiles. We go all the way across the frequency spectrum and we look at
> the effects of the modulations that we think will cause problems, based on
> our experience. When we get an upset, that is when we say a system starts
> to be susceptible."[54]

The work commands the highest security classification, for if a weakness is
found in a system it is important to keep it secret until there is a cure.

Radio frequency interference is an insidious foe, and it can enter a system
via the most unexpected of paths. One system that might have come to grief
when it went into action, had it not been for vigilance of the Directorate, was
the AGM-114 Hellfire anti-armor missile carried by the AH-64 Apache attack
helicopter. The SLAD team ran its usual range of radio frequency interference
tests on the laser guided weapon, without expecting any reaction. To their
surprise, Hellcat proved vulnerable to high-powered radar-type signals in the
J band from the Gun Dish radar that controlled the Soviet ZSU 23-4 mobile
anti-aircraft gun. Tom Reader commented:

> "We looked at the Hellfire missile, and found it was driven off track by
> signals from the Gun Dish radar. The missile was specifically designed to
> attack tank columns defended by the ZSU 23-4. But if the Hellfire flew
> towards a tank, and a Gun Dish radar beam swept through it, that drove
> the missile right off target. In conjunction with the missile people, we
> developed a technique to prevent that happening. A very fine mesh in the
> dome was sufficient to keep out the RF energy, while still allowing the IR
> energy to come in. That worked just fine. What really astonished us was
> the frequency match between the Gun Dish radar frequency, and the
> vulnerable point in the Hellfire. It was a good thing we caught that!"[55]

The pay off for making vulnerability assessments early in a program is that
corrections are relatively easy to make. Comprehensive testing on these lines

is not cheap but the alternative, ignoring the problem, can be very expensive indeed.[56]

The use of ever-more-powerful computers to analyze data has allowed scientists, engineers and military personnel to assemble and manipulate huge quantities of information. However, it also became clear that using these systems to pass classified information posed a potential security risk. The early computers lacked shielding and radiated a plethora of signals which a diligent enemy might pick up and exploit. Once this became known, the Department of Defense launched the so-called Tempest program to establish shielding criteria for computers and transmission systems carrying classified information.

President Reagan's bid to outspend the Soviets militarily caused a predictable reaction, and when Communist states tried to match the move their weaker economic systems came close to bankruptcy. That wrecked the previous balance of power. Within a few months in 1989 the Communist governments in across Eastern Europe were ousted. The Warsaw Pact, the military alliance of Communist states in Europe, simply fell apart.

The process of disintegration did not stop at the borders of the Soviet Union. During 1990 and 1991 fourteen republics seceded from the Union and gained their independence. Russia herself, and the rump of republics that remained with her, turned to the west for aid. The Cold War was over. Before we consider the effects of that political shift, however, we need to step back in time to examine the long running US program to produce aircraft with low observables features.

References to Chapter 14

1. Gershanoff, Hal, "Peace is our Profession," *Journal of Electronic Defense*, February 1985
2. *Ibid*
3. Interview Vern Luke
4. Interview Stan Alterman
5. *Ibid*
6. *Ibid*
7. *Ibid*
8. *Ibid*
9. *Ibid*
10. Interview Monte Correll
11. *Ibid*
12. *Ibid*
13. White Paper, *Airborne Self Protection Jammer*, Burdeshaw Associates Ltd, Bethesda, Maryland, 1993

14. *Ibid*
15. *Ibid*
16. Interview Alfred Victor
17. *Ibid*
18. *Ibid*
19. "Joint Service/Joint Venture; A Management Challenge," *Program*, September–October 1988
20. Victor
21. *Ibid*
22. *Ibid*
23. *Ibid*
24. *Ibid*
25. See Van Brunt, Leroy, *Applied ECM*, EW Engineering Inc, Dunn Loring, VA, 1978
26. Interview Paul Westcott
27. *Ibid*
28. Taylor, William, "Understanding the Infrared Threat," *Journal of Electronic Defense*, Feb 1999
29. *Ibid*
30. *Ibid*
31. Interview Dick Curtis
32. *Ibid*
33. *Ibid*
34. *Ibid*
35. Interview John O'Brien
38. *Ibid*
37. *Ibid*
38. Interview Frank Klemm
39. *Ibid*
40. *Ibid*
41. *Ibid*
42. Morgan, Rick, "VAQ129: a Heavy Past, an Electronic Future," *The Hook*, summer 1990
43. *Ibid*
44. Lake, Jon, "On the Prowl," *Air International*, September 1999
45. Interview Jerry Proctor
46. *Ibid*
47. Interview Frank Ernandes
48. Internet Websites http://members.aol.com/_ht_a/tgreatnstr/airdef. "Military Equipment of the Former USSR, Air Defense." Also www.fas.org/man/dod-101/sys/missile/row.htm, http://homwtown.aol.com/threatmstrairdef.htm
49. Interview Gene Starbuck
50. *Ibid*
51. *Ibid*
52. *Ibid*
53. *Ibid*
54. Interview Tom Reader
55. *Ibid*
56. *Ibid*

Chapter 15

THE QUEST FOR STEALTH

1964 to 1990

"They seek him here,
They seek him there,
Those Frenchies seek him everywhere.
Is he in Heaven? – Is he in Hell?
That damned elusive Pimpernel."
Baroness Orczy *The Scarlet Pimpernel*

Stealth, or very-low-observables as knowledgeable proponents like to call it, is an integral part of electronic warfare. Any discussion of this technology needs to start by considering the ways a vehicle can be detected. The "deadly signatures," like the deadly sins, are seven in number. In approximate order of importance for detecting aircraft they are: radar, infrared, electromagnetic radiation from the plane, visual, contrails, engine smoke and acoustic.

Radar is the most effective method for the long-range detection of aircraft or ships. So this sensor receives most attention when it comes to reducing a vehicle's signatures. Work on reducing radar signatures began in the late 1950s, in the laboratories at Wright-Patterson AFB. As discussed in Chapter 1, early in the 1960s the CIA's Lockheed A-12 reconnaissance plane (predecessor of the SR-71 Blackbird) was the first manned aircraft to incorporate signature reduction features at the design stage. The plane was shaped to reduce to a minimum reflections from the front and side aspects, and radar absorbent material (RAM) covered many parts of the airframe.[1]

For their time the signature-reduction features applied to the A-12 were a fine effort. Yet, as also described in Chapter 1, Project Palladium revealed that the Soviet air defense system could have tracked A-12s flying through its coverage.[2]

Project Palladium also established the radar signature reduction necessary, if planes were to fly over the Soviet Union unseen.[3] The figure remains classified, but the reduction had to be in excess of 98 percent of a normal aircraft's signature. In this account aircraft with the "98 percent plus" signature reduction will be termed "very low observable" or "stealthy." Those with lesser reductions in signature will be termed "reduced observables."

From the early 1960s the signature reduction features developed at Wright-Patterson AFB, the University of Ohio Radiation Laboratory and other centers found their way into the designs of conventional combat planes. Although these did not come close to giving the planes very low observable properties, they brought clear advantages. If the radar signature of a plane or other vehicle is reduced by a certain proportion, the jamming power necessary to shield it falls by the same proportion.

The radar cross section (RCS) of a plane depends on its shape and the electromagnetic properties of its external surfaces. A major source of radar echoes is the engine air intake. Another is from inside the radome covering the plane's radar scanner which has to be radar-transparent. Behind the radome is the radar reflector which rotates or flips from side to side. Each time the reflector faces the enemy radar it gives an excellent return signal. Other echoes come from crew positions covered by radar-transparent (as well as optically transparent) glass.[4]

Reducing a conventional plane's total signature can be achieved incrementally in several ways. Radar signals entering the engine intake usually bounce off the side walls more than once before they reach the rotating compressor disk. After being reflected off the disk, the signals again bounce off the walls on their way back to the radar. A lining of RAM on the walls of the engine air intake will attenuate the signals at each bounce off the structure. The plane's own radar scanner can be "tuned" to the frequency of its radar, making it opaque in that frequency band but transparent to those from radars in other frequency bands.[5] Also the plane's radome can be "tuned" to admit only signals in the same frequency band as the plane's own radar, and appear opaque to radar signals in other bands. Glazed areas around cockpits can be covered in an ultra-thin layer of gold film to make them opaque to radar signals but transparent to light.[6] Taken together these moves will reduce the radar echoes from individual parts of the plane.

An early application of this technology was to the AGM-28 Hound Dog air-to-surface missile carried by B-52s. It was found that a RAM coating inside the engine air intake gave a useful reduction in RCS from the head-on aspect. Following successful tests, during the 1960s SAC's inventory of AGM-28s was modified in this way.[7]

At Wright-Patterson AFB, theoretical work on reducing aircraft radar signatures had advanced during the 1960s and 1970s. During this period Bill Bahret was the leading visionary on very low observable techniques. He recalled:

"If you do the arithmetic, it becomes clear that to really hurt a hostile radar you have to do heroic things in reducing a vehicle's signature. In simple English, it takes a 95 percent reduction in signature to reduce a radar's detection range by 50 percent. It takes a 99 percent reduction in signature to reduce the radar's detection range by 67 percent."[8]

The methods of securing a major reduction in an airplane's radar signature fell into three broad categories: the treatment of specific parts of the plane (already discussed), shaping, and the application of RAM to the external surfaces.

To reduce the radar signature of a plane to anything approaching the magic 98 percent level, the machine had to be shaped to conform with the principles of very low observables. Bill Bahret again:

"Shaping is an extremely powerful tool. I can get a lot more radar echo reduction that way, than I could using the world's best radar absorbent material. Shaping has broadband applications, but there are limits to what you can do. It all depends on how much you are willing to compromise the design, in order to get a low radar cross-section. I used to tell Air Force guys, 'If you want a really low radar cross-section, go build a flying saucer!' The biggest echoes from a flying saucer are when you look straight down at it, or when you look straight up at it. Otherwise, you are not going to see very much. Now people might say 'When you go directly over the top of radar, he is going to see you.' But who in his right mind builds an early warning radar that looks vertically upwards?"[9]

On the development of RAM for aircraft applications, Bill Bahret went on to comment:

"The reflection from a surface is proportional to the dielectric constant of that surface. The material with the lowest dielectric constant that we know of is something like polystyrene foam. If you had an infinitely thick sheet of that material, any energy that went into it would never come back out. But you would still get an echo off the front face, because you have a discontinuity where the air meets the foam…

You can build absorbing materials that will reduce the radar reflection, and you can do some pretty nice things. But you want to make the material as broad band as possible, you don't want some narrow band solution. Also, when you put absorbent materials on an airplane, you have to worry about the other guys' needs. The structures guy, he wants it to have a certain amount of physical integrity, because it has to stand up to the environmental conditions. The aircraft designer wants it to be zero thickness, zero weight—and preferably zero cost!"[10]

The Air Force laboratory took the lead with radar and infrared signature reduction programs, but other services soon entered this field. Before the advent of radar-homing anti-ship missiles, warship designers gave little thought to reducing ships' radar signatures. Traditionally the parts of a ship's superstructure met each other and the decks at right angles; that looked nice. However, that created an efficient corner-reflector at each intersection in the structure, and those echoes added up to produce a huge radar signature.

With the appearance of radar-homing anti-ship missiles, RCS reduction became important for warships. One fruitful area was the eradication of corner-reflectors in the superstructure, so modern warships have the angles between structural intersections set at 95 degrees or more, rather than 90 degrees as previously. That greatly reduced the corner-reflector effect in new warships. In existing vessels this effect was partially achieved by inserting metal fillets at intersections. Also, RAM was applied to surfaces likely to produce large echoes. On-deck metallic clutter has been reduced to a minimum. Of course such changes did not come close to giving a warship very low observable characteristics. Their principal value lay in the improving the effectiveness of warships' jamming and decoy systems.[11]

Another significant area of warship signature-reduction has been in the infrared spectrum. This became important when anti-ship missiles entered service with dual-headed seekers operating in both the radar and the infrared parts of the spectrum. By cooling or screening engine exhausts and other hot spots on the superstructure, warships' infrared signatures were also greatly reduced.[12]

In the Army the reduction of the visual, engine smoke, electromagnetic and acoustic signatures of equipment had long been a major objective. Attacking the various radar and infrared signatures came much later.

During the closing stages of the Vietnam War, Army helicopters faced a major threat in the shape of the SA-7 shoulder-launched IR missile. We have seen that Army aviation engineers developed a makeshift metal diffuser to fit around the helicopters' engine exhausts, "The Toilet Bowl." That deflected the hot gasses into the cool downwash from the rotor, giving rapid mixing of the air and a marked reduction in the helicopter's IR signature.[13]

Later Army battlefield helicopter types, like the AH-64 Apache, were fitted with more-effective exhaust suppressors. The helicopter's cockpit canopy has flat slabs of toughened glass, to reduce the IR "glint" caused by reflected sunlight. The non-glass external surfaces are covered in a special anti-IR paint that gives a useful reduction in IR emissions. In combination these passive measures greatly reduce the vulnerability of Army helicopters to IR weapons.[14]

Where appropriate, the Army has also applied these principles to reduce the radar and IR signatures of other items of equipment.

In 1974 the Defense Advanced Research Projects Agency (DARPA) solicited bids for design studies for manned experimental airplanes with very low observable characteristics. In the fall of 1975 Lockheed and Northrop each received a contract to design and build a full-scale non-flying demonstrator incorporating the available very low observable features.

The design work at Lockheed had not gone far when that company received help from an unexpected quarter. In 1962 the Soviet mathematician and physicist Piotr Ufimtsev of the Moscow Institute of Radio Engineering had published a learned paper giving formulae for calculating the RCS of two-dimensional shapes. Ufimtsev's paper aroused little interest in his own country, but when Lockheed discovered its existence it was manna from heaven. Denys Overholser, a mathematician and radar expert, later commented:

> "Ufimtsev has shown us how to create computer software to accurately calculate the radar cross section of a given configuration, as long as it's in two dimensions… We can break down an airplane into thousands of flat triangular shapes, add up their individual radar signatures, and get a precise measurement of the radar cross section."[15]

Ufimtsev's paper provided a reliable method of predicting the RCS of a plane before it was built, something that had not previously been possible.

In the mid-1970s computers were insufficiently powerful to run Ufimtsev's RCS calculations for three-dimensional designs.[16] So Overholser built his stealthy plane from a large number of individually flat panels; that gave it the distinctive "faceted" appearance. Wherever possible the facets were aligned to reflect radar energy away from the radar looking at the plane.

Lockheed engineers determined that the optimum shape for a stealthy vehicle would resemble a beveled diamond, and their entry won the "pole-off" competition at Holloman AFB. In March 1976 Lockheed received a contract to build two proof-of-concept manned demonstrator aircraft under the "Have Blue" program.[17]

Although the beveled diamond performed impressively during RCS measurement tests, a plane of that shape would have uncontrollable in flight. The challenge was to build a controllable airplane that did not compromise too many of the very low observable principles. Have Blue's outer wing was extended to produce a notched delta shape with just over 72 degrees of sweepback. At the rear it sprouted two vertical stabilizers canted inwards, looking from the front like an inverted "V." Mesh screens covered the engine air intakes, to make these appear on radar as solid surfaces that could be treated as separate facets.[18]

The Have Blue prototype quickly took shape at Lockheed's Skunk Works at Burbank, California. Intended to test only aerodynamic handling, the odd-looking machine lacked many very low observable features—the RCS tests would be conducted using the second prototype. The plane was 47 feet 3 inches long and the wing spanned 22 feet 6 inches. Fully loaded it weighed 12,500 pounds. Have Blue used components from existing aircraft types wherever possible. Power came from two General Electric J85 turbofans giving 2,850 pounds thrust, as fitted to the T-2B Buckeye trainer. The landing gear came from the Northrop F-5 fighter, the pilot's side-stick control from an F-16.[19]

Have Blue made its first flight from the secret airfield at Groom Lake, Nevada on 1 December 1978. In the next five months the aircraft flew thirty-six times. The computer-controlled fly-by-wire system kept the plane in the air, but handling was never easy. Ben Rich, the pilot, commented that the take-off performance of Have Blue was akin to that of "a fully laden Boeing 727."[20]

On 4 May Rich made a heavy landing in the aircraft, which hit the ground hard and bounce high. Rich pushed open the throttles, retracted the landing gear and accelerated to regain flying speed; but by then the damage had been done. When Rich extended the gear in preparation for another landing attempt, only the left leg had extended. All attempts to lower the right leg failed, so Rich climbed to 10,000 feet and ejected. As the cockpit canopy lifted off it struck him on the head and knocked him unconscious. That and a back injury suffered during the same incident ended Rich's career as a test pilot, though he remained with the company in a non-flying post.[21]

Meanwhile the second Have Blue was nearing completion. Carrying the full RAM coating it flew for the first time on 20 July 1978. Over the next twelve months the plane made more than fifty flights and demonstrated its very low observable capability against a range of domestic and foreign radars. On 11 July 1979 the second Have Blue prototype crashed after suffering an in-flight fire.[22] By then, however, the two Have Blue prototypes had performed their allotted tasks. They had shown it was possible to build, fly and control an aircraft employing almost the full range of low observable features.[23]

Following the success of Have Blue, Lockheed received an order to develop a stealthy subsonic attack plane to carry a 5,000-pound payload over a radius of action of 400 miles. The aircraft received the codename "Senior Trend."[24]

Senior Trend was essentially a scaled-up version of Have Blue, with some additional features. To improve low-speed handling the wing sweepback was reduced to 67 degrees. The nose was shorter and the attachment points of the vertical stabilizers were moved inboard and canted outwards instead of inwards.[25] Senior Trend had internal weapons bays to accommodate either two 2,000-pound free-fall bombs or two B-61 thermonuclear weapons. Laser designators above and below the plane's nose would allow the pilot to acquire targets at a reasonable range and deliver the attack in level flight.[26]

As mentioned at the beginning of this chapter, the signatures an aircraft needed to counter are: radar, infrared, electromagnetic emissions from the plane, visual, contrails, engine smoke and acoustic. Having discussed radar, we shall now look at the others in turn.

On the subsonic Senior Trend the main sources of infrared emissions were the engine exhausts. To reduce these emissions the plane had flattened tailpipes to ensure rapid mixing with the cool surrounding air.[27]

To eliminate an electro-magnetic signature when near or over enemy territory, the aircraft would employ passive systems for navigation and attack, and observe strict radio silence except in an emergency.

Confining operations to the hours of darkness greatly reduced the plane's visual signature. Contrails were avoided by flying below or above the band of altitudes where these formed. The engine, the General Electric F-404, was a non-augmented turbofan which produced scarcely any smoke and was relatively quiet.

The full-scale development program for Senior Trend called for the construction of five experimental prototypes and fifteen production aircraft.[28]

We left Northrop's work in 1976, following the award of the Have Blue contract to Lockheed. Shortly afterwards the Defense Advanced Research Projects Agency requested that Northrop conduct a very low observables study for a different role.

An important project at that time was "Assault Breaker," intended to halt a Soviet armored thrust into Western Europe. Assault Breaker employed a surveillance aircraft carrying a synthetic aperture radar to pinpoint concentrations of enemy tanks and other vehicles. The latter would then be attacked with air-to-ground and ground-to-ground missiles.[29]

The aircraft was to carry a low-probability-of-intercept radar. That might sound like a contradiction in terms, but the designers had several tricks up their sleeves. The radar transmissions were spread over a broad slice of the frequency spectrum, with varying waveforms so the signals merged with those from other radars in the area. The signals also carried pseudo-random noise modulation to make detection difficult.[30]

For this scenario the radar surveillance aircraft needed to spend long periods flying close to the battle line, which led to the requirement for the Battlefield Surveillance Aircraft Experimental (BSAX), to be a very low observables design, to fly much of its mission unseen on enemy radar. The radar returns collected by the plane would be conveyed by data link to a ground station.[31]

Design work on the BSAX was complete by the end of 1977 and in the following spring Northrop received a contract to build a prototype code-named Tacit Blue. The resultant single-seat plane was certainly odd-looking. Viewed from the side, the upper part of the fuselage resembled an old-fashioned iron bathtub mounted upside-down. Low-set straight wings protruded from each side, and at the rear was a V-tail. Power came from two Garrett AiResearch ATF3 turbofans buried in the rear fuselage, drawing air through a flush intake set into the top of the fuselage.[32]

The unusual plane flew several times in the early 1980s. Then the Assault Breaker program was cancelled, and thereafter interest in the BSAX waned rapidly.

While Tacit Blue was under construction, Northrop became involved with a considerably more ambitious project. In 1979 the Air Force looked to very low observables to maintain the survivability of its manned bomber force. Northrop received a study contract for a stealthy long-range penetrating airplane, which led to a detailed design study for the Advanced Strategic Penetration Aircraft.[33]

In September 1980 the Air Force asked for proposals to build its next generation Advanced Technology Bomber (ATB). Northrop teamed with Boeing to offer the "Senior Ice" design, a flying wing with moderate wing sweep. Between 1975 and the end of the decade computer power had increased enormously, and now it was possible to design a very low observables plane in three dimensions rather than just two.[34]

Before the Air Force picked the winner of its Advanced Technology Bomber competition, the government changed. The 1980 election swept President Reagan into power, with a raft of proposals to strengthen the nation's defenses. In the following October there were two major political decisions affecting Strategic Air Command. First, as recounted in the previous chapter, President Reagan announced that he wanted to re-instate the B-1 into production. Secondly, with no fanfare at all, Northrop received a secret contract to design and build six ATBs (later designated the B-2), with an option for a further 127.[35]

To return to the B-1B for a moment, one set of alterations incorporated in the bomber before it re-entered production is relevant to this chapter. North American Rockwell incorporated several changes to reduce the RCS of the B-1B. Sherm Mullin at Lockheed's Skunk Works, one of those involved with this work, commented:

> "Years earlier we had discovered that you can't Band-Aid signature reduction features on to an existing design and make a plane stealthy. On the other hand, even if you can't get a huge reduction in signature, a smaller reduction is still worth having. Nobody would call the B-1B a stealthy airplane. But the pay off with signature reduction comes when it is used in conjunction with electronic countermeasures. From many aspects, the B-1B has a signature little bigger than that from a fighter-type plane. So, the B-1B can be protected by fighter-type countermeasures systems of lower power, lower weight, and lower cost than those normally fitted to bombers. Now [in the year 2000] we get the B-1B being protected by the ALE-50 towed decoy designed to protect the A-6 Intruder. Signature reduction and countermeasures can be

complementary technologies, and the synergy of the two is outstanding."[36]

The process of radar signature reduction has also been applied to a greater or lesser extent on almost all the non-stealthy US combat aircraft types; in the B-1B Lancer we see one of the clearest example of its effectiveness.

As detailed design work for the ATB commenced at Northrop, the initial batch of Senior Trend aircraft neared completion at Lockheed's Skunk Works. In June 1981 the first prototype made its maiden flight from Groom Lake. By the spring of the following year, all five development prototypes had joined the test program.

The Groom Lake testing ground was a good place for testing secret aircraft, but it lacked the facilities necessary for the operation of a regular Air Force unit. Accordingly the Air Force activated the nearby remote airfield at Tonopah, Nevada, to receive the new plane. Tonopah airfield lies about 140 miles northwest of Las Vegas and adjacent to the weapons range of the same name.[37]

In February 1982 Sherm Mullin became Program Manager for the Senior Trend program. He described some of the unique problems he had to overcome:

> "The structure of the stealth fighter required mechanical tolerances way beyond those of any conventional military or commercial airplane. For example, in a commercial airplane if the skin is not exact, let's say here and there it is out by maybe ¼ inch in a 150-foot wing span, that does not cause any particular problem. For the stealth fighter the structure had to be accurate to a maximum tolerance of around one-hundredth of an inch. And those flat facets had to be really flat, as flat as you can measure. There were a lot of problems getting the tooling to achieve these extremely tight tolerances."[38]

The first production Senior Trend was delivered to the Air Force's 4450th Test Group at Tonopah in August 1982. Further aircraft followed at one-month intervals. In October 1983, on the arrival of its fourteenth plane, the Test Group attained its initial operating capability.[39]

In April 1984 the 4450th passed its first operational readiness inspection. During the next 4½ years, in the course of which Senior Trend acquired the designation F-117A, the program remained under tight security wraps and the planes flew only at night.

Only in November 1988 was the existence of the F-117A finally revealed. At a Pentagon press conference Assistant Secretary of Defense Daniel Howard showed an in-flight photograph of the F-117A taken from the starboard quarter. Although too grainy to show details of the facetted exterior, the image revealed the plane's unusual outline and aroused considerable interest.[40]

Contrary to copious media reports, very low observable features do not make a plane "invisible" on radar. If such a plane ventures close enough to a radar, it will be seen. The value of stealth is that it drastically reduces the effective range of an enemy's defensive radars. To exploit its capabilities to the full, a stealth aircraft needs to pick its way through the gaps in the coverage of the radars and SAM defenses.

One further stealth program, for the US Navy, requires mention at this point. In 1978 Lockheed's Skunk Works designed a proof-of-concept very low observables ship. Named *Sea Shadow*, the vessel was a catamaran 160 feet long and 70 feet wide, displacing 560 tons and with a crew of four. The superstructure resembled an upturned bathtub and flat panels of radar-absorbent material covered the structure above the waterline.[41]

The stealthy vessel began sea trials in 1981 but the need for security caused severe problems. A barge with a structure like an aircraft hangar hid the unusual craft from prying eyes during the day. For each test the barge was towed out to sea from its base at Long Beach. After nightfall, provided no unauthorized craft was in the area, *Sea Shadow* emerged. The craft had to be back in her special barge by one hour before dawn, then the barge and its cargo were towed back to Long Beach.[42]

One role foreseen for the low observables warship was that of covert mobile anti-aircraft missile battery. Positioned up-threat from a task force or an important convoy, the craft could engage and disrupt enemy air attacks.[43] The Navy saw operational difficulties with the concept, however, and took the idea no further.

In November 1988 the prototype Northrop Advanced Technology Bomber, the B-2, was revealed to the press. The B-2 was a larger and more formidable fighting machine than the F-117A; its maximum take-off weight was about seven times greater, and its maximum weapon load was twelve times greater, than that of the smaller plane.[44]

At its unveiling the B-2 lacked engines and other major components, and was far from ready to fly. Its maiden flight was in the following July, two years later than originally planned. We shall return to this program in a later chapter.

With the F-117A revealed to the public, it could be assigned to a regular Air Force unit. Accordingly, in October 1989, the 37th Tactical Fighter Wing assumed responsibility for stealth fighter operations.[45]

One development made over several years played a vital role in making the F-117A into an effective combat plane: the reduction in maintenance hours per flight hour. In 1983 the plane required about 150 hours' maintenance for each flight hour, compared with just over 19 hours for the F-16. Much of the problem stemmed from the need to restore the RAM covering whenever a panel was opened. By 1989 the F-117A averaged 45 maintenance hours per flight hour.[46] While it would never be easy to maintain, it was now much closer to the figure for a conventional fighter.

On 20 December 1989 the F-117A flew its first operational missions. There was evidence that Panamanian dictator Manuel Noriega allowed drug smugglers to use his country as a staging point to the US. Operation Just Cause, the invasion of Panama, was mounted to remove Noriega from power. Six stealth fighters of the 37th TFW took off from Tonopah, refueling in the air five times during the flight to Panama and back. Two planes were to support an operation by Special Forces to capture the dictator. Two more were to drop bombs near a barracks housing troops loyal to him, to cause confusion rather than casualties. The remaining two planes were reserves, in case planes assigned to the two main operations had to abort.[47]

The operations did not go according to plan. The Special Forces' operation was aborted, leaving two F-117As without a target. Then, due to a misunderstood order, the aircraft assigned to "shake up" the barracks missed their intended aiming points by several hundred yards. The planes in reserve did not attack anything. Thus four of the six planes returned with their bombs and those from the remaining two planes fell in the wrong place.[48] The news of the F-117A's seeming failure during its first operational mission drew howls of derision from the press. Yet the miscarriage of its operation had nothing to do with the plane's stealth capabilities or lack of them.[49]

In July 1990 Lockheed delivered the fifty-sixth and last production F-117A. The 37th Tactical Fighter Wing now possessed its full complement of planes and personnel, and it was eager to show what it could really achieve in combat. As we shall observe in the next chapter, that opportunity would occur much sooner than anyone anticipated.

References to Chapter 15

1. Interview Gene Poteat
2. *Ibid*
3. *Ibid*.
4. Whitford, Ray, "Fundamentals of Fighter Design, Part 10: Stealth," *Air International*, September 1997
5. *Ibid*
6. *Ibid*
7. Aronstein, David, and Piccirillo, Albert, *Have Blue and the F-117A*, American Institute of Aeronautics and Astronautics Inc, Reston, Virginia, 1997, p 7
8. Interview Bill Bahret
9. *Ibid*
10. *Ibid*

11. Interview Admiral Julian Lake
12. *Ibid*
13. Interview Tom Reinkober
14. *Ibid*
15. Quoted in Rich, Ben, and Janos, Leo, *Skunk Works*, Little, Brown and Company, Boston, MA, 1994, p 20 *et seq*
16. Lake, Jon, "Lockheed Martin F-117A," *Air International*, August 1998
17. *Ibid*
18. *Ibid*
19. *Ibid*
20. Dorr, Robert, *Lockheed F-117A Nighthawk*, AIRtime Publishing, Westport, CT, 1995, p 11 *et seq*
21. Aronstein, pp 44, 45
22. Dorr
23. *Ibid*
24. *Ibid*
25. *Ibid*
26. *Ibid*
27. Lake
28. *Ibid*
29. Hewish, Mark, "The Assault Breaker Program," *International Defense Review*, 9/1982
30. *Ibid*
31. Sweetman, Bill, *Inside the Stealth Bomber*, MBI Publishing Co, Osceola, Wisconsin, 1999, p 14
32. *Ibid*
33. *Ibid*, p 26
34. *Ibid*, p 30
35. *Ibid*, p 31
36. Interview Sherm Mullin
37. Dorr, p 19
38. Mullin
39. Dorr, p 22
40. *Ibid*, p 39
41. *Ibid*
42. Rich, p 271 *et seq*
43. *Ibid*
44. Sweetman, p 125
45. Dorr, p 66
46. *Ibid*, p 40
47. Aronstein, pp 150–2
48. Dorr, p 40
49. Giangreco, D, *Stealth Fighter Pilot*, Motorbooks International, 1993, p 65

Chapter 16

DESERT STORM: THE AIR CAMPAIGN

August 1990 to February 1991

"The race is not always to the swiftest nor the fight
to the strongest. But that's the way you bet."
Attributed to Samuel Goldwyn

On 2 August 1990, Iraqi dictator Saddam Hussein implemented his plan to annex the neighboring state of Kuwait. Iraqi troops crossed the border and advanced rapidly through the small country. In response the United Nations Security Council passed Resolution 660, which demanded an immediate and unconditional withdrawal by Iraqi forces.

The first US plane from outside the Gulf to reach the area was an RC-135 Rivet Joint aircraft from the 55th Strategic Reconnaissance Wing on detachment at Hellenikon, Greece. Within hours of the invasion the plane flew over Egypt and Saudi Arabia to a point south of Kuwait, from which it monitored radio traffic from advancing Iraqi troop units. At the end of the mission the RC-135 returned to Hellenikon.[1]

The invasion sparked a flurry of diplomatic activity. On 6 August President Bush ordered the implementation of Operation "Desert Shield" to counter a feared continuation of the thrust into Saudi Arabia. The largest military airlift of all time began, to carry combat units, equipment and supplies to the Persian Gulf area.

Brigadier General Larry Henry, Inspector General of Tactical Air Command, was soon on his way to the Air Force Command Center at Riyadh to join the staff of General Chuck Horner, the US air commander. Once there Henry assembled a team of officers to plan SEAD (Suppression of Enemy Air Defense) operations to support US air strikes, should Iraqi forces push into Saudi Arabia. In the days to follow the required SEAD units—EF-111 Ravens, Wild Weasel F-4Gs and EC-130 Compass Call aircraft—arrived in the theater.[2]

As the Allied buildup accelerated the force moved from defense to offense. Larry Henry and his staff began working on a SEAD plan to support air strikes on targets in Iraq itself.

Initially the main intelligence target was the Iraqi air defense system, created by French engineers in the 1980s. With France a member of the Coalition, the planners at Riyadh had a rare insight into the enemy's air control system. The hub was the National Air Defense Operations Center near Baghdad. Subordinated to it were five sector operations centers which directed the activities of interceptor fighters and missile and gun batteries, within their assigned geographic areas. Each sector, in its turn, controlled a number of intercept operations centers responsible for directing local air defense in their areas.[3] The system employed a range of different radars, providing considerable frequency diversity and redundancy. There was a similar diversity and redundancy in communications between the elements of the system.

US intelligence sources estimated the Iraqi night and all-weather interceptor force comprised about 160 fighters; MiG-23s, MiG-25s, MiG-29s and Mirage F1s. Covering Baghdad, the most heavily defended part of the country, were some 550 SA-2, SA-3, SA-6, SA-8 and Roland missile launchers and more than 1,200 guns of calibers from 23 mm to 85 mm.[4] Other important areas, notably the H-2 and H-3 military bases and the cities of Mosul, Talil/Jabilah and Basra, possessed less strong but still menacing SAM and AAA defenses.[5]

To expose weaknesses in the Iraqi air defense system the Coalition sent fighters on "needling" missions close to the Iraqi border, while RC-135s and other intelligence collectors observed the Iraqi response. Larry Henry explained:

> "During Desert Shield we sent aircraft in close to the border—real close—and watched what the Iraqis did. I wanted to see the timeliness of their reaction, and track the way they passed on the information. I wanted to see how their sector operations centers and intercept operations centers would operate if we actually went in. Would they act independently, or would they just pass the data up the chain of command? We found that in most sectors the passage of information was pretty good, it was passed up the chain of command and also to the adjacent sectors. They alerted each other.
>
> Then we found one intercept operations center where the information went only up the chain of command, never sideways. It seemed that those guys did not talk to their counterparts on either side. That was the weak point in the system we had been looking for… If that center went down, those on either side of it wouldn't be alarmed if they heard nothing. They did not expect to hear from them anyway."[6]

The plan to reduce the Iraqi air defense system would open with attacks on the national air defense center and key sector and interception operations buildings. Simultaneously there was to be an elaborate attack to neutralize the missile batteries around Baghdad. Earlier in his career Larry Henry had studied the June 1982 Israeli attack on Syrian missile batteries in the Bekaa region of Lebanon (described in Chapter 12). Now he planned to use this as a model for his attack on the Iraqi system.[7]

First, all intelligence sources were to be used to assemble a detailed picture of the layout of the enemy defenses and its operating procedures. Secondly, on the night of the initial attack, drones masquerading as attack fighters would fly over defended areas to lure the missile batteries into action. Thirdly, EF-111As and EA-6Bs would jam the missile acquisition radars, forcing missile batteries to use their narrow-beam target tracking radars to locate the drones. Fourthly and finally, Wild Weasel F-4Gs and Navy and Marine EA-6Bs and F/A-18s would attack the missile control radars with HARMs (High Speed Anti-Radiation Missiles).[8]

By early October 1990 Larry Henry had finished work on his plan, but then he had to return to the US to take up another appointment. Brigadier General Glenn Profitt took over the defense suppression command cell, but kept Henry's plan with few changes.

United Nations Security Council Resolution 678 stated that unless Iraqi troops withdrew from Kuwait by 15 January 1991, member states could use "all necessary means" to dislodge them. The Baghdad government ignored the deadline.

Throughout Desert Shield relays of E-3 Sentry and E-2 Hawkeye radar surveillance planes, usually supported by RC-135 Rivet Joint and EP-3 SIGINT aircraft, flew around-the-clock patrols to observe Iraqi air activity. Backing these were standing patrols by fighter planes. When the deadline passed the patrols continued as before. It was important that the Iraqis should not detect that anything unusual was in the offing.

H-hour for Operation Desert Storm, the start of the co-ordinated series of attacks, was 0300 hours on 17 January (times in Baghdad local time).

By 0215 hours (H minus 45) waves of attack planes were heading towards the Iraqi border: F-117As, F-111s, F-15Es, A-6s and British Tornado GR 1s. Escorting them were F-14s, F-15s and F/A-18s. Each jet entering hostile territory carried the regular self-protection electronic defense suite: radar warning receiver, active jamming equipment and chaff and IR decoy dispensers. EF-111 and EA-6B jamming support planes accompanied the raiding forces. EA-6B Prowlers, F-4G Phantoms, F/A-18 Hornets and A-7 Corsairs, all carrying AGM-88 HARMs, also headed for their assigned target areas.

Also at this time seven B-52s, each carrying five AGM-86 air-launched cruise missiles, reached their designated launch points over Saudi Arabia. These planes had taken off from Barksdale AFB, Louisiana, more than sixteen hours earlier, The heavy bombers launched their weapons at eight separate targets, then returned to Barksdale. The 34-hour flight would be the longest operational bomber mission ever flown.[10]

USAF, USN and USMC EW Aircraft in the Persian Gulf[9]
20 January 1991

Location	Service	Type	No
At Taif, Saudi Arabia	USAF	EF-111A	18
Incirlik, Turkey	USAF	EF-111A	6
Aircraft carriers	USN	EA-6B	27
Shaikh Isa, Bahrain	USMC	EA-6B	12
Saudi Arabia, various bases	USAF	EC-130H	15
Incirlik, Turkey	USAF	EC-130H	3
Shaikh Isa, Bahrain	USAF	F-4G Wild Weasel	48
Incirlik, Turkey	USAF	F-4G Wild Weasel	12
Incirlik, Turkey	USAF	F-16C HARM carriers	13
Jeddah, Saudi Arabia	USN	EA-3B	2
Bahrain Itnl	USN	EP-3E, P-3B	3
Masirah, Oman	USN	EP-3E	
Total			160

Note: Although the table gives the figures for 20 January, the number of planes available was little different on the night of 17 January when the air offensive began. The table does not include the strength of the RC-135 contingent, which was not included in the published list.

As the leading attack planes neared the Iraqi border, Larry Henry's defense suppression plan unfolded. Thirty-eight Northrop BQM-74 decoy drones, launched from Saudi Arabia, headed for Baghdad flying at medium altitude in fighter-type formations. Simultaneously Navy A-6s launched scores of Tactical Air Launched Decoys (TALDs) and these, too, began heading towards defended areas.[11]

Iraqi surveillance radars watched the incoming drones and decoys. As these came within range, the missile batteries received the order to engage. Missile control radars tracked the intruders and the batteries launched salvos of SAMs. The SAMs picked off several drones and decoys, and there was great excitement at the launch sites. Not to be outdone, the AAA gunners joined in firing many thousands of unaimed tracer rounds into the darkness.

Once the SAM batteries had been drawn into action, the second phase of the attack opened. Flying behind the decoys came the defense suppression packages. One such package, heading into the Baghdad air defense zone, comprised twelve F-4G Wild Weasels, two EA-6Bs, ten F/A-18s and eight A-7s, all carrying HARMs. Three EF-111As and two EA-6Bs provided jamming protection.[12] These planes swept in behind six BQM-74 drones and thirty-two TALD decoy gliders. As the Iraqi missile batteries swallowed the bait, on the screens of their special receivers SEAD crews observed signals from numerous SAM control radars. They locked HARMs on to individual radars, then sent the deadly weapons on their way. During one period that night no fewer than two hundred HARMs were in flight and heading for active enemy radars.[13] Several HARMs detonated on or near enemy missile control radars, putting these firing sites out of action.[14]

The next act opened at 0238 hours, H minus 22. Eight AH-64 Apache attack helicopters of Task Force Normandy, 101st Airborne Division, arrived in the vicinity of their targets: two early warning/ground controlled intercept (EW/GCI) radar stations some 50 miles inside Iraq and about 70 miles apart. These radars were subordinated to the intercept operations center at Nukhayb, which Larry Henry had chosen as the weak link in the Iraqi system.[15]

The helicopters launched their Hellfire missiles from ranges of around three miles, then moved in closer to engage with unguided rockets and 30 mm cannon.[16] In less than two minutes both radar stations had been reduced to wrecks, then the helicopters turned for home.

By that time several Tomahawk cruise missiles, launched from US warships in the Persian Gulf and the Red Sea, were heading for selected electricity switching stations in Iraq. As it passed low over its objective, each missile released small spools which unwound to produce serpentine trails of carbon fiber. When a length of fiber fell across high voltage electric transmission lines, it caused a short circuit which tripped out the protective circuit breakers and cut power to the surrounding area.[17] The Iraqi air operations centers normally ran on power from the national electricity grid. For a brief time the centers in the affected areas blacked out, until their back-up electrical generators came on line—but in the interval the air defense computers had "crashed," losing vital information on the unfolding air action.

Simultaneously F-117A Nighthawk stealth fighters from the 37th TFW headed for key targets in defended areas. Major Gregory Feest was briefed to hit the interceptor operations center at Nukhayb, the weak link in the enemy defensive chain. At 0251 hours, (H minus 9 minutes) Feest released a 2,000-pound laser guided bomb and watched on his screen as it disappeared into the roof of the bunker. A column of hot smoke spurted out the entry hole. Then, as if kicked by some enormous boot, the heavy steel entrance doors tumbled away from the front of the building.[18] Obviously that particular bunker would not control fighters for a long time to come.

There was a brief pause, then Nukhayb's defenses sprang to life with a vigorous gun barrage. Tracer rounds streaked past the stealth fighter, yet as Feest headed away from the area the tracers did not follow. Obviously the gunners were firing blind. The F-117A left the scene and headed for its second target, the sector operations center at H-2 airfield in western Iraq.[19]

At 0302 hours an F-117 hit the central telephone exchange in Baghdad. The success of that strike was observed in real time in the operations center at Riyadh. Officers watching the live CNN broadcast from the Iraqi capital, showing tracer rounds arcing across the night sky, saw the transmission end in mid-sentence and the picture dissolve into "snow." That night the Nighthawks attacked thirty-seven precision targets in defended areas.[20]

At 0306 hours the first of the Tomahawk cruise missiles carrying high explosive warheads reached Baghdad. These struck the Presidential Palace, the Ba'ath Party headquarters and the missile storage complex at Jaji.[21] Simultaneously the B-52s' cruise missiles began exploding on communications, air defense and airfield targets around Mosul in northern Iraq.

With the Nukhayb intercept operations center and two of its important radars out of action, a safe corridor had been blasted through the Iraqi air defenses. Like sand streaming through an egg timer, conventional attack planes sped through the corridor making for their assigned targets. At the SAM sites that might have engaged the planes, many had their control radars wrecked or damaged by HARMs. At other sites where the control radars had survived, the ready-use missiles had all been launched against the drones and decoys. When the attacking planes swept past, on the ground the missile crews were still toiling in the darkness to re-load their launchers.

Wing-Commander Ian Travers Smith, leading three British Royal Air Force Tornados running in for a low altitude attack on Al Sad airfield, saw dramatic proof that his arrival was unexpected:

"I had a few problems with my autopilot so I had to fly the aircraft manually. I was head-down in the cockpit as we turned on the IP [initial point] for the target run, which was almost along the line of a valley. Then I looked up and I couldn't believe my eyes: all the runway and taxiway lights were on, the entire airfield was lit up. We really had caught them by surprise."[22]

As the cratering munitions detonated across the taxiways, the airfield's lights suddenly extinguished. Before the defensive barrage could begin, the Tornados were clear of the target.

Elsewhere, attack planes had to pass through areas where the alerted defenses laid on spectacular displays of tracer. When Lieutenant Colonel

Tommy Crawford led six F-111Fs of the 48th TFW to attack Ali Al Salem airfield in Kuwait, Iraqi troops in the desert hosed the sky with their automatic weapons, and initially Crawford found this disconcerting:

> "Our intention was to run in at 1,000 feet until SA-6 signals on the radar-warning receiver forced us down. But there was so much AAA, I couldn't believe how much there was. We crossed the border at 2,000 feet and that was where we stayed until we delivered the bombs. It seemed like every 50 yards a guy with a gun was shooting at us, it was the damdest 4th of July show you ever saw. As we approached the border it looked like a solid wall of fire, but you had no perception of depth so it looked a lot worse than it really was. Once we had crossed the border, it seemed the flak opened up in front of us as we flew along. Then it seemed as if it was worse to the sides and behind than it was in front."[23]

It soon became clear that those visual displays were far less dangerous than they seemed.

So Operation Desert Storm was launched on its deadly course. The initial attacks knocked out important parts of the Iraqi air defense system and inflicted damage at a score of military airfields.

The Iraqis' light-and-sound shows were relatively harmless, as evidenced by their lack of results. That first night the Coalition flew 671 manned aircraft sorties over Iraq and Kuwait. The sole aircraft lost, a Navy F/A-18, fell to an Iraqi fighter.[24] The rest returned safely, though a few bore superficial scars. The so-called "walls" of unaimed tracer were ineffective in terms of aircraft damaged or destroyed, or in crews deterred from hitting their briefed targets.

The Wild Weasel force in the Persian Gulf area comprised forty-eight F-4G Phantoms of the 35th TFW (Provisional) based at Sheik Isa AB, Bahrain. In the west, operating out of Incirlik in Turkey, the 23rd TFS operated twelve F-4Gs with a similar number of F-16s able to carry and launch, but not target, anti-radiation missiles.[25]

Since the end of the Vietnam War the Wild Weasel units' equipment had been much improved. The F-4G Phantom with its APR-47 receiver suite was a more effective radar hunter than the F-105G. Moreover the F-4G's primary weapon, the HARM, was longer ranging and considerably more lethal than the Shrikes and Standard ARMs it replaced. HARM weighed 790 pounds, which included a 145-pound pre-fragmented high explosive warhead.

Lieutenant Colonel Ed Ballanco took off on his first operational Wild Weasel mission from Sheik Isa soon after dawn on 17 January. In one of a dozen F-4Gs, he was to support F-16s attacking the airfields at Ali Al Salem and Ahmed Al Jaber in Kuwait. F-15s flew top cover while EF-111s provided jamming support. The F-16s ran in at altitudes around 20,000 feet, the Weasels at 28,000 feet and the EF-111s and F-15s above that.[26]

"To avoid having to deconflict our targeting, we targeted the SAMs by type of missile and by airplane. So we had one aircraft going after SA-6s, another engaging SA-3s, somebody else looking for SA-2s. I was after SA-6s. I launched a long range HARM into the target area and I think it was a good shot.

Then other missile sites in the area become active, suddenly we found ourselves in a target-rich environment. I fired HARMs at two separate radars as the F-16 flights were coming off the target. Then we got an indication of a missile launch directed at somebody else. We turned to point directly at the site and got off our shot within a few seconds. The missile's time of flight was short, about 25 seconds, then the radar went off the air. We reckoned we killed that one, too."[27]

The pace of initial fighting between the Iraqi missile batteries and the Wild Weasels was too fast and furious to continue for long, and it did not.

On the evening on 17 January, just eighteen hours into the conflict, a Weasel Flight flew over Kuwait in company with an attack force. They passed several Republican Guard SAM units but the latters' radars remained silent. The surviving Iraqi missile control radars had received orders not to radiate.[28]

The reports that the Iraqi target tracking radars remained off the air posed an unexpected problem for Major General John Corder, General Horner's senior operations officer:

"After about the fourth day of the war the Iraqi Electronic Order of Battle [EOB], our understanding of the disposition of their forces, was in a shambles. We did not know how many radars we had destroyed, we did not how many were sitting there not emitting, we didn't know where the systems were that were worth going after, we didn't know if they were waiting out there in the weeds."[29]

Yet the more the general thought through the evidence, the better the picture it painted.

"The big bosses, people like General Schwarzkopf and Chuck Horner, they wanted to see briefing charts showing the locations of all the active SAM sites. I said to them, 'Look, we don't know where they are. But let me tell you this, if I was able to tell you the positions of all their active SAM sites at this stage and we had not been able to knock them out, it would probably mean we were losing. We're not losing many airplanes. We've got a grip on things. This is what it feels like when we're winning!'"[30]

Chuck Horner and John Corder had haunting memories of friends lost over Vietnam, and strong views about the over-use of the low altitude penetration tactic. Now the Iraqi fighter force and the long range missile defenses were in tatters, with little capability against targets flying at 15,000 feet and above. From now on US planes flying over defended areas would do so above that altitude, unless there were sound operational reasons for going below it.

With the change in penetration altitudes came a major change in Wild Weasel tactics, as Ed Ballanco explained:

> "After the first few days we gave up flying regular direct support missions, going in with or ahead of a particular strike force. Instead, we flew mainly indirect support missions, nicknamed the 'Weasel Police.' Beforehand we would go through the frag [the operational order for the day] and mark down the kill boxes where attack planes were going to be active. Then we positioned our flights in the optimum locations to support those forces. The 'Weasel Police' had free reign to support attack missions as we thought best."[31]

US aircraft carriers operating in the Red Sea and the Persian Gulf carried a total of twenty-seven Grumman EA-6B Prowler jamming support planes. A further twelve Marine Corps Prowlers flew from Sheik Isa, Bahrain.

Lieutenant Commander Rick Morgan flew as an ECM officer with VAQ-141 aboard the USS *Theodore Roosevelt* in the Persian Gulf. During combat missions these aircraft normally flew with one ALQ-99 pod under each wing and one under the fuselage, a HARM on the port inboard station and a fuel tank on the starboard inner station. Morgan outlined their usual mode of operation:

> "With their self-defense jammers, chaff, flares and evasive maneuvers, the attack planes could handle the terminal threats. We in the Prowlers were there to jam the early warning and missile acquisition radars. That made it harder for missile control radars to find their targets, so they had to spend longer on air doing it. And that made them more vulnerable to attack from HARMs."[32]

The eighteen EC-130H Compass Call aircraft in the theater operated from King Kahlid International Airport, Riyadh, and Incirlik in Turkey. This communications jamming plane carried a crew of thirteen: a flight crew comprising two pilots, navigator and flight engineer and a mission crew consisting of mission commander, two operators, five linguists and an airborne maintenance technician.

The EC-130Hs jammed VHF, UHF and higher bands used by special command and control systems. The jamming system could be programmed to employ specific types of modulation to counter enemy signals, depending on their characteristics.[33] Lieutenant Chris Bakke, an EWO with the 41st Electronic Combat Squadron, described the way his system operated:

"The system received signals, it searched for and filtered through those that met the criteria we had set. Then the operators got the signals, they filtered them further and designated the targets. Once a signal had been designated as a target, it was routed to the mission commander for jamming. The linguists assisted the mission commander to classify targets by the type of weapon system they were associated with, by their location, by whatever other criteria we wanted to use."[34]

When on station in their allocated areas, the EC-130Hs flew racetrack patterns at altitudes around 20,000 feet. The jamming could be radiated either to port or to starboard, selected by switching the antennas. While jamming the planes flew straight runs perpendicular to the threat axis, typically about 15 minutes (75 miles) long.[35]

If Compass Call aircraft were to be used to the full, much depended on having effective control over the jamming. During the Vietnam War, absence of such effective control had led to an NSA veto on most communications jamming. Captain David Long, another EWO with the 41st, explained how control was achieved during Desert Storm:

"It was a co-operative effort between NSA, the Air Force and the intelligence community. Do our folks jam it, or do we exploit it and gather the information? That is a major dilemma that had to be worked on before we could use our system. During Desert Storm we had an electronic combat communications net with an EC controller who controlled us using a secure voice link. If there was a departure from the frag order, he decided whether or not we could jam. Also we had an electronic combat co-ordination officer on board the AWACS plane, he would provide liaison between Compass Call, the RC-135s and other planes."[36]

In time of war fratricide can take many forms. Chris Bakke described a rare, possibly unique, instance of electronic warfare—Psyops fratricide:

"On one occasion I was on orbit conducting jamming operations, and we knew an EC-130E Commando Solo aircraft was in the area putting out [psychological warfare] broadcasts to Iraqi troops. But we didn't know the frequencies or the times when it was operating. A linguist misidentified a broadcast, we targeted it and we ended up jamming it. We discovered the mistake only after we landed."[37]

Those aboard the Compass Call plane could only hope they had not done a good job on that occasion! Following this discovery there was a tightening of procedures to prevent a recurrence.

During Desert Storm the Rivet Joint RC-135Vs and RC-135Ws played an important role collecting SIGINT intelligence on enemy activity. These planes did not control air battles; their forte was to collect and analyze the information on actions and report this by secure link to the Air Force Operations Center in Riyadh.[38] Rivet Joint aircraft kept clear of Iraqi territory, and so avoided confrontation with the enemy.

Major General Corder had the clout to shrug off embarrassing questions concerning the number of Iraqi radars remaining, but those lower down "the food chain" could not. Lieutenant Colonel Mike Kemerer was at the Intelligence Office at Riyadh, trying to make sense of the enemy electronic order of battle (EOB):

> "The Constant Source [secure data relay terminal] screen gave near real-time updates on Iraqi radar emissions. During the first couple of days of the war, I saw lots of radar activity. Then I could see that our guys were tearing down the Iraqi integrated air defense system, and by the end of the war I saw very little radar activity.
>
> We knew the Wild Weasels were very effective, because we had SIGINT collection taking place at times when the Weasels were up. A radar would be up and emitting, tracking an airplane. A HARM would be fired and several seconds later the radar would go down. And it would not come back up again. So we had good SIGINT indications that that radar had been put out of action."[39]

Yet as any good cop will testify, knowing a thing to be true is quite different from being able to prove it. There were clear signs that HARMs destroyed a significant proportion of the Iraqi missile control radars, but finding evidence "admissible in court" was another matter. Mike Kemerer continued:

> "Our EOB data was based primarily on SIGINT. At the start of Desert Storm, there were about two hundred radars in the Iraqi EOB. As the war progressed, there was a major problem because we had no good way of doing EOB deletions. Guys would go out and bomb a radar or shoot a HARM at it. But unless there was imagery confirmation, that radar could not be deleted from the official list. Also, when the Iraqis moved a radar from one place to another, SIGINT would plot the radar in the new location and report it as a new radar. So the official EOB just kept growing, it never got smaller."[40]

The intelligence officers begged for photography of attacked radar sites, but the aerial reconnaissance effort was limited. SAM sites that might or might not be operational came way down the list of priorities.[41]

The conflict had witnessed the most intensive and successful radar-wrecking campaign in history. Yet, paradoxically, when the fighting ended the official US estimate of the Iraqi EOB listed more radars than it had at the beginning of Desert Storm.[42]

Having examined the part played by electronic warfare in its various forms in support of the air actions during Desert Storm, it remains to assess what they achieved. Twenty-seven US Air Force, Navy and Marine fixed wing planes were lost in combat during Desert Storm (Army losses are covered in the next chapter). The breakdown of losses is given in the table below. The loss rate approximated to that of a relatively quiet month over North Vietnam in 1966.

Fixed wing losses to enemy action during Desert Storm[43]			
Cause of Loss	*Air Force*	*Navy/Marine*	*Total*
Fighter	0	1	1
AAA	3	4	7
SAM (Radar)	3	2	5
SAM (IR)	7	5	12
Other	1	0	1
Unknown	0	1	1
Total	**14**	**13**	**27**

For most of the Vietnam War US combat pilots had only one type of SAM to worry about, and there were never more than two. The Iraqis fielded ten different SAM systems in quantity, which should have been able to make the skies at medium and high altitude dangerous for any plane that came within range.[44]

The fact that they did not was due to the successful employment of electronic warfare systems. The table shows the relative lethality of the threats facing aircraft during Desert Storm. SAMs caused the destruction of seventeen (70 percent) of the US fixed wing aircraft lost. Splitting those losses between IR-guided and radar-guided weapons, puts the nature of the modern threat into sharper focus. The newer generation Soviet IR weapons proved dangerous adversaries and caused twelve (44 percent) of all US fixed wing losses. The main culprits were the SA-9 Gaskin, the SA-13 Gopher and the shoulder-launched SA-14 Gremlin and the SA-16 Gimlet. These weapons gave little or no indication of their presence before launch, and once in flight they were difficult to detect, particularly in daytime.

During the first few days of Desert Storm a significant proportion of Iraqi missile control radars were destroyed or damaged. Thereafter the survivors rarely came on the air. As a result, radar-guided missile systems accounted for only five (18 percent) of all US fixed wing aircraft destroyed.

AAA (including small arms fire), mostly optically aimed, accounted for seven (26 percent of) losses. That was a poor showing considering the huge number of automatic weapons the Iraqis fielded. The reason for these low losses was that Coalition fixed wing planes usually kept above 15,000 feet when over the combat zone.[45]

Only one US plane was lost in air-to-air combat, the F/A-18 which fell on the first night.[46] The 32:1 victory ratio by US fighters during Desert Storm confirmed the superiority of US fighter pilot training and equipment. It also showed the value of the enhanced situational awareness given to fighter pilots by AWACS aircraft and RC-135 Rivet Joint SIGINT aircraft. Once they were airborne, their enemy counterparts received little or no reliable assistance from their battered and jammed air defense infrastructure.

References for Chapter 16

1. Interview Bill Strandberg
2. Interview Brigadier General Larry Henry
3. Cordesman, Anthony, and Wagner, Abraham, *The Lessons of Modern War*, Volume IV: *The Gulf War*, Westview Press, Boulder, Co, 1996, p 133–4
4. *Ibid*
5. *Ibid*
6. Henry
7. *Ibid*
8. *Ibid*
9. "Final Report to Congress: Conduct of the Persian Gulf War," Department of Defense, p 161
10. Coyne, James, "Plan of Attack," *Air Force*, April 1992
11. Henry
12. Cordesman and Wagner, p 411
13. Unattributed article "US Air Force Target Drones Baffled Iraqi Defense Radars," *Aviation Week*, 19 August 1991
14. Henry
15. *Ibid*
16. Flanagan, Lt Gen Edward, *Lightning; the 101st in the Gulf War*, Brassey's Inc, McLean, VA, 1994, p 128
17. Fulghum, David, "Secret Carbon-Fiber Warheads Blinded Iraqi Air Defenses," *Aviation Week*, 27 April 1992
18. Coyne, James, "A Strike by Stealth," *Air Force*, March 1992
19. *Ibid*
20. *Ibid*
21. Atkinson, Rick, *Crusade*, Houghton Mifflin, 1993, p 37
22. Interview Ian Travers Smith
23. Interview Tommy Crawford

24. Unpublished manuscript, Deur, John, "Wall of Eagles," pp 8–10
25. Interview Ed Ballanco
26. *Ibid*
27. *Ibid*
28. *Ibid*
29. Interview Major General Corder
30. *Ibid*
31. Ballanco
32. Interview Rick Morgan
33. Interview Chris Bakke
34. *Ibid*
35. *Ibid*
36. Interview David Long
37. Bakke
38. Hopkins, Robert, *Boeing KC-135 Stratotanker, More than Just a Tanker*, Speciality Press, North Branch, MN, 1997, p 133 *et seq*
39. Interview Mike Kemerer
40. *Ibid*
41. *Ibid*
42. *Ibid*
43. Cordesman p 402
44. *Ibid* p 437
45. Cordesman and Wagner, p 417
46. Atkinson, Rick, *Crusade*, Houghton Mifflin, New York, 1993, p 47

Chapter 17

DESERT STORM: LAND AND NAVAL ACTIONS

August 1990 to February 1991

"In the long run, luck is given only to the efficient."
Helmuth von Moltke

The land and naval actions in the area around Kuwait and Iraq during the 1991 war have been covered in several publications. This account will confine itself to the electronic warfare and related aspects of the story.

When the Iraqis invaded Kuwait, Army Colonel Tom Reinkober had recently been appointed Program Manager for Aircraft Survivability Equipment (ASE). From his office at St Louis he and a staff of some fifty officers and technicians oversaw the self-protection EW systems fitted to Army helicopters and fixed wing aircraft. Normally they had few requests for assistance but now, as Army Aviation units prepared to move to the Mideast for possible combat, that changed. Demands for help to bring EW equipment to operational status suddenly became both numerous and strident.[1]

On paper the Army Aviation helicopters and aircraft had a good electronic warfare capability (see table overleaf). Yet, as Tom Reinkober now discovered, the truth was rather different:

"When Desert Shield began, if you were to categorize the level of knowledge of electronic warfare in the Army Aviation units between one and ten, ten being good, I would say that generally the knowledge of EW was about in the two range. Very few colonels really took EW to heart. That was something they didn't train for. They didn't use their jammers, they didn't use their radar warning receivers. Most of them thought those things were a pain in the butt to have in their aircraft. Systems like the ALQ-144 were classified, which meant that when the helicopter was on the ground it had to be kept under guard. So, many units flew without the ASE equipment fitted."[2]

EW Equipment: Army helicopter and slow fixed wing types	AH-64	UH-60	EH-60	CH-47	OH-58	OV-1E
ALQ-144 IR jammer	•	•	•			
ALQ-136 Pulsed radar jammer	•					
ALQ-162 CW radar jammer	•		•			
APR-39A Warning Receiver	•	•	•	•	•	•
APR-44 Warning Receiver						•
M-130 Chaff & Flare Dispenser	•	•	•	•		•
ALQ-151 Quick Fix			•			
ALQ-156 Missile Approach Detector			•			
ALQ-133 ELINT System						•
IR Emission Suppressor	•	Part of Force				

Reinkober's teams did their best, but there was not time to bring every helicopter to full combat standard before it left the US. Accordingly he dispatched a 15-man team to Saudi Arabia, to meet each unit as it arrived and complete the task.

As well as restoring existing EW systems fitted to Army aircraft, Tom Reinkober's office had to introduce a new one into service. The Iraqis had purchased large numbers of new-generation Soviet SA-14 Gremlin and SA-16 Gimlet shoulder-launched IR missile systems. The Sanders ALQ-144 active IR countermeasures system was only marginally effective against these and its replacement, the ALQ-144A, was still in the development stage. Tom Reinkober continued:

"It was imperative to get the ALQ-144A into the attack helicopters before they went into combat. We didn't have any of those jammers when Desert Shield began. We got permission to put the ALQ-144A into production even before it got through its testing. Everybody knew that against the newer types of IR missile the ALQ-144A was better than the ALQ-144, we didn't need to go though all the wickets to find out how much better it was. Fortunately, Saddam Hussein co-operated immensely by not starting the war early. By the time Desert Storm began, two-thirds of the Apaches in the theater had ALQ-144As fitted."[3]

Before the ground war began, the new jammer had also been installed in a large proportion of the OH-58D Kiowa Warriors and UH-60 Blackhawks.

For the first time, helicopters carrying electronic warfare suites were to go into action in large numbers. Only after battle had been joined, would their proponents learn whether or not these systems were effective.

US forces launched a large-scale reconnaissance effort, using every type of sensor, to determine the positions and identities of Iraqi combat units in the likely battle area. Once the air war began, the emissions from the Iraqi Army air defense radars added new pieces to the jigsaw picture. Army Colonel Charles Thomas, deputy commander of the Joint Intelligence Center at Riyadh, explained:

> "The ELINT collected from Iraqi Army air defense units helped us to understand, on the basis of which types of radar lit up, what type of gun or missile battery they belonged to. For example, signals from Straight Flush radar meant an SA-6 missile battery was present. We knew that certain types of air defense unit were co-located with certain echelons of command. Thus, an SA-6 battery indicated that a division or higher echelon headquarters was positioned nearby. The next step was to figure out what kind of division it might be associated with, and which elements of the division or the corps the SA-6 unit might be positioned to defend."[4]

Three battalions of Guardrail aircraft deployed to Saudi Arabia, two with Improved Guardrail V and one with the older Guardrail V system. Guardrail operations began in mid-January and units flew at maximum effort from 23 February, the day before the ground offensive opened. These planes flew missions round the clock, placing heavy demands on both men and machines.

Early in February General Schwarzkopf ruled against an amphibious landing on the coast of Kuwait. From then on, however, Marines carried out much-publicized landing exercises to strengthen Iraqi fears of such a move. Also warships repeatedly approached Iraqi-held coasts, as if covering a mine clearance operation.

After the bulk of the Coalition armored units moved west to their start points along the Iraqi border, units remaining in the east mounted deception operations to draw attention upon themselves. A fake headquarters put out spurious message traffic, and psychological warfare experts employed a range of tricks to make the forces remaining behind appear far larger than was the case.[5]

Over Vietnam the B-52 had gained an awesome reputation for delivering huge quantities of high explosive on enemy troop positions. The Coalition psychological operations campaign exploited Iraqi fears of such a bombardment. Colonel Jones, commander of the US Army's 4th Psychological Operations Group, explained:

> "Most of the alternating leafleting and bombing was done inside Kuwait. We did drop leaflets on the Republican Guards with B-52s, but the massive leafleting of specific divisions was really along the front in Kuwait and it was designed to do several things. First, to let them know that our intelligence system was good enough to target specific divisions by number. But we did not just leaflet that particular division. We dropped a million and a half leaflets each time, all along the front over every single division and told them that tomorrow we were going to bomb the 20th Division or whatever. We also announced it on the radio. And then we did exactly what we told them we were going to do. We scheduled with the Air Force, generally [sending in] flights of 4 or 6 B-52s, each carrying 72 x 750 lb bombs apiece. We dropped leaflets in the dark, so that when the Iraqi soldiers woke up in the morning the leaflets were all over the ground to tell them that there was an alternative. It wasn't just that were going to bomb them but the alternative was to get away from their equipment, to desert, to come across the border. There was an alternative to death and that was an important message to get across. It was in fact a leadership substitute, and it was a warning. We alternated leafleting them (giving them 24 hours to think about it), bombing them, leafleting them again, saying that we told you so, that we are going to do it again tomorrow and those of you who are left who didn't pay heed to our warnings before, had better watch out next time, and then bombing them again."[6]

Broadcasts from EC-130E Commando Solo aircraft of the 193rd Special Operations Wing strengthened that message. These planes transmitted US-produced "Voice of the Gulf" broadcasts on the HF and VHF bands. The planes flew missions lasting up to fourteen hours, orbiting over friendly territory.[7]

Iraqi military leaders greatly exaggerated the capabilities of the US SIGINT exploitation systems. Iraqi units were ordered to pass most signals traffic by landline, and use radio as little as possible. That approach fell apart when units moved and had to abandon their landlines. When they had to use radio to communicate, their lack of familiarity with it became evident. Colonel John Black, Intelligence Operations Officer with the US Third Army, commented:

> "We were amazed at the extent of their EMCON [electronic emission control]. They hardly used their radios at all. Later we asked Iraqi senior officers taken prisoner why they had not used their radios more. They said that if they pressed their talk button, they expected to have enemy artillery shells bursting round their heads within a couple of minutes. They greatly overestimated our capability to intercept their signals, take

and plot bearings and bring immediate artillery fire down on them. They must have read our press releases and believed every word!"[8]

Immediately before the launching of the ground attack, Coalition tactical aircraft and long range artillery struck at ten of the fourteen major Iraqi communications centers located in and near Kuwait. The remaining four, in the northern sectors with Republican Guard, were left intact to see if they would yield useful intelligence.[9]

On the morning of 24 February, as Coalition armored columns streamed into Kuwait from the south, US amphibious forces staged a major demonstration off the coast. The battleship *Missouri* bombarded targets with her mighty 16-inch guns. Then the helicopter carrier *Okinawa* launched CH-53E troop carriers which headed towards the coast as if running in to land Marines. Then, about three miles short of their apparent objective, they turned around and returned to their carrier. Early the next day there were similar feints to reinforce the threat.[10]

Throughout this time the Army Guardrail crews flew their monotonous orbit patterns round-the-clock. Yet for much of the time there was little Iraqi signals activity. Even when the land battle started, the intelligence haul was far less than had been hoped. Major Gary Long, commander of the Guardrail Company, 1st Military Intelligence (MI) Battalion, explained:

"There was never the density of communications that we had expected. But some key things did happen. We picked up indications that some Iraqi units were thinking of doing something different instead of retreating. They had stopped and were talking in plain language. We got low level chatter between individual tanks and units. Things like 'I think the Americans are over there,' 'We need help over here,' or 'I'm short of gas.'"[11]

Once the land battle began, the Army's ground SIGINT collection units were also unable to achieve much. Colonel Susan Browning was Executive Officer of the 533rd MI battalion, part of the 3rd Armored Division in the "Hail Mary" outflanking maneuver:

"Once the advance began, we were moving forward so fast. For its security, the MI battalion had stay tucked in close behind the leading tank brigade in the division. We had to keep up with the lead brigades because as we advanced, we saw Iraqi vehicles and troops we had bypassed on either side. When our leading tank battalions stopped to engage in fire fights with Iraqi tanks, we were about 3 km behind them. We could see the flashes from their guns as they fired.

The MI battalion commander took the decision not to deploy the [SIGINT collection] antennas when we stopped, it was just too dangerous. To get an acceptable bearing on an enemy emitter, the antenna baseline needs to be about as wide as the target is deep. Typically, that would mean setting out an antenna baseline 15 to 20 km wide. That was out of the question when we simply had no idea what was on our left flank, what was on our right flank. So, no, we were not able to provide useful intelligence for the division during its rapid advance."[12]

Had Iraqi troops brought the Coalition armored thrust to a halt, those intelligence troops would have laid out their antennas and established the composition and location of the enemy units. But once the Coalition *Blitzkrieg* got into its stride, no power at Iraq's command could stop it. So long as the advance continued at that rate, victory for the Coalition was inevitable.

Supporting the US Army's attack were large numbers of combat helicopters. As mentioned earlier, for the first time in a major engagement, individual helicopters relied on their EW systems to protect them from guided missiles and radar controlled AAA. Army helicopter combat losses during Desert Storm amounted to one AH-64 Apache, two UH-60 Black Hawks and one UH-1.

The AH-64 was lost to an SA-14 Gremlin man-portable IR weapon, during a daylight action on 25 February when Apaches hovering at about 25 feet were engaging Iraqi vehicles. Later examination of gun camera tapes showed an Iraqi soldier rise from a foxhole about 1,500 yards in front of the helicopters. There was a flash and a backblast, and 3–4 seconds later the missile struck the AH-64 in the engine compartment and the warhead detonation wrecked the helicopter. The crewmen suffered minor injuries and were rescued soon afterwards. That AH-64 was one of the few not fitted with the new ALQ-144A(V) infrared jammer.[13]

The other three helicopters succumbed to small arms fire. Seven AH-64s were damaged; in five cases by small arms fire, in one case by a missile fragment, and in the remaining case the hit was from either a small arms or a AAA round. Given the huge number of sorties flown, that minimal loss rate is little short of astounding.[14]

Army helicopter crews reported having been engaged by Iraqi short-range missiles on only eight occasions, with a total of seventeen missiles fired, during the entire war. Of the missiles fired, nine were believed IR-guided while the remaining eight were radar-guided.[15]

The ubiquitous man-portable IR homing missiles—SA-7 Grail, SA-14 Gremlin and SA-16 Gimlet—achieved only one successful attack on a helicopter. During the other seven attacks these missiles missed their targets, probably due to a combination of IR jamming and the use of IR decoys.

The feared radar-guided missiles, and the ZSU-23/4 radar-laid AAA system, failed to down a single Army helicopter. The combination of nap of the earth flying tactics, timely warning from warning receivers and the deployment of chaff and jamming from ALQ-136 or ALQ-162 equipments defeated the threat on every occasion.

The report of only seventeen short-range missiles launched, during the entire land battle, suggests the threat from these weapons was negligible. That was not the case. Before launch the guided missiles needed an IR or radar lock-on. There were numerous occasions when missile crews tried to achieve lock, but the helicopters' EW systems prevented it and the missile failed to leave its launcher. Also there were many occasions when the radar warning receiver provided a timely indication of the threat, allowing the helicopter pilot to descend behind a fold in the ground.[16]

Army Aviation has every reason to be pleased with the performance of its electronic warfare systems during Desert Storm.

During the land battle US Army and Marine units deployed TLQ-17A communications jamming equipments, carried in light trucks and in a couple of dozen EH-60 Quick Fix helicopters. When Iraqi units started using radio, jamming was permitted against high level digitally encrypted signals which could not be read easily or quickly. These signals were more vulnerable to jamming than voice communications, forcing Iraqi commanders to transmit important messages "in clear." The latter were left unjammed, to provide a rich harvest for the US eavesdroppers.[17]

On 25 February the commander of the Republican Guard *Tawalkana* Division came on the air, ordering his troops to form a defensive line to halt the Allied onslaught. As the division moved into position early on the 26th, a senior Republican Guard commander warned the *Tawalkana* that they were violating communications security. The irate *Tawalkana* commander angrily replied that the American attack was under way and he had little security left to protect![18]

The US listeners followed the squabble from afar and relayed the messages to Riyadh. Then, as Charles Thomas described, SIGINT provided the first evidence of the Iraqi withdrawal from Kuwait:

"Once the Coalition forces were committed, we needed to know whether the Iraqis would stand and fight. The initial elements of US forces were closing on locations where Republican Guard units were known to be in position. Then SIGINT gave the first clear indication that the Republican Guard did not intend to stay and fight. There were indicators that they were moving forward their big [Austrian built] Steyr artillery tractors, used to tow their high value artillery. We knew that only the Republican Guard units were issued with that artillery. Soon afterwards we got indications that they were moving forward tank transporters too. It seemed clear to us that the *Nebukedneza* division and the rest of the *Tawalkana* division were pulling back."[19]

Those reports, coupled with the analysis of radar pictures from the Boeing E-8 JSTARS aircraft, confirmed the pattern of the Iraqi withdrawal and later rout.

Electronic warfare made two major contributions to the land battle against Iraq. First, it allowed US Army helicopters to operate with minimal losses. The second major success was the enforcement of "EMCON suicide" on Iraqi military commanders. Charles Thomas commented:

> "In my view a most significant electronic warfare success was on the first day of the land battle, when we breached the Iraqi lines without suffering casualties. We had eight or nine very narrow breach lanes. A division with 5000 vehicles flowing through three breach lanes took the better part of eighteen hours to push through. Although many of the vehicles were armored, most were not. For every ten Abrams tanks there needed to be a 5,000-gallon tanker close by, to keep them supplied with fuel. There were never better targets for the Iraqi artillery, our casualties could have been horrendous.
>
> It was obvious where the breaches were, there were huge dust clouds. The Iraqis had both rocket and tube artillery within range. Although there were futile attempts to do so, their forward observers failed to direct accurate artillery fire on those breach lanes.
>
> By ordering their troops to avoid using radio, the Iraqi leadership committed EMCON suicide. Their soldiers were so afraid of our perceived capability to locate transmitters accurately, and deliver counterstrikes immediately they came up on the nets, that they stayed off the air. I hold that up as a major success for our electronic warfare troops."[20]

In the related fields of deception and psychological operations, US forces scored other major successes. The feint operations by the Navy and Marines off the coast of Kuwait achieved their aim of holding Iraqi Army units in place. Until Saddam Hussein ordered the pull out from Kuwait, no units moved away from the coastal areas threatened by feints.

The attack on Iraqi troop morale produced the most spectacular result of all. About 400,000 Iraqi troops were deployed in Kuwait and adjacent areas in Iraq. Estimates vary on the number killed, the most likely being between 10,000 and 25,000 (between 2.5 and 6.25 percent of the total).[21] Yet, carefully exploited, that relatively small percentage loss led to a collapse of fighting spirit. That collapse is the more remarkable if one considers the Iraqi troops' confident mood just a few weeks earlier. The air attacks did not deal out death and destruction uniformly among the Iraqi Army units. A few ill-fated divisions suffered far more heavily than the average, others suffered a great deal less. Yet, thanks to the Coalition propaganda campaign, the worst effects of the aerial pounding were known to all. Significantly, when the collapse came, it affected the entire force and not just those units hardest-hit.

References to Chapter 17

1. Interview Tom Reinkober
2. *Ibid*
3. *Ibid*
4. Interview Major General Charles Thomas
5. Cordesman, Anthony, and Wagner, Abraham, *The Lessons of Modern War*, Volume IV: *The Gulf War*, Westview Press, Boulder, CO, 1996, p 586
6. Quoted in Lambert, Group Captain A., "The Psychological Impact of Air Power in the Gulf War," *Air Clues*, March 1995
7. *Air Force*, October 1998, p 64
8. Interview John Black
9. Atkinson, Rick, *Crusade*, Houghton Mifflin, 1993, p 439
10. *Ibid*
11. Interview Garry Long
12. Interview Susan Browning
13. Desert Storm Survivability Equipment After Action Comments, declassified Army report
14. Reinkober
15. GAO "Operation Desert Storm: Apache Helicopter was Considered Effective in Combat, but Reliability Problems Persist," quoted in Cordesman and Wagner, p 736
16. Reinkober
17. Thomas
18. Atkinson, p 439
19. Thomas
20. *Ibid*
21. Cordesman and Wagner, p 344

Chapter 18

RELATIVE CALM AFTER THE STORM

1991 to 2000

"Right in itself is powerless; in nature it is Might that
rules"

Arthur Schopenhauer

In September 1991, six months after the end of the Gulf War, President George Bush announced a major shift in the US military posture. Following the end of the Cold War he ordered US strategic bomber, tanker and ICBM units to cease their alert status. Strategic Air Command was to disband as a separate force and merge with Tactical Air Command to form the new Air Combat Command. The newly formed US Strategic Command would control nuclear forces in time of war.

With no discernible military threat to the nation, the stage was set for the military equivalent of a harsh stock market "correction." The military budget was slashed by nearly 60 percent and the procurement budget by over 70 percent. By December 1998 the Army's combat power had been reduced by half, the Navy's fighting ships had been reduced by nearly half and the Air Force's fighter wings had been reduced by more than one-third.[1]

The Air Force's dedicated electronic warfare units were among the first to feel the pinch. The Wild Weasel F-4Gs were expensive unit items in the inventory, and on cost grounds it was decided to phase out them out of service in 1995.[2]

The replacement for the F-4G was the F-16CJ Fighting Falcon carrying a podded HARM Targeting System. The consensus was that the single-place fighter would be far less effective than a two-seater for this task. The crucial question, however, was whether the new machine would prove effective enough in combat.

The EF-111A Raven followed the F-4G out of service, for the same cost-cutting reasons. The Air Force had said its minimum EF-111A requirement was twenty-four aircraft. The Navy was about to dispose of twenty-five elderly EA-6B Prowlers. So Department of Defense officials ordered the Air

Force to phase out its EF-111As, and the Navy to retain its EA-6Bs and provide jamming support for Air Force strike forces.[3]

In the Air Force the sole electronic warfare support plane remaining in the inventory was the EC-130H Compass Call communications jamming aircraft, and that fleet was reduced from thirteen to ten.[4]

With the huge reduction in the B-52 fleet and the phasing out of most dedicated electronic warfare units, large numbers of electronic warfare posts disappeared. The pool of operational EW experience, painstakingly built up during the Cold War, ebbed away rapidly.

The Northrop B-2 program was another victim of the new mood. Originally 132 of these aircraft were to be procured, later reduced to 75 then to sixteen. In 1992 Congress was persuaded to provide money for five more B-2s, to bring the production run to twenty-one planes.[5] And there it has remained.

In December 1993, the first production Northrop B-2 Spirit arrived at Whiteman AFB, Missouri, to join the 509th Bomb Wing. Two years elapsed before the unit possessed its first eight bombers. The first bomber with the definitive Block 30 configuration was delivered in November 1997, and the remaining aircraft in the fleet were also modified to that standard.

After more than a decade of development, Raytheon put the ALE-50 towed decoy system into limited production early in the 1990s. Originally it was to be carried internally by the A-6 Intruder, but after that aircraft was phased out of service the Navy targeted the ALE-50 for its new F/A-18E/F attack fighter. The Air Force evaluated the ALE-50 aboard the F-16 and the B-1B and, suitably impressed, ordered the system into full production.[6]

Among the first units to receive the towed decoy were F-16 units based in Italy. That installation comprised a combined launcher and control unit fitted to either side of two of the weapons pylons. That gave a total of four decoys per plane, without reducing the ordnance or fuel loads it could carry.[7]

The B-1B Lancer's ALE-50 installation consisted of a four-decoy dispensing unit on either side of the rear fuselage beneath the horizontal stabilizer, giving a total of eight decoys.[8]

At the end of 1998 there was a resurgence of air strikes on Iraq to police the no-fly zones there. During these actions the Lancer made its combat debut, twelve years after entering service.[9] That it received protection from a system intended for the A-6, points out the success of the signature-reduction modifications applied to the B-1B. As pointed out earlier, for each reduction in an aircraft's radar signature, there is a proportionate reduction in the jamming power needed to screen it. After more than a decade in limbo, the long-range bomber assumed its proper place in the US combat inventory.

The burden of providing escort jamming support for the Air Force, as well as its own strike forces, placed the Navy's EA-6B Prowler fleet under heavy pressure. To ease the situation, in August 1995 the Navy formed five extra squadrons of Prowlers using the machines previously earmarked for phasing out.

The last of the 170 Prowlers had come off the production line in 1991; at the time of writing about 120 are left. At any time about forty are undergoing overhaul or are in storage ready for issue. The remaining 80 aircraft are sufficient, just, to meet the commitments with little margin for attrition.[10]

We left the ALQ-165 Airborne Self Protection Jammer in 1993, after Congress decided to cut off further funding. The majority of the 136 systems built had gone straight into storage.

The next conflict to see serious US air involvement was that in Bosnia in 1995. On 2 June a Bosnian Serb SA-6 missile battery shot down Captain Scott O'Grady's F-16. The pilot ejected and, after six days evading capture, was picked up by a Marine rescue team.[11]

After that incident the Marine air commander in the area requested ALQ-165 jammers for his planes. A few systems had the software updated to include new information on threats and additional countermeasures techniques. These underwent a re-evaluation process flying against threat systems at medium altitude, and passed with flying colors.[12] Subsequently the ALQ-165 became the jammer of choice for F/A-18C and F-14D units operating over Bosnia and Iraq. The 136 production systems are now fully utilized, and as units leave the conflict zones they pass these jammers to those replacing them.[13] Thus a serendipitous chain of events has saved the ALQ-165 from an otherwise inglorious ending.

To protect Navy warships from radar homing anti-ship missiles, the latest countermeasure is Nulka. This active seduction decoy is about 6 inches in diameter and 7 feet long. It weighs about 100 pounds at launch and employs a hovering rocket system. Frank Klemm at the Naval Research Laboratory described its working:

> "The decoy is powered by a solid fuel rocket. For control there are three metal tabs at 120-degree intervals around the periphery at the base, that can be extended into the efflux of the rocket. When a tab enters the efflux it spoils the thrust on that side, allowing the decoy's height and direction of flight to be controlled. Pull all the tabs out, there is an excess of thrust over weight and Nulka goes up. Push all the tabs in, there is less thrust than weight, and Nulka goes down. Push in one tab, and Nulka tilts over and heads in that direction."[14]

Nulka is an end-game system, launched when an enemy missile nears the warship. The decoy climbs to a pre-set altitude and moves away from the warship, and repeats the missile's radar signals to provide a more attractive target. The Nulka rounds are carried in two additional launching tubes mounted near the Super RBOC launchers.[15]

In the mid-1990s the Army fielded Guardrail Common Sensor, its newest airborne SIGINT collection system. Advances in microelectronics allowed it to include the capabilities of the earlier Guardrail and also the Quick Look ELINT system carried in RV-1D Mohawk aircraft. Guardrail Common Sensor uses time-difference-of-arrival and differential Doppler techniques to produce highly accurate bearings on signal sources.

The Beechcraft RC-12K aircraft carrying the new system has more powerful engines than its predecessor, enabling it to cruise at 35,000 feet. To exploit the increased pick-up range, Guardrail Common Sensor aircraft fly in three-plane teams rather than in two-plane units as before. When the new system entered service, the RV-1D Mohawks were phased out.[16]

Major Gary Long served at the Guardrail program office at Fort Monmouth, New Jersey, early in the decade. He used a series of briefing charts to illustrate the spectacular improvements to the system over the years:

> "The first graphic showed a map of Washington, DC. With early Guardrail, we could determine the location of an enemy transmitter to within an area about the size of that city. With the improved Guardrail V, we could narrow the location to an area about the size of the White House grounds. With Guardrail Common sensor we can say the source of the signals is somewhere in an area about the size of the East Wing of the White House."[17]

Once the target is found it can be engaged with the Multiple Launch Rocket System to a range of 32 km, or the Army Tactical Missile System out to a maximum range of about 85 km, with a good chance of scoring a hit with the first missile launched.[18] At last, the US Army has a signals location system that measures up to the Iraqis' assessment of its abilities prior to the Gulf War!

By the early 1990s the Army's Crazy Horse RC-12G aircraft, used in low-intensity operations in Central and South America, needed replacement. That came in the shape of the four-turboprop RC-7 using the same airframe as the Bombardier Dash 7 fifty-seat airliner. For the Airborne Reconnaissance Low (ARL) mission the RC-7 carries sensors tailored to the particular operation. The suite might include optical cameras, an infrared linescan equipment, a moving-target indicator radar, a SIGINT collection system, an electro-optical video system, or a selection of these.[19]

During the 1990s a new family of threats was added to the list confronting helicopters and low flying aircraft: laser systems. Today laser designators, laser range-finders and laser beam-riding missiles represent potent threats. To warn of these, Raytheon produces the AVR-2A passive receiver for Army AH-64, OH-58D and MH-47E helicopters. Like earlier helicopter receivers, the AVR-2A employs a voice synthesizer to tell crews of the threat and its direction.[20]

The proliferation of man-portable IR missiles and their ready availability poses a severe potential threat to civil air transport. Already these weapons have destroyed airliners over Angola, the Sudan and the one-time Soviet republic of Georgia. Yet because these incidents occurred in areas remote from the West they failed to receive the publicity they deserved.

To counter this menace, Lockheed Martin Electro-Optical systems has produced the ALQ-204 Matador system. Installed in more than twenty "head of state" VIP aircraft, including the US Presidential Plane "Air Force One," it employs active pulsed IR jammers, one per engine, to confuse IR seeker heads.[21]

It would indeed be a sad turn of events if the IR missile threat to commercial air traffic moved from the potential to the real, and it became necessary to make such installations general.

Following the break-up of the Soviet Union, that nation's distribution of free weaponry to political allies abruptly ended. If there is a common denominator of the nations likely to come into armed conflict with the USA, it is that they operate mainly 1960s and 1970s vintage Soviet air defense weapons. These center on the SA-2, the SA-3, the SA-6, the SA-7 and the SA-8 SAM systems. A few states also possess the SA-5 and the later shoulder-launched SA-14 and SA-16 weapons. Their main AAA control radars are the Flap Wheel and Gun Dish equipments. In every case, examples of these have undergone exhaustive testing in the USA. But that is not the end of the story.

In recent years a thriving industry has emerged, to update Soviet-made air defense and other systems. France, Israel, South Africa and Russia herself are active in this field, and the process includes replacing outdated electronic systems with more capable modern ones. In the case of air defense radars, it results in systems with electronic "observables" differing markedly from those of the original system.[22]

An example of this so-called "Gray Threat," the linkage of one-time Soviet hardware with newer foreign electronics, is the NATO code-named "Tiger Song" missile system deployed by Iraq. This uses the missiles, launchers and other parts of the SA-2 system, with French- and Chinese-built radars replacing the Spoon Rest and Fan Song equipments.[23] Initially, when US planes over Iraq picked up signals from Tiger Song, their automated warning systems failed to identify it as a threat. Luckily there were no shootdowns before the threat was recognized and electronic defensive systems were reprogrammed to take it into account.[24]

The inexorable march of technology has produced a raft of new possibilities for electronic warfare systems. These will be addressed under the headings of power sources and digital signal processors.

In a radar or jamming system, the power source produces a high powered output at the required radio frequency. Back in the mid-1960s, countermeasures systems employed magnetrons, backward-wave oscillators (carcinotrons) or travelling wave tubes (TWTs) with efficiency levels of around 10 percent. So 90 percent of the power that entered the jammer, remained behind in the form of heat. A heavy duty cooling system was needed to remove and dissipate that heat, and the resultant thermal stresses were a major cause of failures of vacuum tubes and other components.[25]

At the end of the 1970s, the new-generation TWTs gave higher gain, greater bandwidth, greater power output and much higher efficiency levels. That process has continued. Paul Westcott at the Air Force Research Laboratory at Wright-Patterson outlined the capabilities of the recent systems:

"Since the mid-1990s a family of mini-TWTs has appeared. These new systems are much smaller than their predecessors. Instead of a package the size of a small suitcase or a shoebox, a microwave power module would fit into a lady's small evening handbag. Current devices provide in excess of an octave of bandwidth, have output powers in excess of 150 watts, and have efficiencies in excess of 35 percent."[26]

The rise in efficiency from 10 percent to 35 percent has significantly reduced the problem of retained heat. That in turn has led to significant increases in TWT reliability. Paul Westcott described other advantages:

"With the small air-cooled microwave power modules, we can pack several of them side-by-side. We configure them in a linear antenna array and, 'Voila!' we can steer the beam in azimuth to direct the power where we want it to go. For most applications azimuth beam steering is enough, most modern jamming systems are configured that way. But if necessary we could mount the microwave power modules in a planar array, and steer the beam in both azimuth and elevation. We can even divide the power so that the jammer radiates multiple beams simultaneously. It is merely a matter of having the right control circuitry."[27]

Next let us turn to digital signal processors. Radar warning receivers, for threat warning and power management, have made startling progress over recent decades. Paul Westcott again:

"The signal processing systems carried in a fighter plane in the late 1980s measured their processing capacity in hundreds of kilobytes. Today we are substituting commercial derivatives of processing systems with a capacity of several gigabytes [several thousand million bytes]. That means we now have much more ability to do things…

Think of the signal processor as a funnel. You've got billions of grains of sand, and of those billions there are about a hundred that are a different color. Those are the only ones you are interested in. As the grains of sand go through the funnel, a few at a time, it will take time before you find the grains with the color you are looking for. With today's processors, it is as if the funnel is opened right up. Even though the sand is running through the neck in a torrent, you can pick out exactly what you need because of the tremendous capacity of the modern processor."[28]

The aim, as always, is to build receivers that provide warning of real threats, without the false warnings that have dogged systems in the past. As we have seen, anything that reduces the false alarm rate will be a hit with aircrew.

References to Chapter 18

1. Geshanoff, Hal, editorial in *Journal of Electronic Defence*, January 1999; also April 1999 issue, p 48
2. Interview General John Corder.
3. Interview Ken Krech
4. Interview Andy Vittoria
5. Sweetman, Bill, *Inside the Stealth Bomber*, MBI Publishing Co, Osceola WI, 1999, p 126
6. Interview Fred Paxton
7. *Ibid*
8. *Ibid*
9. "Military Affairs," *Air International*, February 1999
10. Lake, Jon, "On the Prowl," *Air International*, September 1999
11. Correspondence Captain Larry Kaiser.
12. *Ibid*
13. *Ibid*
14. Interview Frank Klemm
15. *Ibid*
16. Interview Gary Long
17. *Ibid*
18. Interview "Butch" Erikson
19. *Ibid*
20. *International Countermeasures Handbook*, 1996, p 52
21. *Ibid* p 99
22. Fulghum, David, "Improved Air Defenses Prompt Pentagon Fears," *Aviation Week*, 6 July 1998
23. *Ibid*
24. *Ibid*
25. Interview Paul Westcott
26. *Ibid*
27. *Ibid*
28. *Ibid*

Chapter 19

EAVESDROPPING FROM SPACE

1960 to 2000

"Space isn't remote at all. It's only an hour's drive away if your car could go straight upwards."
Sir Fred Hoyle

ELINT and SIGINT collection satellites are heavily shrouded in secrecy, and even after the passage of more than four decades since they came into service little hard information has been released on them. This chapter has been assembled from open source literature, with general comments from people associated with ELINT satellites. It discusses in broad terms the strengths and weaknesses of these vehicles when supporting electronic warfare. It also outlines the ways in which satellites contribute to the general intelligence picture.

The first US ELINT satellite to reach orbit was GRAB (standing for Galactic Radiation And Background experiment). That title was not entirely fictitious, for instruments in the ELINT satellite measured X-ray and other types of solar radiation. The Thor Able Star launcher carrying GRAB and a Navy Transit navigation satellite lifted off from Cape Canaveral on 22 June 1960. The satellite entered a 330-mile by 573-mile elliptical orbit inclined at 67 degrees to the equator.[1] That was some way off the intended circular orbit, but was close enough for ELINT work.

GRAB, designed and built at the Naval Research Laboratory in Washington, weighed 42 pounds. Little bigger than a basketball, it carried a wide-band crystal video receiver operating in the 1550 to 3900 MHz band. Electrical power came from six solar panels spaced around the periphery of the satellite. As radar signals were picked up they were immediately re-transmitted to a ground station.[2]

The primary targets for GRAB were the Soviet Token (P-20) EW/GCI radar then being widely deployed, and the Gage acquisition radar associated with the SA-1 missile system. Over a period the satellite overflew almost the entire territory of the Soviet Union and her allies.[3]

Surveillance radars did not radiate signals straight upwards, so the satellite did not receive these when it was directly above the radar. If radar signals were being received clearly, then suddenly disappeared and reappeared a little later, that indicated that the satellite had passed over the radar. Since the satellite's orbit pattern was known exactly, that effect was used to establish the radars' positions.[4] The US Navy's ground station at Bremerhaven, Germany, was a major collection point for data from GRAB.

Considering it was a first-generation proof-of-concept system, GRAB 1 performed remarkably well. On 6 August 1961, more than a year after launch, it produced an unexpected windfall. Cosmonaut Gherman Titov was making the second Soviet manned space flight, and his controlling ground station temporarily lost radio contact with the capsule. To maintain track on it the Soviets turned on every available space search radar, including a new anti-ballistic missile radar unknown to western intelligence. GRAB collected its signals.[5]

GRAB 1 continued to pass back useful information until August 1962.[6] Although that first ELINT satellite performed almost faultlessly, its immediate successors did not. GRAB 2, launched from Patrick AFB, Florida, in November 1960, failed to reach orbital velocity. Embarrassingly the rocket came down in Cuba, where it demolished a cow in its path.[7]

GRAB 3, launched in June 1961, was a partial success. It launched with a Transit satellite and a research satellite. All three satellites went into orbit and the Transit separated as planned. GRAB 3 and the research satellite failed to separate, however. Both satellites worked, but GRAB's telemetry transmissions interfered with those from the research satellite and vice versa. The ground controllers arranged a system of time sharing and, despite this limitation, GRAB 3 passed back some useful signals.[8] GRAB 4, launched in January 1962, failed to achieve orbital velocity and crashed into the Atlantic.[9] GRAB 5, launched in April 1962, suffered a similar fate and crashed into the Pacific.[10]

In the meantime the Air Force had also become heavily involved in the ELINT satellite business. During 1961 that service launched five SAMOS (Satellite And Missile Observation System) satellites, most of which were unsuccessful. According to some published reports, a small ELINT satellite accompanied the SAMOS on some launches and, after release, a rocket boosted the ELINT satellite into its higher orbit.[11]

The small ELINT sub-satellites were valuable collection vehicles, but larger and more capable systems were also needed. The so-called "heavy ELINT satellite" weighed about a ton and required a launcher to itself. It is believed that the first successful heavy ELINT satellite launch took place in June 1962.[12] In the decade that followed at least thirteen heavy satellites followed it, together with some forty of the lighter ELINT sub-satellites.[13]

As satellites became more capable the transceiver method of operation no longer matched the collection opportunities. Later satellites used the "store and dump" method, recording signals as they passed over areas of interest and replaying them later when they came within range of their ground stations.

Compared with an ELINT aircraft, an ELINT satellite can overfly unfriendly nations without causing an international incident. ELINT satellites do not get tired, they never switch off and they do not need to land to refuel. ELINT satellites can remain in orbit for very long periods, collecting radar signals and relaying them to ground stations.

Rich Haver, from the Office of Naval Intelligence, outlined other advantages of satellites for the ELINT collection role:

> "Another great advantage is the inability of an enemy to conceal things from satellites for long. When an airplane appears off his coast, or a ship comes into view, he can shut down his sensitive systems. When a satellite flies past every ninety minutes or so, depending on its orbit, after a time it becomes very hard to be that disciplined. If he wants to train people, if he wants to experiment, if he wants to test his systems, he has to radiate."[14]

Against that, the early ELINT satellite systems suffered some serious limitations. Rich Haver continued:

> "First there is the problem of command and control. There was no human operator in the satellite to run it. The early satellites were rudimentary analogue systems, slow in operation. Basically, the satellite was a dumb machine. The receivers and transceivers were relatively limited in terms of bandwidth, as were the command uplinks and downlinks.
>
> Antennas were another problem. If people wanted to intercept VHF radar signals, the satellite needed to put out a [1 meter long] VHF antenna. That was a fairly difficult contraption to stick inside an object little bigger than a basketball, and get it to unfold when it was in orbit. Unfolding things in space was something that had to be invented."[15]

Launch weight, internal space and electrical power were strictly limited in the early satellites. If a designer wanted to add an additional item inside the vehicle, something else had to be left out. In the case of receivers carried in a satellite, it was necessary to strike a difficult balance between the frequency spectrum covered and receiver sensitivity.

Reliability was another major problem, as Rich Haver commented:

> "In the early days many of the devices were unreliable. If an airplane receiver breaks, you land and fix it. If it breaks in space, it's gone. So, reliability and durability were at a very high premium. People learned the need to test things exhaustively before putting them up there. That took time and it required scrupulously monitored test procedures. And it was

expensive, it could be as expensive as designing the system in the first place."[16]

The next major series of SIGINT satellites was Jumpseat, operated by the National Reconnaissance Office. This satellite flew in the so-called Molnya orbit, shaped like an elongated ellipse flattened at one end. That orbit gave optimum coverage over areas at high latitudes, like the northern areas in the Soviet Union.

The first Jumpseat launched in March 1971, carried aboard a Titan 23B Agena D vehicle. The satellite's orbit was inclined at 63 degrees to the equator, with an apogee of 21,200 miles and a perigee of 177 miles. Six Jumpseats followed, between March 1971 and April 1981, one of which failed to achieve orbit.[17]

By the early 1970s, advances in space technology produced far-reaching improvements in satellite capability. The introduction of more-powerful launch vehicles made it possible to place larger and heavier satellites in orbit. If required those larger satellites could be lifted to higher orbits than previously, reducing their rate of speed decay and lengthening their operational lives. The simultaneous evolution of microelectronic systems brought about major advances in sensors, giving greatly increased capability combined with reduced weight, bulk and power requirements.

Following these new systems' entry into service a new possibility appeared, the so-called geostationary orbit. A satellite positioned on an equatorial orbit 22,300 miles high completes its orbit in exactly 24 hours. Since the earth rotates at that same rate, the satellite appears to remain almost stationary above a point on the equator. The geostationary orbit has many advantages for SIGINT collection, giving continuous coverage of areas in the lower latitudes.

The physical laws for signal collection do not change because a receiver is in space. For a radio receiver to pick up signals, the power entering the antenna cable has to exceed a certain threshold. So an ELINT satellite in a higher orbit has to compensate for the reduction in signal power, due to the increased distance the signals have to travel. One way is to increase the sensitivity of the receiver, another is to use a large directional antenna focused on the source of the signals. Both methods are employed.

Canyon, developed in a combined NSA/USAF program, was the first US COMINT satellite to use a geostationary orbit. Reportedly the satellite weighed 500 pounds and was targeted at the Soviet internal communications system. The first Canyon went into orbit in August 1968, carried aboard an Atlas Agena D vehicle. Between then and May 1977 six more Canyon satellites followed.[18]

Next came the CIA's Rhyolite system, designed and built by TRW Defense and Space Systems to perform telemetry intelligence (TELINT) collection. Rhyolite fitted into a cylinder about 20 feet long and 5 feet in diameter and it weighing 606 pounds. Once the satellite was in orbit a radio command from the ground deployed the 70-foot diameter openwork dish antenna. The dish increased the sensitivity of satellite's receivers, enabling them to pick up low powered telemetry transmissions from within its angle of view. The satellite also deployed smaller antennas to collect radar and communications signals on shorter wavelengths.[19]

The first Rhyolite went into orbit in June 1970 carried aboard an Atlas Agena rocket. From its geostationary orbit position over the Horn of Africa, it picked up transmissions from a large swathe of the central and southern USSR. These signals were relayed to a ground station near Alice Springs in Australia. The second Rhyolite was launched in March 1973 and it went into orbit in the same general area as the first.[20]

Rhyolite would be fully effective only so long as the "eavesdropees" were unaware of its capabilities. That changed in 1975 when TRW employee and small time drug user Andrew Lee and drug dealer Christopher Boyce formed an unholy alliance to fund their respective habits. They sold the secrets of Rhyolite and other US satellites to the Soviet government. Boyce delivered several packages of documents to the Soviet Embassy in Mexico City, before the pair were apprehended in January 1977. Both were convicted of espionage; Lee received a life sentence and Boyce got 40 years.[21]

The pair had done immense damage to the US intelligence collection effort. Afterwards the Soviets encrypted their more important missile performance parameters, to sever a long running and lucrative conduit for information.[22]

Following the betrayal of Rhyolite, the program was renamed Aquacade and the last two satellites in the series were launched in May 1977 and April 1978. From a geostationary orbit over Borneo they monitored signals coming from China, North Korea and eastern areas in the Soviet Union.[23]

The successor to the Canyon COMINT satellite was Chalet. Launched aboard a Titan IIIC, the first Chalet went into geostationary orbit in June 1978. When an article in the *New York Times* compromised that code-name, the system was renamed Vortex. In 1987 Vortex was itself revealed and the system was renamed Mercury. Six Chalet/Vortex/Mercury satellites were launched, the last going into orbit in May 1989.[24] Little has been released on this system though it appears it uses larger openwork dish antennas than earlier systems.[25]

To exploit the latest advances in micro-electronic technology TRW and E-Systems built the Magnum SIGINT satellite, the first of which took off aboard the space shuttle *Discovery* in January 1985. According to one report

Magnum weighed about 9,000 pounds and it carried an extendable dish antenna some 330 feet in diameter to pick up telemetry, radio and radar signals and telephone calls.[26]

After Magnum was compromised, later in the 1980s, it was renamed Orion. Later Magnum/Orion satellites were carried aloft by Titan 4 launchers. The fifth and most recent Magnum/Orion satellite to be revealed went into space in May 1995.[27]

A further new SIGINT satellite, Trumpet, was launched in May 1994 followed by a second in July 1995.[28] The most recent launch of this system to be mentioned publicly was in November 1997.[29] Trumpet used the Molnya orbit and it is believed to be a more capable development of the earlier Jumpseat. Reportedly the satellite weighs around five tons.[30] In addition to receivers to pick up ground and space voice communications, the satellite is believed to carry an infrared early-warning payload for a Defense Support Program.[31]

At the other end of the scale, there have been reports that the National Reconnaissance Office plans a constellation of smaller, more numerous satellites on lower orbits to collect signals.[32] In 1998 that organization announced its intention to combine COMINT, ELINT and TELINT collection using an Integrated Overhead SIGINT Architecture (IOSA) satellite. By exploiting new technology in data processing and other areas, it is said the new system will provide improved performance at lower overall cost.[33]

Today, space-borne SIGINT systems provide essential support for US military operations. Because satellite systems have limitations, the intelligence derived from them needs to be combined with that from aircraft, ships, submarines, ground stations and other sources. That combination makes it extremely difficult for an enemy to conceal major signals activity for any length of time. The only way to be sure that no useful information is betrayed, is not to transmit. Yet, as the Iraqi Army discovered during Desert Storm, "EMCON suicide" significantly reduces one's ability to employ military forces effectively.

References to Chapter 19

1 Day, Dwayne, "Listening from Above: The First Signals Intelligence Satellite," *Spaceflight*, August 1999
2. *Ibid*
3. *Ibid*
4. *Ibid*
5. *Ibid*

6. *Ibid*
7. *Ibid*
8. *Ibid*
9. *Ibid*
10. *Ibid*
11. Peebles, Curtis, *Guardians*, Ian Allan Ltd, Shepperton, Surrey, England, 1987, p 191
12. *Ibid*
13. *Ibid*, p 192
14. Interview Rich Haver
15. *Ibid*
16. *Ibid*
17. McDowell, Jonathan, "US Reconnaissance Satellite Program," unpublished paper
18. Clark, Philip (editor), *Jane's Space Directory 1997-8*, Jane's Information Group, Alexandria, VA, 1997, p 178
19. Peebles, *Guardians*, p 199
20 For a full account of this espionage story see Lindsey, Robert, *The Falcon and the Snowman*, Jonathan Cape Ltd, London, 1980
21. Peebles, *Guardians*, p 201
22. SIGINT Overview on Internet, at http://www.fas.org /spp/military/
23. Interception Capabilities 2000, Document on Internet at .Iptvreports.mcmail.com/ic2kreport.htm
24. Peebles, *Guardians*, p 204–5
25. Interception Capabilities 2000
26. *Jane's Space Directory 1997-8*
27. "Military Satellite Directory," *Flight International*, 5 June 1996
28. McDowell
29. "Military Satellite Directory," *Flight International*, 5 June 1996
30. *Ibid*
31. McDowell
32. "Military Satellite Directory," *Flight International*, 5 June 1996
33. Herskovitz, Don, "A Sampling of SIGINT Systems," *Journal of Electronic Defense*, June 1999

Chapter 20

THE METAMORPHOSIS TO INFORMATION WARFARE

1991 to 2000

"Though fraud in other activities be detestable, in the management of war it is laudable and glorious. And he who overcomes an enemy by fraud is as much to be praised as he who does so by force."

Niccolo Machiavelli

Information Operations (IO) and Information Warfare (IW) are slippery terms and those who try to define them face a dilemma. Precise definitions are wordy and legalistic in tone, while short definitions tend to be loose generalizations devoid of meaning.

In 1998 the long-awaited US government-wide definitions of Information Operations and Information Warfare were finally approved:[1]

Information Operations: "Actions taken to access and/or affect adversaryinformation systems, while defending one's own information and information systems."

Information Warfare: "Information Operations conducted during time of crisis or conflict to achieve specific objectives over a specific adversary or adversaries."

Those banal definitions would not ignite fires in anyone's belly, yet it took a long time to get even that far. At the heart of the problem was the debate on who should control IO and IW, and thereby receive the resources that went with that coveted position. No fighting service or government agency was willing to allow a definition to gain official currency, if that definition did not cover its particular slant on the subject.

Daniel Kuehl, a professor of Information Warfare at the National Defense University, stressed the importance of a wide-open approach to this subject.

"Information as an environment may be a difficult concept to grasp, but there is no arguing that there is a physical environment in which information is uniquely related: cyberspace. Cyberspace is that place where computers, communications systems, and those devices that operate via radiated energy in the electromagnetic spectrum meet and interact. A radar or radio jammer is an IW device; an implanted computer code that affects an adversary's computer system via a 'logic bomb' is an IW device; and a videotape altered via computer 'morphing' to influence an adversary's political stability is an IW device. Note the synergies between IW and other forms of warfare… disabling an enemy air defense computer with either a bomb or a virus can be both air and information warfare, given the means employed and the effect sought."[2]

The origin of Information Warfare cannot be attributed to a single person, authority, or causative element. Yet, by the end of 1991, the new perception had taken root. Given the overwhelming US superiority in electronic warfare and computer technology, IW seemed uniquely tailored to US talents and capabilities. Influential members of the US military-industrial establishment gave their support to the concept and a number of politicians joined their cause. Information Warfare become "The New Big Idea" in defense circles.

Information Warfare needed a tangible place within the military establishment, and that soon came. In September 1993 the Air Force Electronic Warfare Center at San Antonio was renamed the Air Force Information Warfare Center. Within months the Army and Navy had followed suit with their own Information Warfare Centers.[3]

Information Warfare is a strategy, not an operational art in itself. It was an evolutionary development from Command and Control Warfare (C^2W) which co-ordinated electronic warfare, deception, psychological operations, physical destruction (of the enemy command and control network) and operational security. IW took those five elements and added three more: computer network attack, civil affairs and public affairs.

As we observed earlier, Information Operations describes the use of these techniques by the military or government, or both, when no hostilities exist. Like military intelligence, IO are part of a continuing process that takes place both in war and in peace. IO may take either offensive or defensive forms.[4]

When discussing Information Warfare it is important to appreciate the enormous flow of information necessary to support a modern military operation. This has shortened the military decision cycle—the ability to observe, orient, decide and then act—beyond recognition.

During the War of Independence, General Washington's observations were limited to what he and his staff saw through a telescope. He orientated his force in weeks, decided on his course of action in months, and the resultant operation took up much of the fighting season. In the Civil War, General Grant got much of his information via the telegraph. He orientated his force in days, decided on his course of action in weeks, and went into action with a month. In World War II, General Patton received his information via radio and landlines. He orientated his force in hours, decided on the course of action in days and opened the action within a week. In the Gulf War, General Schwarzkopf observed the situation in near-real time through intelligence gathering assets like the E-8 JSTARS battlefield radar surveillance aircraft, Guardrail and a host of other systems. He orientated his forces in minutes, decided on the course of action in hours and began his operation within a day.[5]

Victory usually goes to the side with the shorter decision-making cycle. The aim of IW is therefore to deny, degrade, pollute or manipulate the flow of information entering the opponent's headquarters. If successful, that will lengthen his decision cycle and may cause him to deploy forces in the wrong place. None of that is new, of course. Over the centuries military and naval commanders have sought ways to get inside their enemy's decision cycle. What is new is the effect of recent advances in technology on this process.

With the new line of thinking, a new term entered the military lexicon, Information Superiority. General John Thomas, commander at the Army Intelligence and Security Command (INSCOM) at Fort Huachuca, Arizona, explained the concept:

"Information on the battlefield is made up of two pieces on either side of an equation. It is our knowledge of ourselves and our knowledge of the enemy. And on the enemy side it is his knowledge of himself and his knowledge of us. In IO, our goal is to affect that equation in our favor. So we want to have more information on ourselves and on the enemy, than the enemy has. The difference between the two, we call Information Superiority. We can affect that equation by increasing our knowledge of ourselves and of our enemy. We can also affect it by decreasing the enemy's knowledge of himself and of us. Communications jamming can play a part in that, by limiting his command and control capabilities and his ability to get status information on his forces. When it comes to his knowledge of us, this can be reduced by the application of security and deception measures."[6]

One attraction of Information Operations is that, compared with other aspects of warfare, they are relatively cheap to mount. During a major operation only a minute proportion of a force will be directly involved with the IO process. Yet, given the right circumstances, the IO troops may have an effect out of all proportion to their numbers. Either side can play the

Information Warfare game, of course, so it is prudent to expect an opponent to exploit the opportunities, too.

Information Warfare could be more about preventing wars than fighting them. Fred Levien, lecturer at the US Navy Postgraduate School at Monterey, California, has commented:

> "The job of our military used to be 'to break things and kill people.' But now it is important to avoid casualties, not only to ourselves but also to our opponents. The way you do it is to avoid going to war. You make your enemy do what you want him to do, without shooting at him. That is very big change in thinking for the military of this country."[7]

In such operations the aim is to suppress perceived threats rather than engage them head-on. If the strategy of coercion fails to prevent an armed conflict, the Information Warfare staff will shift gear and take up a more aggressive stance.

In August and September 1995 we saw an effective use of this strategy in Bosnia. The main body of the Bosnian Serb Army comprised about 65,000 troops in static defensive positions. Supporting them were four mechanized rapid reaction brigades, each numbering about 4,000 men. To control these rapid reaction forces the Serbs benefited greatly from having the use of the telecommunications network in Bosnia, which depended on fourteen radio relay stations positioned at strategic points on high ground. These well-equipped troops moved quickly to threatened sectors, to defeat attacks by more numerous but less-well-equipped Bosnian Government and Croatian forces. In short, the Serbs enjoyed the advantage of operating inside their opponents' decision-making cycle.

Following a particularly flagrant breach of a cease-fire, NATO air force units went into action against Serbian forces. On 30 August 1995 the initial air operations followed the now established pattern with attacks on the air defense system. Having subdued a major part of the air defenses, NATO planes struck at the Serbian communications networks and military command centers. Key elements of the command, control and communications system were knocked out.

Suddenly the Serbs' advantage of possessing the shorter decision-making cycle disappeared. Exploiting their newfound tactical advantage, Bosnian Government and Croatian forces launched powerful offensives into the Serb-occupied territories. Lacking adequate communications, Serb commanders were unable to re-deploy their mobile forces in time to meet the thrusts. Resistance crumbled, and in the ensuing rout the Serbs were ejected from large areas in Croatia and Bosnia.

Following the cease-fire, the IO staff resumed its peacetime role. Lieutenant Colonel Mark Ashton, onetime instructor at the Air Force Information Warfare Center at San Antonio, Texas, described the situation in Bosnia in 1997:

"In northeast Bosnia [friendly] political leaders were being undermined in
their attempts to keep to the [peace] accords, because of the radio and TV
[propaganda] broadcasts from the former warring parties. The opposition
had to be convinced that it was in their best interest to avoid conflict with
our forces, due to our ability to control the decision cycle."[8]

NATO forces ended the hostile broadcasts by sending ground forces to
disable the offending transmitters, or by jamming those transmitters that
could not be reached.

It was important to put something in the place of the silenced transmitters,
so in September 1997 three EC-130E Commando Solo radio and TV
transmitting planes arrived in Italy. Their broadcasts, beamed into Bosnia,
made the population aware of NATO's aims and the restraints it was ready to
apply. That did much to calm the situation.

Cyber attacks on computer networks are part and parcel of Information
Operations. The US armed forces and government agencies have been
reticent about their own cyber attack capabilities, though undoubtedly much
thought and effort have been devoted to these.

In today's global economy, the military and commercial infrastructures of
any developed nation rely heavily on their computer networks. An
imaginative cyber attack might shut down a section of that infrastructure,
with devastating effects on both the military capability and the economy.

From the military viewpoint, geography has been especially kind to the US.
Throughout the twentieth century, in every major armed conflict her
opponent lay thousands of miles from her shores. Provided her forces
maintained control over the seas and skies around her, the US homeland was
safe from an enemy attack.

That cozy position no longer pertains. When the US military planners
looked at possible cyber attacks on enemy computer networks, they found
themselves gazing into an open Pandora's Box. For the US is more dependent
on information transmission and computer network systems than any other
nation on earth. The inescapable conclusion was that the US is potentially the
most vulnerable nation to cyber attack.

With today's global electronic network connectivity it is possible to gain
access into unprotected or poorly protected computer systems on the other
side of the planet. Once the computer has been broken into, its information
can be tapped, or it can even be reprogrammed to obey the commands of the
hacker (or his far more dangerous professional counterpart, the cracker).[9]

The first computer networks were easy for hackers or crackers to
penetrate. Today the problem is better understood and penetration is more
difficult. Computer networks carrying classified or sensitive information
employ elaborate defensive layers, "firewalls," to keep intruders out. Yet
computer hardening does not come cheap. Unless there are good reasons for

incurring that added expense, most commercial enterprises do little in that respect.

A cyber-hit on a major target in the US might take many different forms. During a period of military tension, for example, an opponent might wish to interfere with the process of mobilization. It is not necessary to take on the hardened military systems, hitting the supporting civilian infrastructure could achieve disruption with less effort. Retired Navy Captain Roc Caldarella, an Information Operations specialist with the Scitor Corporation, outlined some possibilities:

> "They could impact the supply of blood for transfusions in the US, just by confusing the data base. Supposing, for example, someone got into the database and changed the dates of the donations. The entire blood supply would then became suspect. If that happened during the mobilization for an Iraq-type conflict, the effect could be serious.
>
> Take another example. Most service people who deploy overseas make allotments of money to their wives. That information is held in an open source unclassified computer database. If someone manipulated that data so the wives did not get their checks, what effect would that have? What is the impact on readiness if you have 50,000 irate wives who have not received their checks? Probably you would have 50,000 very irate soldiers, sailors, airmen and marines. Those are simple things to do, an enemy would not have to do anything sophisticated."[10]

The point is that a large-scale deployment of US forces requires a huge civilian infrastructure in support. And within that diverse infrastructure are many thousands of unprotected or poorly protected computer systems.

An attack aimed at US society as a whole would probably not be restricted to military related targets. With these dangers in mind, in 1997 President Clinton ordered the establishment of the National Infrastructure Protection Center in Washington.[11] The NIPC's task is to examine critical elements of the US national infrastructure to determine their vulnerability to outside interference. In support of this effort, the CIA assembled a strong team of experts to assess the threat and the nature of possible foreign cyber attacks.

Infrastructure failures resulting from equipment breakdown, human error, the weather or other natural causes are a separate matter. However, a clever opponent might use one of these to camouflage or enhance the effect of a cyber attack. Until the cause is established, each major failure has to be examined carefully to see if it is a cyber attack.

Although a concerted cyber attack from a foreign nation might represent a serious threat to US computer systems, this is not the only source of danger. At the other end of the scale are the amateur computer hackers. The newspapers love stories of single-minded youngsters who throw a one-fingered-salute at authority by attacking government and military computer systems. Jim Gosler at the CIA's McLean facility discussed the threat they posed:

> "Kids that are very good at computer hacking are obsessed with it. They breathe, eat and live it... It is not uncommon for these kids who are so obsessed with computer technology to lack some of the basic skills— vocabulary, reading, writing, mathematics and interpersonal skills. But they can get into a system and take the ones and zeros out of it. A week later they can tell you exactly how it works, even though they hadn't seen it... That is one class of hacker. There is another class and those are basically information gatherers. They can't create an attack because they have not got that depth of understanding. But they collect everyone else's approaches, become masters of those approaches and how to use those tools."[12]

Fortunately for the victims, the motivation for most hackers is the esteem of their peers. Thus, having made a successful penetration, the amateur hacker feels compelled to publicize it. The victim organization can close the loophole and the system becomes harder to enter in the future.

At the other end of the threat scale, there is the professional team of crackers bent on insinuating its way into a computer network for military, commercial or criminal gain. This can be a formidable adversary.

As mentioned earlier, electronic warfare is now regarded as one of the constituent elements of Information Warfare. Abandoning its earlier independent status met resistance from those who were comfortable in their niche and saw no reason to change. Such sentiments persist in parts of the EW community, though most have come to accept the new order.

The strength of Information Warfare is that it views its opponent as a total system, with information flowing up and down its control structures. Information Warfare attacks the vulnerabilities of that system, regardless of the method used. If the attack were confined to jamming radars or communications system, in the classic electronic warfare sense, the damage would be confined to the outer layers of such a system. An Information Warfare assault penetrating to the inner layers of a system could achieve a great deal more and achieve it more rapidly.[13]

Lieutenant Colonel Mark Ashton was one of those who initially sought to resist the change in the status of electronic warfare. Now he has changed his mind:

> "I have come through 180 degrees on the issue of electronic warfare's relationship with Information Operations. When I participated in C²W development in 1992, I was concerned about the loss of identity that electronic warfare would suffer by being included in the C²W/IW/IO evolution. I was skeptical that Information Warfare as a unifying strategy

would help electronic warfare in operations, and that EW might get lost in the shuffle.

In hindsight, I can see that I was wrong. Electronic warfare as a part of a coordinated strategy of Information Operations retains all of its original impact on the battlefield, and it attains a status it never had before. It goes from being a supporting player to being a very important part of a key warfighting strategy. Electronic warfare is further enhanced by the synergy with the other aspects of Information Operations. I have seen electronic warfare discussed in operational planning with a new sense of importance as an operational art. I can assure you that, as we fight the battles of the future, electronic warfare will be a vital part of Information Operations. We need not fear for electronic warfare, as long as we are a part of the Information Operations revolution in military affairs."[14]

There are wide differences in the perception of what constitutes Information Warfare. It depends on whom you talk to. Some commentators go so far as to advocate Information Warfare as a means of driving wedges between sections of society and government. They cite a couple of examples from recent history to support that view.

Professor George Stein, Director of International Security Studies at Pennsylvania State University, discussed the proliferation and influence of protest organizations and ideological and religious pressure groups. He wrote:

"All this suggests that the military or governments of a traditional nation-state might not be the only serious threat to our security or the driver of our national security politics... Let us take a look at this in a context we think we're familiar with: propaganda as an effort to influence national morale and support for the nation's armed forces. The Vietnam War taught us the consequences of winning every battle in the field and losing the information war on the home front."[15]

The defeat in Vietnam was traumatic for the US nation, but it had little effect on the course of world history. Far greater were the effects of the collapse of the Communist bloc, a decade and a half later. After the event Soviet military leaders asked themselves how that could have happened. They commanded huge armed forces that had been powerless to stop or even slow the process. The world's most feared military machine was quite unable to safeguard the system it had pledged to defend. Admiral Baltin, formerly commander of the Soviet Black Sea fleet, has written:

"We have every reason to talk of a third world war that broke out, and has almost died out, before our very eyes. It was not a classic but a 'velvet' war... This war can be deemed to have begun physically with the destruction of the Berlin Wall. The essence of the 'velvet' third world war is an information-strategic offensive in which the main role is played by well-honed psychological operations"[16]

There was no one single reason why the Communist bloc imploded when it did and in the way that it did. In the perception of Admiral Baltin and other Russian military leaders, a significant factor leading to that collapse was the long running Information Warfare attack by the west on the populations of the Soviet Union and her allies.

References to Chapter 20

1. Joint Publication 3-13 "Joint Doctrine for Information Operations," dated October 1998
2. Kuehl, Dr Daniel, *Defining Information Power*, National Defense University, Strategic Forum No 115, June 1999
3. Interview Mark Ashton
4. *Ibid*
5. Rose, John, *et al*, *War In The Information Age*, Brassey's, Dulles VA, 1997, p 230
6. Interview General John Thomas
7. Interview Fred Levien
8. Ashton
9. Interview Jim Gosler
10. Interview Roc Caldarella
11. Presidential Decision Directive 63, May 1998
12. Interview Jim Gosler
13. Kopp, Carlo, letter in December 1997 issue of *Journal of Electronic Defence*
14. Correspondence from Mark Ashton
15. Stein, Professor George, "Information Warfare," 1997 *Air Power Supplement to Air Clues*, p 26
16. Quoted in Rose, *War In The Information Age*, p 75

Chapter 21

THE KOSOVO CONFLICT

March to June 1999

"I am sorry that the movements of the armies cannot keep pace with the expectations of the editors of papers."

General Robert E. Lee

By the late 1990s the break-up of Yugoslavia was almost complete. Four of the original six states—Croatia, Slovenia, Bosnia and Macedonia—had declared independence. Only Serbia and Montenegro remained in the Federal Republic of Yugoslavia (FRY). Yet the inter-racial enmities built up over hundreds of years continued to plague the area.

In the westerly Serbian province of Kosovo, the Belgrade government used armed force to maintain dominance over the ethnic Albanians comprising nine-tenths of the population. That oppression led to calls for independence there, too. Following provocative attacks by Kosovar guerrilla fighters, FRY military and special police units retaliated. Police supported by army tanks and artillery launched several one-sided actions against the guerrillas, while Albanian civilians suffered atrocities.

The crisis dragged on into 1999, with NATO governments becoming increasingly vocal in condemning Serbian actions. NATO demanded the Serbian military and paramilitary forces withdraw from Kosovo. When talks broke down, NATO air force units were ordered into action. As with the conflicts discussed in earlier chapters, this account will confine itself to those aspects relevant to the history of US electronic warfare.

Most FRY air defense weaponry had been manufactured in the Soviet Union during the Cold War. The mix of radar-guided surface-to-air missiles comprised "the usual suspects": the SA-2 Guideline, the SA-3 Goa, the SA-6 Gainful and the SA-8 Gecko. The arsenal of short-range IR missiles comprised the man-portable SA-7 Grail, the SA-14 Gremlin and SA-16 Gimlet, and the vehicle-borne SA-9 Gaskin. The air defense fighter force consisted of fourteen modern MiG-29 Fulcrums and about sixty obsolescent MiG-21 Fishbeds. The Federation possessed the usual range of Soviet AAA weapons and their associated gun control radars, as well as some locally manufactured 20 mm and 30 mm weapons.[1] Most of the radars were from the Soviet union, though there were also a few TPS-63 and TPS-70 surveillance sets from the US.[2]

Operation "Allied Force," the air action against the FRY, began on the night of 24/25 March 1999. Spearheading the attack were Tomahawk Land Attack Missiles targeted at the air defense system.[3] Planes from thirteen NATO nations then delivered follow-up attacks.

Phase 1 was to establish air superiority over Kosovo, create a no-fly zone in the south and degrade the integrated air defense system.[4] To keep outside reach of man-portable IR weapons, attacks would be delivered from altitudes above 15,000 feet.[5] Each attack force entering enemy territory had a covering force usually comprising four air superiority fighters (F-14s, F-15Cs, F-16s, F/A-18s or French Mirage 2000s), two EA-6B jamming support planes, at least two F-16CJs or German Air Force Tornados carrying HARM missiles, and an EC-130H Compass Call communications jamming aircraft.[6]

Initially the attackers expected the main threat to come from ground launched missiles, but FRY officers had studied earlier NATO defense suppression operations and the SAM batteries remained silent. Instead, the FRY Air Force scrambled several MiG-29s hoping to catch the raiders by surprise. The attacking packages were well able to look after themselves, however, and the first night's operations cost the FRY Air Defense Corps three MiG-29s or nearly a quarter of its fleet.

Meanwhile several flights of F-15E attack fighters headed for targets in Kosovo. Each Strike Eagle carried an offensive armament of two GBU-10 2,000-pound laser guided bombs. Weapon Systems Officer Captain Don Jones of the 494th Fighter Squadron, 48th Tactical Fighter Wing, was aboard one of the F-15Es heading for the airfield at the capital, Pristina:

"There was not a lot to see, it was night and we had our lights off. There was not a lot of light on the ground, though we did see scattered fires where villages were burning. Our targets were a tunnel built into a hillside to house airplanes, and a barracks. We attacked these with our LGBs.

The mission was a lot easier than we had expected, no missiles came up at us that first night. We had expected a lot more reaction from the defenses. My guess is that perhaps they thought we would send in a whole lot of target drones, as we had against Iraq. Maybe they thought we were drones and that was why they didn't shoot at us."[7]

Supporting the attack packages were EC-130H Compass Call aircraft of the 43rd Electronic Combat Squadron, orbiting clear of the defenses at altitudes around 24,000 feet. Captain Kathy Maloney, the only female Compass Call mission crew commander, commented:

"I had been looking forward to doing the job for real. We arrived on station in time to support the first allied air strikes going in. The AWACS was reporting details of unfriendly fighters that had taken off, but I did not feel particularly threatened. There was a big air strike going in, there were a lot of planes between me and the bad guys. Any enemy fighter that got airborne had too much to deal with, to think about attacking our plane."[8]

Compass Call operational missions lasted between twelve and fourteen hours, which included an in-flight refueling half way through the mission. Such missions, flown three days out of every four during the weeks to follow, imposed considerable strain on crews.

Major Chris Bakke, another Compass Call mission crew commander with the 43rd, had flown in the aircraft eight years earlier during Desert Storm. From his viewpoint, what were the main differences between the two conflicts?

"Professionally, the biggest difference between the two campaigns was the density of the signal environment. The Yugoslavs had a more sophisticated communications network than the Iraqis, and they were very much smarter in the way they used it...

We jammed their AAA and SAM systems as much as possible, to protect the NATO strike aircraft. If Yugoslav fighters took off, we also jammed their communications. As a result of the various countermeasures, and the aggressive combat air patrols, the Yugoslav air defenses were no more effective than those over Iraq."[9]

The first night of Allied Force saw the combat debut of two important US systems. The first was the Northrop B-2 Spirit. Two bombers from the 509th Bomb Wing took off from Whiteman AFB, Missouri, to strike at targets in FRY. After delivering their attacks the B-2s returned to Whiteman to complete their 31-hour missions.[10]

The second new system making its debut was the 2,000-pound Joint Directed Attack Munition (JDAM) weapon. Each B-2 carried sixteen of these free-fall weapons. Equipped with GPS-guidance, the near-precision JDAM could hit targets regardless of weather conditions.[11]

The ALE-50 towed decoy system, which had previously seen combat over Iraq aboard a few B-1Bs, again went into action aboard F-16 attack fighters.

The FRY government's reaction to the NATO air attacks was brutal, ordering Army and special police units to expel the entire ethnic Albanian population from Kosovo. Tens of thousands of refugees poured across the borders into Albania and Macedonia. TV news broadcasts showed heart-rending scenes of men, women and children standing on barren hillsides without food, water, sanitation or shelter. The refugees brought with them horrific stories of random killings to force them to leave their homes, which were then looted and in many cases burned.

There was harsh international condemnation for the Belgrade government's actions. Yet, by themselves, NATO air attacks could do little to ease the refugees' suffering. The most they could achieve was a disruption of daily life in the FRY, to make its leaders realize there was a price to pay for their chosen course of action.

During Allied Force there were fears that the Yugoslav Air Force might attack NATO troop positions in Bosnia or aircraft flying over it. To meet that potential threat, fighters maintained round-the-clock standing patrols over the republic.

Late on the afternoon of 26 March, three days into Allied Force, a pair of F-15C fighters, Dirk flight from the 493rd Fighter Squadron 48th Tactical Fighter Wing, was on patrol over Bosnia. Each fighter carried the regular air superiority armament load of four AIM-120C Advanced Medium Range Air-to-Air Missiles with active radar guidance, two AIM-7M Sparrows with semi-active radar guidance, two AIM-9M Sidewinder with infra-red guidance and a 20 mm cannon. An hour into the patrol, as dusk was falling, Dirk flight was near Tusla at 28,000 feet, when the leader, Captain Jeff Hwang, observed a radar contact on a plane some 40 miles to the east and inside Serbia. His wingman, Captain Joey McMurry, saw the contact at about the same time.[12]

Hwang reported the contact to the supporting E-3 AWACS aircraft, but the latter had not seen it. The approaching plane was not on a pleasure flight, as Hwang observed:

"The contact was doing over 600 knots at about 6,000 feet, which was much faster than I would expect any non-fighter type aircraft to be going. At the time we were close to the Bosnia/Serbia border, it didn't make sense to continue heading east. For one thing, it would have taken us over enemy territory and too far from our supporting assets."[13]

If there was to be an engagement, Hwang wanted to run it on his terms. That meant putting more distance between himself and the approaching plane. Accordingly the two F-15Cs turned west and accelerated to supersonic speed. When he had the spacing he needed, Hwang and his wingman turned to face the potential enemy. By now the AWACS had also made radar contact with the unidentified plane, and as they rolled out of their turns the two US pilots also regained radar contact. Jeff Hwang continued:

"He was heading west, directly towards us. We were running at way above supersonic speed, and the indications [on the F-15C's classified air-to-air identification system] were that the contact was a MiG-29 and it was flying supersonic, too. We were closing at more than 20 miles per minute.

The sun was setting in the west. I had not planned it that way, but the sun was on our backs and I knew the MiG pilot would have the sun in his eyes. I think maybe his ground control had told him where we were, or perhaps he was going after one of the tankers."[14]

Under the US rules of engagement, pilots had normally to obtain AWACS clearance before they engaged a plane they could not identify visually. The F-15C pilots were awaiting that clearance when events removed the need for it. The contact was closing fast and it would soon be in missile range of the F-15Cs. Hwang and his wingman were under threat and under their Rules of Engagement they were permitted to strike the first blow.

Hwang cleared his wingman to open fire, and watched the AIM-120 streak out in front of his F-15C. At that moment the AWACS called to say the radar contact had split—there were two planes ahead. Then Hwang's radar screen also showed the two contacts. He locked his radar on the leader, then selected narrow scan so he could see both contacts. Flying just below 30,000 feet, Hwang was 16 miles from his target when he launched his first AIM-120. Once that missile was on its way, he shifted the marker to the second contact and pressed the firing button a second time. Now three AIM-120s were heading through the twilight in front of the US fighters, but it seemed nothing much was happening.[15]

As the F-15Cs came within 10 miles of the contacts, Hwang asked his wingman to check his radar-warning receiver for signs that the approaching planes might be trying to target them.

"I called 'Naked!' [not being targeted], my wingman called 'Naked!' also. So we continued with the attack, descending rapidly to try to get a visual on the MiGs. Then against a broken cloud deck, just below the horizon, I picked up black dot ahead but a fair way off my nose, about 8 miles away. It was a MiG which I assessed to be the trailer. Still there had not been any explosions, the missiles launched earlier had not 'timed out.' I was starting to think about engaging with Sidewinders when, just outside my heads-up display, I saw an explosion. It looked just like a torch being swung through the air at a Hawaiian Luau party. That was not the plane I had seen, but another that I assessed was the leader. I returned my attention to the trailer, and a couple of seconds later he exploded into flame in the same way as the first."[16]

From the time of the initial radar contact, until the second MiG went down, was just four minutes and that included the initial turn away from the MiGs to open the range.

After the shootdowns the F-15Cs swept the area with radar to ensure there were no further planes. Finding no contacts, the F-15Cs returned to their CAP line. They still had weapons and their replacements were not due to arrive for another 2½ hours.[17]

Both MiG-29s fell on open ground a few miles inside Bosnia, close to the border with Serbia. Later analysis of data recordings revealed that Jeff Hwang's missiles had brought down both MiGs.[18]

On the night following Jeff Hwang's shootdowns, 27 March, the NATO air forces initiated Phase 2 of the air campaign. This expanded the list of targets to include military objectives in Kosovo and reinforcement routes.[19]

At the opening of the new phase the defenders enjoyed a rare taste of success, when they brought down an F-117A stealth fighter near Belgrade. The F-117A pilot ejected and reached the ground safely, and was picked up in a daring combat rescue operation. According to one source,[20] the aircraft had completed its attack when it was engaged by three or four SA-3 Goa missiles. Missile fragments blasted the plane inflicting severe damage, and it fell out of control. The source attributed the loss to a combination of a flight route used previously, inadequate jamming cover from an EA-6B that was too far away, and luck on the part of the SA-3 crew.

It appears likely the Low Blow missile control radar was cued to search in the correct part of the sky by one or more long wavelength acquisition radars, probably a Spoon Rest B (P-18). The source also mentioned that SA-3 batteries had been moved into positions under known F-117A flight routes. Given the propaganda value from an F-117A shootdown, almost certainly the missile crews involved were the best available.

By then the F-117A had flown about 1,400 combat missions over Iraq and FRY without loss or an instance of serious damage. Given that the stealth fighters' targets usually lay in the most heavily defended areas, even after the loss its combat record was substantially better than any other attack fighter type. Thereafter the F-117As used more varied routing and enjoyed more effective screening from the EA-6Bs. These moves appear to have been successful, for no more stealth fighters were lost in action during the conflict.

After the first week's fighting the FRY radar-guided missiles became more aggressive. One who noticed the difference was Major James McGovern of the 494th Fighter Squadron, 48th TFW. His F-15E was part of a force making a daylight attack on an army barracks near Obrava in the south of Serbia.

"We dropped our bombs, two GBU-10s [2,000-pound LGBs]. The back seater was designating for the bombs when a missile control radar illuminated us. On the ALR-56 warning receiver, we could see it was an SA-3 tracking radar. We dropped chaff and commenced an evasive maneuver. That forced the WSO to stop designating the target. We evaded the first missile. Then I rolled out to get a visual on the second missile and saw it was well clear. The [laser designating] pod gave us a countdown to impact. We needed between 8 and 12 seconds of level flight to correct the final part of the bomb's trajectory. As we rolled out I looked at the clock, and there happened to be 12 seconds left before impact. Fortunately my

WSO was thinking exactly the same thing, as we rolled out. He resumed designating. I held the plane straight and level, looking out to see that no more missiles were coming for us. He guided in the weapons and shacked [scored a direct hit on] the target. Then we resumed our evasive maneuvers and egressed the area."[21]

From 1 April, five B-1B Lancer bombers joined in the attacks on FRY, flying from Fairford in England. Like the F-16s, these aircraft carried ALE-50 towed decoys.

B-1Bs flew more than fifty missions during the Kosovo conflict, many of them against defended targets. According to one report these aircraft had an estimated thirty missiles fired at them. Of that thirty, it is believed ten locked on to the bomber/decoy combination before they were seduced away by the decoys.[22]

When Phase 2 of the air campaign failed to bring the FRY government into meaningful negotiations, Phase 3 was launched. This expanded the target list to include high-value military and security-related targets throughout FRY territory. On 3 April, for example, the first of several cruise missiles struck Belgrade, hitting Interior Ministry buildings. From 5 April bombers attacked fuel storage depots and oil refineries, halting operations at the latter.

During the early morning darkness of 2 May an F-16 Fighting Falcon was shot down over FRY, again by an SA-3 battery. The pilot landed by parachute and was rescued soon after he reached the ground. No information has been released on whether the aircraft had a ALE-50 decoy deployed at the time it was hit.

On 3 May the attack opened against the FRY electricity grid. The weapon used was the CBU-94 cluster munition, a development of the carbon-fiber-wire device that disrupted the Iraqi electricity grid nearly a decade earlier. Like its predecessor the CBU-94 was designed to cause temporary shutdowns. The individual submunitions, each about the size of two beer cans stacked one on top of the other, were carried in a tactical munitions dispenser dropped from the aircraft. At low altitude the dispenser opened and the submunitions spilled out, each stabilized in its fall by a small parachute. Then small explosive charges expelled the reels of specially treated wire, which unwound to produce long lengths. When wires fell across high voltage power lines, that section of the electricity supply system was unusable until the offending wires had been removed.[23]

To look at the work of the EA-6B Prowler force let us follow a typical action, one on the night of 7 June. The composite Navy and Marine EA-6B wing at Aviano sent two Prowlers to support a strike on the main Belgrade power station.

Each Prowler carried the standard external stores for Allied Force: a jamming pod under each wing and one under the fuselage, a fuel tank on the starboard inboard station and a HARM on the port inboard station. Each EA-6B was to launch its HARM pre-emptively at a set time from a set point, to suppress the missile defenses as the strike force ran in. Air Force Captain Jeff Fischer, an EWO on an exchange with Navy squadron VAQ-138, flew in one of the EA-6Bs:

> "The Yugoslavs had imposed a blackout throughout the country. As we ran in we knew Belgrade was about 50 miles away on the nose, but we could see no lights from the city or from the countryside. It was very serene, very quiet.
>
> As we neared the designated firing point we began the countdown for the HARM launch. The missile came off the rail and lit up the night sky like a beacon. After the launch, we turned away. When we looked down, we saw that three AAA sites were firing tracers at us. It was the first time I knew I had been shot at, and for the pilot it was the first time she knew she had been shot at. The airplane was not hit, but it was very uncomfortable until we got clear. As we were driving outbound, with our jamming antennas pointed aft, we looked back and saw SAMs coming up and exploding in the sky.
>
> Suddenly the sky above Belgrade lit up as if it was daytime. I looked at my watch I saw it was the TOT [time on target], somebody's bombs were exploding on the power plant. When the flash died down there was a warm yellow glow in the sky, with flashes from secondary explosions. We remained on station for about ten minutes until the last of the attacking planes had left the danger area. Then we went home."[24]

At the end of 1988, when the situation in Kosovo came to the boil, the 1st Aerial Exploitation Battalion with RC-12K Guardrail Common Sensor aircraft was at Taszar in Hungary supporting US forces in Bosnia. Army Colonel Susan Browning described the relocation of her Guardrail unit for the new conflict:

> "I was told to look at ways of supporting possible US operations in Kosovo, as well as those in Bosnia. We looked at several options, and decided we could support both operations from bases in Italy. At short notice we redeployed the Guardrail aircraft to Naples, and moved the Integrated Processing Facility (IPF) to Brindisi in the south of the country...
>
> During each mission the planes had first to make a one-hour flight to Brindisi, where the crews received their briefings. Then they flew to their orbit stations over Albania. With the flights out and back via Brindisi, the Guardrail planes had only about two hours on station for each mission. Normally the unit would have had eight RC-12Ks, but it had lost one during a training exercise in 1998. With only seven planes, and having to

fly so many missions, we could afford to put up only two planes at a time [instead of the preferred three]. So, we lost a bit of accuracy. Even so, Guardrail was the most prolific collector of intelligence available to the Army in the theater."[25]

The RC-12Ks established a base line over Albania, about 160 miles from their ground processing facility. Operating at altitudes close to their limit of 35,000 feet, the RC-12Ks located numerous signal sources in Kosovo and the FRY.[26]

By the end of May 1999 the cumulative damage from NATO planes had halted much industrial activity in the FRY. This, combined with wide-ranging trade sanctions, had brought the economy was close to collapse. President Milosevic finally acceded to NATO's demand to withdraw his army and special police units from Kosovo, and the air campaign ended on 10 June.

According to US records, during the conflict FRY forces fired 266 SA-6s, 174 SA-3s, 106 shoulder-launched IR weapons and 126 unidentified missiles. AAA was intense throughout the bombing campaign, especially around Belgrade.[27]

During nearly 14,000 strike and defense suppression missions over FRY territory, Allied losses, as we have seen, were an F-16 and an F-117A.[28] Both pilots were rescued. In addition several unmanned reconnaissance vehicles were lost in action or from accidents.

There have been unconfirmed reports that both sides carried out information warfare attacks aimed at their opponent's computer systems. Neither side has "claimed responsibility" for such actions, however, nor has anyone admitted suffering damage.

The air war over the FRY was a David-and-Goliath struggle, but Allied Goliath had the superior sling and was more proficient in its use. The "bottom line" for the air campaign provides a ringing endorsement of the potency of modern air power. The action lasted 78 days and cost no NATO lives and only two manned planes in combat.

Much has been written about the failure to inflict significant damage on Serbian military and paramilitary forces in Kosovo. Yet by definition, the bombing campaign inflicted sufficient damage to force President Milosevic to accede to NATO demands. Aspects of the conflict could have been handled better, but that can be said for any war.

The loss of two aircraft, both apparently to radar-guided missiles, was too few to allow meaningful statistical analysis. It is however certain that the decision to remain above 15,000 feet over hostile territory was effective in neutralizing the otherwise dangerous IR missile systems.

The Kosovo conflict is too recent for detailed conclusions on the effectiveness of the various electronic warfare systems to appear in any unclassified account. Yet there is no question that these held aircraft losses to such a low figure.

References to Chapter 21

1   Ripley, Tim, *Operation Deliberate Force*, Centre for Defence and International Security Studies, Lancaster, England, 1999, pp 77, 78; also Aeroflight Database, "Yugoslav Air Force," www.Flight2000.com/hangar/aeroflight
2. DoD Report Kosovo/Operation Allied Force, After Action Report, pp 7, 8
3. *Ibid*
4. *Ibid*
5. *Ibid*
6. *Ibid*
7. Interview Don Jones
8. Interview Kathy Maloney
9. Interview Chris Bakke
10. "B-2 ESM Passes First Test," *Journal of Electronic Defense*, May 1999
11. *Ibid*
12. Interview Jeff Hwang
13. *Ibid*
14. *Ibid*
15. *Ibid*
16. *Ibid*
17. *Ibid*
18. *Ibid*
19. DoD Report, pp 7, 8
20. Fulghum, David, "Pentagon Gets Lock On F-117 Shootdown," *Aviation Week and Space Technology*, 19 April 1999.
21. Interview James McGovern
22. "Washington Outlook," *Aviation Week and Space Technology*, 31 May 1999
23. Fulghum, David, "Electronic Bombs Darken Belgrade," *Aviation Week and Space Technology*,10 May 1999
24. Interview Jeff Fischer
25. Interview Susan Browning
26. *Ibid*
27. Major General Chuck Wald, Department of Defense news briefing
28. DoD report, p 69

Chapter 22

TOMORROW AND THE DAY AFTER

From 2001

"**Future**: That period of time in which our affairs prosper, our friends are true and our happiness is assured."

Ambrose Bierce, *The Devil's Dictionary*

This chapter overviews US electronic warfare programs in progress at the time of writing, intended to produce systems for the decade ahead. Almost certainly, some of the programs listed will fail to reach fruition. Despite this caveat, it is hoped that the account which follows will serve as a map, albeit an imperfect one, to chart the future path of US electronic warfare development.

The next generation self-protection system, intended for small- and medium-sized combat aircraft, is the joint service ALQ-214 IDECM (Integrated Defensive Electronic Countermeasures) equipment. Built by ITT and Lockheed/Martin/Sanders, it is in advanced development. This internally mounted system uses state-of-the-art technology and features the latest techniques in deception. Due to technical problems, the system's scheduled in-service date has slipped beyond the originally quoted 2005.[1]

The follow-on system for the ALE-50 towed decoy is the Lockheed/Sanders ALE-55, which radiates twice the power. While the ALE-50 merely retransmits incoming radar signals, the ALE-55 will operate as an adjunct to the ALQ-214 with signal modulations from the latter fed along a fiber-optic line to the decoy. The ALQ-214 and ALE-55 combination is scheduled initially for installation in the B-1B Lancer and the F/A-18E/F Super Hornet.[2]

During the mid-1980s the Air Force set out its requirements for the air superiority fighter to replace the F-15. Early in 1991 the Lockheed F-22 Raptor won the Advanced Tactical Fighter competition. The F-22 carries the Integrated Electronic Warfare System (INEWS), built by General Electric and

Lockheed/Sanders. INEWS provides warning of radar, IR and laser threats, it processes the incoming signals and produces the necessary jamming response and, in a novel departure, it also handles the plane's communications.

Between 1988 and 1993 Dr Hugo Poza headed the Avionics Division at Lockheed/Sanders and was heavily involved with INEWS:

> "INEWS is an integrated system tailored to the F-22. It cannot go in any plane other than the F-22. The capability of the electronic warfare system is many times greater than that currently available on the F-15 in terms of defense, in terms of jamming, in terms of targeting.
>
> The F-22 has many stealth features. But it is a myth to think that a stealthy aircraft does not need EW systems. It is important to blend the plane's stealth capability with its EW system; they have to be carefully matched. There needs to be a passive EW system to detect the direction from which the threatening radar signals are coming. Then the pilot can present the plane's most stealthy aspect to that direction, to try to remain undetected. During an engagement it is likely that for most of the time the pilot will not to jam at all, preferring to stay passive. But occasionally it may be necessary to jam, and INEWS includes a jamming system. On a stealthy airplane, a little jamming power at the right time can achieve a great deal."[3]

During the 1991 war in the Persian Gulf, infrared homing missiles caused the majority of aircraft losses. Currently there are about 600,000 man-portable IR missiles in circulation[4] and the potency of this threat is increasing: future IR weapons will be far less vulnerable to countermeasures than their predecessors.

To counter modern IR missiles, Raytheon is working on a towed IR decoy as an alternative load for the ALE-50.[5] The IR decoy is designed to produce a signature similar to an aircraft and to defeat the current discrimination systems in IR missiles.

The development of IR homing heads continues apace, however. The next generation of IR missiles will use imaging IR seeker heads, which generate a moderate-resolution thermal image of the target airplane and lock on to a part of it. Thus the imaging seeker head will differentiate between an aircraft and the most sophisticated flare.[6]

Countering a missile with an imaging IR seeker head poses a severe technical challenge; there is no simple way to do it. One answer currently undergoing tests is the AAQ-24 "Nemesis," a directed infrared countermeasures (DIRCM) system. Produced by Northrop/Grumman in partnership with Marconi in Great Britain, it is intended for installation in helicopters and large fixed-wing planes. In one form Nemesis employs four passive ultraviolet detectors positioned around the aircraft to detect, locate and track the incoming missile. If the missile is seen as a threat, the system automatically radiates a narrow beam of energy in that direction to dazzle the seeker and disrupt its guidance system. Against the shorter wavelength homing heads, IR energy is used; against the longer wavelength homing heads laser energy is used.[7] The Air Force intends to fit the AAQ-24 initially in the MC-130 Combat Talon and the AC-130U Spectre aircraft.

A later system along the same general lines, for installation in smaller combat aircraft, is the ALQ-212 Advanced Tactical IR CounterMeasures (ATIRCM) system. Under development by Lockheed/Sanders, this uses an infrared or ultraviolet system (both are under consideration) to detect the missile and determine whether it is a threat. If it is, ATIRCM aligns the laser or IR head on the weapon and beams energy in that direction.[8]

For the protection of helicopters and slow fixed-wing types, ITT is currently working on the ALQ-211 SIRFC (Suite of Integrated RF Countermeasures) to replace the APR-39 warning receiver and ALQ-136 pulse radar jammer currently in service. The new system will provide improved situational awareness in locating, identifying and countering pulse, pulse-Doppler, and continuous-wave threats in the C through M bands. As with the earlier warning system, SIRFC uses a synthetic voice generator to transmit warnings to the crew. SIRFC, together with the ALQ-212 ATIRCM, is scheduled for retrofiting into Army AH-64 Apache helicopters.[9]

To maintain the EA-6B Prowler's capability against the newest threats a further enhancement of electronic warfare capability is planned. The ICAP-III (Improved CAPability III) upgrade is scheduled to begin testing in 2002. A new ESM system from Litton will replace the current receiver suite and the jamming transmitters will incorporate a range of new techniques with revised software to counter the latest threat radars. Also, there will be a new low band jammer to counter long wavelength radars which have sometimes been able to track stealthy aircraft.[10]

At the time of writing, the Navy has a requirement for more than one hundred jamming support planes to replace the EA-6Bs. One contender for the role is a dedicated jamming variant of the Boeing F/A-18F Super Hornet two-seater.[11]

There is recognition in the Air Force that the dissolution of the EF-111A Raven force cannot be reversed. That service is now looking for a new jamming support aircraft and it has several options under consideration.

Up till now the suppression of enemy air defenses (SEAD) mission has been mainly reactive—enemy radars were attacked only after they came on air. The future may see pre-emptive attacks on missile batteries before they transmit. The success of such engagements will hinge on accurate intelligence to locate such targets, and near-real-time transfer of that intelligence to attacking planes in flight. The new Joint Stand Off Weapon (JSOW), employing the global positioning system for guidance, is accurate enough to perform the hard-kill part of that operation.[12]

The SLQ-32 shipborne defensive system has rendered good service over the years, but events have overtaken it. The Navy has shifted away from "blue water" operations and now focuses its attention on operations close to the enemy littoral. Inshore the threats to warships are more numerous and the response time is far shorter.

At the end of 1997 the Navy selected the team to build its next generation EW system for its surface vessels, SLY-2 Advanced Integrated Electronic Warfare System. Lockheed Martin Ocean Radar and Sensor Systems is prime contractor.[13] The SLY-2 is due to replace the SLQ-32, the WLR-1H and the SSQ-82 intelligence gathering system in some newer warships. The system is designed to cope with the dense radar environment likely to be encountered during inshore operations.[14]

Currently the Army is finalizing its requirements for Aerial Common Sensor, the system to replace both Guardrail and Airborne Reconnaissance Low at the end of the decade. Colonel William Knarr, at the Training and Doctrine Command at Fort Huachuca, Arizona, commented:

> "As we develop our requirements for the follow-on to Guardrail Common Sensor and Airborne Reconnaissance Low, we are looking at a possible mix of manned and unmanned aircraft. The Department of Defense asked us if we could do everything we needed using unmanned aircraft. My answer was, it depends on the time frame. The visionaries say we may be able to do that in the year 2020. I think that for 2010, we will need to have the capabilities of both systems. The manned system gives flexibility of response. We don't yet know the full capabilities of the unmanned systems. But we do feel that using an unmanned vehicle gives more freedom of action. If necessary, it can be sent over enemy territory to pick up signals from low powered transmissions. UAVs [unmanned air vehicles] are not throwaway items, they are not expendable. But if the situation requires, they can be attritable."[15]

In recent years, the US armed forces have become increasingly dependent on the global positioning system (GPS) for navigation and self-location. GPS is the key guidance element in a number of new precision attack systems, notably the Joint Direct Attack Munition (JDAM), the Joint Stand Off Weapon (JSOW) and the ship-launched Tomahawk land attack missile. If GPS can be degraded or rendered unusable, it will be a major coup for any state in conflict with the US.

When it was first considered, GPS was intended purely as a navigational aid and there was little thought given to the possibility of jamming.[16] Since the system has come into large-scale use the possibility of intentional interference has had to be addressed. A new term has entered the electronic warfare lexicon: Navigation Warfare or NAVWAR.

Jamming of GPS might be either unintentional or intentional. Johns Hopkins University Applied Physics Laboratory has carried out an independent assessment of the system and concluded that accidental jamming is not a major risk.[17] Intentional jamming poses a major threat, however.

The Aviaconversiya Company in Russia offers a lightweight (just over 6 pounds) low powered (8-watt) jamming system designed to render unusable both GPS and its Russian GLONASS equivalent. According to the manufacturer the device can prevent use of these systems out to distances of "several hundred kilometers," provided the jammer is within line-of-sight range of the victim receiver.[18]

Under tactical conditions, however, it might be difficult to position the jammer within line-of-sight of, say, a fighter delivering bombs on a target. If GPS is operating in one of its jam-resistant military modes, the effectiveness of jamming would be much reduced.[19]

Currently minitubes (mini-Travelling Wave Tubes) are employed as power sources in numerous electronic warfare applications. The next step, the microtube, performs the same power-generation functions but for less size, weight and input power and with a greater operating efficiency. At the time of writing, microtubes little larger than a fountain pen can generate power levels up to 240 watts at efficiency levels of around 50 percent.[20]

Tony Brees, with Northrop-Grumman, believes the microtube will produce another leap forward in the effectiveness of electronic warfare systems:

> "Today a typical power amplifier in an airborne system weighs about 100 pounds and has an output of about 350 watts. That box is big and heavy and it needs cooling. You could take four microtubes in the 6 to 18 GHz family, and gang them together to get that same 350 watts. So, the weight goes down to maybe 20 pounds, and the cooling requirement goes down by a factor of eight. The individual microtubes are more reliable than the minitubes they replace, so the mean time between failures goes up by a factor of about ten."[21]

The microtube's output can be modulated with any type of signal and it is suitable for transmitters working at 2 GHz and above. Like minitubes, microtubes can be grouped together to produce a directional antenna array. However, with its much smaller size, power requirements and heat generation, the microtube array will be far easier to locate within a structure. In an airplane such an array might fit comfortably in a wing tip or at the top of the tail.[22]

This chapter has given a peek at some likely future developments in electronic warfare. Following the end of the Kosovo conflict there is a widespread view that modern warplanes can conduct effective military operations with minimal losses in aircraft and personnel. Whether that ideal can be repeated in future conflicts remains to be seen. There can be little doubt, however, that state-of-the-art countermeasures systems will be necessary if that ideal is to be achieved with confidence.

References to Chapter 22

1. "IDECM Program Moves Back on Track," *Journal of Electronic Defense*, August 1999
2. *Ibid*
3. Interview Hugo Poza
4. Colucci, Frank, "Rotary Wing EW—More than Survival," *Journal of Electronic Defense*, May 1999
5. Herskovitz, Don "The Art of Off-board ECM Protection," *Journal of Electronic Defense*, August 1999
6. Interview Tony Grieco
7. "DIRCM goes Laser," *Journal of Electronic Defense*, July 1999
8. Carroll, Sean, "The Top EW Programs," *Journal of Electronic Defense*, August 1999
9. Colucci, Frank, "Rotary Wing EW—More than Survival," *Journal of Electronic Defense*, May 1999
10. Klass, Philip, "ICAP-3 will Update EA-6B's Capabilities," *Aviation Week*, 26 October 1988
11. Lewis, Paul, "Congress may use Kosovo cash for Prowler replacement Study," *Flight International*, 25 May 1999
12. Spaar, Lt Col Ken, "Future SEAD: A USAF Perspective," *Journal of Electronic Defense*, May 1999
13. Knowles, J., "Navy Awards Shipboard EW Program to Lockheed Martin Team," *Journal of Electronic Defense*, January 1998
14. *Ibid*
15. Interview William Knarr
16. Herskovitz, Don, "And the Compass Spun Round and Round," *Journal of Electronic Defense*, May 1977
17. *Ibid*
18. "Russian GPS Jammer Introduced," *Journal of Electronic Defense*, August 1999
19. Herskovitz
20. Interview Tony Brees
21. *Ibid*
22. *Ibid*

Appendix

Soviet and Russian Land Based Surface-to-Air Missile Systems

SA-1 Guild (S-25)
First generation static air defense system, deployed in Moscow and Leningrad areas in the late 1950s. Gage E-band radar for target acquisition and the Yo-Yo E-band radar for missile command guidance.[1]

SA-2 Guideline (S-75 Dvina)
Second generation air defense system, semi-mobile. Spoon Rest A-band radar for acquisition, Fan Song E-band radar, later G-band, for missile command guidance. Exported to more than 40 countries. About 3,700 launchers and 20,000 missiles built. The Chinese produced a modified copy, the HQ-2.[2]

SA-3 Goa (S-125 Neva).
Complementary system to the SA-2, covering lower altitude bands. Usually employed the Flat Face (P-15) C-band radar for target acquisition. Low Blow I-band radar for missile command guidance. Maximum effective range about 17 miles. Exported to about 30 countries.[3]

SA-4 Ganef (9M8 Krug)
Semi-mobile tactical missile system for the defense of army units in the field. Long Track E-band radar for target acquisition, Thin Skin H-band radar for height finding and the Pat Hand H-band radar for missile control. After the launch the missiles were command guided, and switched to the semi-active mode for terminal homing.[4]

SA-5 Gammon (S-200)
Long range static air defense system. Early warning provided by the Big Back D-band radar (Tin Shield radar used at some sites). Bar Lock E/F-band surveillance radar for target acquisition, Square Pair H-band radar for target tracking and missile guidance. After the launch the missiles were command guided, and switched to the semi-active mode for terminal homing. Exported to North Korea, Libya and Syria.[5]

SA-6 Gainful (ZRK-SD Kub)
Semi-mobile tactical missile system for the defense of army units in the field. The controlling radars and launch units mounted on separate tracked vehicles. Surveillance radar as for SA-4. Straight Flush H-band radar for target acquisition, tracking and target illumination. After the launch the missiles were command

guided, then switched to the semi-active mode for terminal homing. Maximum effective range about 20 miles. Deployed in about 20 countries.[6]

SA-7 Grail (Strella 2, 9M32)

The **SA-7A** appeared in 1966, a first-generation shoulder launched man-portable IR missile. Maximum range of about 2.2 miles. The improved **SA-7B** (Strella 2M) appeared in 1972 and carried simple counter-countermeasures including a filter to reject extraneous IR signals. It had a maximum range of about 3.4 miles. Both variants could engage planes only from the rear aspect. Built in huge numbers and exported to more than 50 countries.[7]

SA-8 Gecko (9M33 Romb)

Semi-mobile tactical missile system for the defense of army units in the field. Firing unit mounted on one self-contained wheeled cross-country vehicle. Surveillance radars as for SA-4. Land Roll H-band radar for target acquisition. The same system included two J-band monopulse radars for target tracking and missile command guidance. Thus it could engage an aircraft with two missiles controlled by radars each working on a separate frequency. Exported to at least 11 countries.[8]

SA-9 Gaskin (Strella 1)

Semi-mobile short-range tactical missile system for the defense of army units in the field. The IR missiles and their launchers were mounted as a self-contained system on a light armored vehicle. The Dog Ear surveillance radar provided target acquisition.[9]

SA-10A Grumble (S-300)

Semi-mobile long range air defense system in the same general class as the US Patriot. Clam Shell CW pulse-Doppler radar provided surveillance and early warning. Big Bird F-band tower-mounted early warning radar was used for the detection of low flying aircraft and cruise missiles. The Flap Lip A and Flap Lip B multi-functional phased-array radar provided target tracking and missile guidance.[10] The missile, launched vertically, carried a hefty 315-pound high explosive blast-fragmentation warhead. The later **SA-10B** (S-300PMU) had greater mobility.[11] Sold to China, Bulgaria, the Czech Republic, Iran and Cyprus.

SA-11 Gadfly (9K3 Buk-1M)

Semi-mobile medium range tactical missile system for the defense of army units in the field, replacement for the SA-6. Able to engage tactical ballistic missiles. Snow Drift (9S81M1) I-band phased array radar provided target acquisition.[12] Fire Dome monopulse target illumination radar mounted on the launch vehicle. Exported to India, Syria and Finland.

SA-12A Gladiator, SA-12B Giant (Soviet designation for both, S-300V)

This unusual system employed two different types of vertically launched missile. The **SA-12A** Gladiator (9M83), the smaller of the two, was optimized against maneuvering aircraft, cruise missiles and short range ballistic missiles. The **SA-12B** Giant (9M82) was a longer range missile to combat ELINT, AWACS, JSTARs and high altitude reconnaissance aircraft, and tactical ballistic missiles. Bill Board (9S15) F-band phased-array radar provided surveillance. High Screen

(9S19) phased-array sector scanning radar for target acquisition. Grill Pan (9S32) phased-array radar provided command guidance for missiles during the initial part of their flight. It also provided target illumination during the final part of missiles' flight, when the latter employed semi-active guidance.[13] Bought for the Ukranian defense forces and ordered by Kuwait.[14]

SA-13 Gopher (Strella-10M3)

Semi-mobile short-range tactical missile system for the defense of army units in the field. The IR missiles and their launchers were mounted as a self-contained system on a light armored vehicle. Dog Ear surveillance radar provided target acquisition. Exported to about 15 countries.[15]

SA-14 Gremlin

Shoulder launched man-portable IR missile to replace the SA-7, appeared in 1978. Compared with its predecessor the SA-14 had a more powerful motor, an improved cooled IR homing head, digital electronics and a larger warhead. The system was considerably more reliable and effective than the SA-7. Credited with a maximum range of about 4 miles, built and exported in huge numbers.[16]

SA-15 Gauntlet (Tor-M1)

Replacement for the SA-8 mobile air defense system. Self-contained firing unit mounted on single tracked vehicle. Employed an advanced G-band pulse-Doppler radar for target acquisition. Used a K-band pulse-Doppler radar for target tracking. Missiles vertically launched, then command guided.[17] Operated in states that had been part of the old Soviet Union and exported to Greece.

SA-16 Gimlet (Igla 1)

Shoulder launched man-portable missile, intended to supplement the SA-14. First appeared in 1984. Employed dual mode guidance with IR terminal homing giving all-aspect engagement capability. Built and exported in large numbers.[18]

SA-17 Grizzly (Ural)

Semi-mobile medium range tactical missile system for the defense of army units in the field, intended as replacement for the SA-11. Had capability to engage tactical ballistic missiles. The guidance system was inertial during the initial flight period, updated by command link. During the final part of the interception the missile used semi-active guidance.[19] Details not available on the radars used with this system.

SA-18 Grouse (9K39 Igla)

Shoulder launched man-portable IR missile, intended as replacement for the SA-16. Fitted with two-channel IR seeker head. Missile said to be able to discriminate between engine exhausts, and flares and other types of decoy.[20] Some of these weapons appeared in Yugoslavia during the Kosovo crisis.[21]

SA-19 Grison (9M311)

The 2S6M Tunguska is a semi-mobile combined gun and missile system for the defense of army units in the field, to replace the ZSU-23-4 Shilka anti-aircraft gun and the SA-9. Mounted on a tracked armored vehicle, the gun turret houses two fast-firing twin-barreled 30 mm cannon. On the sides of the turret are launchers for the SA-19, with eight 9M311 optically aimed command to line of sight (CLOS) missiles which train and elevate with the guns. The Tunguska vehicle carries a Hot Shot (1RL-144M) radar system, with an E-band set for search and J-band set for fire control.[22] Exported to India. [23]

S-400 Triumph

Originally known as the SA-10C. Semi-mobile long range air defense system, believed scheduled for deployment at the time of writing to replace the SA-10. Little hard information has been released, but the vertically launched missiles are known to be the 9M96E and the improved 9M96E2.[24]

References

1. Eustace, Harry, ed., *The International Countermeasures Handbook 1997*, EW Communications Inc, Palo Alto CA, 1997, p 245 *et seq*
2. Zaloga, Steven, "Future Trends in Air Defense Missiles," *Journal of Electronic Defense*, October 1997
3. Ibid
4. Dube, F.P. "Buck", ed., *International Electronic Countermeasures Handbook 1999*, Horizon House, Norwood MA, 1996, p 250
5. Ibid
6. Ibid
7. Cordesman, Anthony and Wagner, Abraham *The Lessons of Modern War*, Volume III: *The Afghan and Falklands Conflicts*, Westview Press, Boulder, CO, 1991, pp 172, 230
8. Dube, p 251
9. *Ibid* p 252
10. "The S-300 PMU-1", unattributed article in *Military Technology*, 11/1993, based on material supplied by the Oboronexport, the Russian export organization for defence equipment
11. Dube, *op cit*
12. "BUK: Setting New Standards in Medium Range Air Defence," *Military Technology*, 9/1993;
13. "S-300V: The ATBM Trendsetter," *Military Technology*, 8/1993
14. Dube *op cit*
15. Zaloga
16. Zaloga
17. "SHORAD SUPREME: The TOR SAM System," *Military Technology*, 12/1993
18. Dube, p 254
19. Fulghum, David, "Improved Missiles Trigger Jammer Need," *Aviation Week*, 27 Sept 1999
20. Zaloga
21. Dube p 255
22. "2S6M Tunguska," *Military Technology*, 7/93
23. Zaloga
24. "Emerging Air Defense Weapons Presented," *Aviation Week*, 6 September 1999

The History of US Electronic Warfare: The Full Story

The outcome of more than twenty years of research by Alfred Price, *The History of US Electronic Warfare* is the most detailed reference work available on this aspect of technological history. In three volumes it traces the evolution of this subject from its beginnings before World War II, to the present day.

Volume I (312 pages) covers developments before and during World War II. It includes detailed descriptions of the electronic countermeasures support for the US bomber offensive against Germany, the D-Day invasion of France, the island-hopping campaign in the Pacific and the bomber offensive against Japan which culminated in the atomic bomb attacks on Hiroshima and Nagasaki.

Volume II (390 pages) covers developments from 1945 to the start of the bombing campaign against North Vietnam in 1964. It describes events during the early days of the Cold War, the Korean War, the Cuban missile crisis and the buildup of Strategic Air Command into a potent force.

War in the Fourth Dimension is a condensed edition of Volume III of the history. The full account (612 pages) also covers developments from 1964 to the present day, but does so in far greater detail than has been possible in this shortened version.

The History of US Electronic Warfare is available by mail order from:

AOC Headquarters
1000 North Payne Street
Alexandria
Virginia VA 22314-1652
USA

Tel: (+1) 703 549 1600
Web: www.crows.org
Visa, American Express, Master Card and Diner's Card accepted.

Index
